COLLABORATIVE ENVIRONMENTAL MANAGEMENT

What Roles for Government?

Tomas M. Koontz, Toddi A. Steelman,
JoAnn Carmin, Katrina Smith Korfmacher,
Cassandra Moseley, and Craig W. Thomas

Resources for the Future
Washington, DC, USA

An RFF Press book
Published by Resources for the Future
1616 P Street, NW
Washington, DC 20036–1400
USA
www.rffpress.org

Library of Congress Cataloging-in-Publication Data

Collaborative environmental management : what roles for government? / Tomas M. Koontz
    . . . [et al.].
        p.   cm.
    "An RFF Press book"—T.p. verso
    Includes bibliographical references.
    ISBN 1–891853–80–5 (alk. paper)—ISBN 1–891853–82–1 (pbk. : alk. paper)
    1. Environmental policy.   2. Environmental management.   I. Koontz, Tomas M.
GE170.C635   2004
333.72—dc21   2004014207

f e d c b a

The paper in this book meets the guidelines for permanence and durability of the Committee on Production Guidelines for Book Longevity of the Council on Library Resources.

This book was typeset in Giovanni and Myriad. It was copyedited by Joyce Bond and typeset by Betsy Kulamer. Cover design by Maggie Powell; cover photo by Tomas Koontz.

ISBN 1–891853–80–5 (cloth)   1–891853–82–1 (paper)

About Resources for the Future *and* RFF Press

Resources for the Future (RFF) improves environmental and natural resource policymaking worldwide through independent social science research of the highest caliber. Founded in 1952, RFF pioneered the application of economics as a tool to develop more effective policy about the use and conservation of natural resources. Its scholars continue to employ social science methods to analyze critical issues concerning pollution control, energy policy, land and water use, hazardous waste, climate change, biodiversity, and the environmental challenges of developing countries.

RFF Press supports the mission of RFF by publishing book-length works that present a broad range of approaches to the study of natural resources and the environment. Its authors and editors include RFF staff, researchers from the larger academic and policy communities, and journalists. Audiences for publications by RFF Press include all of the participants in the policymaking process—scholars, the media, advocacy groups, NGOs, professionals in business and government, and the public.

CONTENTS

PREFACE

A movement is taking root in which governments at all levels in the United States are changing the way they engage in environmental management. After years of attempts by public agencies to implement policy from the top down, these agencies increasingly are using collaboration with a broad range of stakeholders to address environmental problems. Sometimes this collaboration takes place among public agencies. In other instances, collaboration primarily involves actors in the private and nonprofit sectors, with public agencies playing a relatively minor role. Governments fill a wide range of roles, all of which influence both the process and the outcomes of collaborative environmental management. By governments, we mean both the government personnel (actors) who participate in these collaborations and the institutions of government, especially the administrative state. Examining a consistent set of factors across the cases presented in *Collaborative Environmental Management* allows us to gain greater insight into the variety of roles that governmental actors play and the ways that governmental institutions leave their mark on these initiatives.

It is fitting that writing a book about collaboration should be a truly collaborative endeavor. Our goal in crafting a cowritten book reflects our belief in the synergies that are possible when multiple authors write, read, reflect on, and rewrite text together. We sought to integrate concepts across a diverse array of cases, drawing lessons and identifying patterns from a variety of contexts. Each of the authors has been actively studying collaborative environmental management since the 1990s. Our disciplinary backgrounds range from political science and public policy to environmental planning, environmental science, natural resource management, and organizational theory. We have combined our insights from various disciplines in writing this collaborative volume about collaborative environmental management.

From the outset, we wanted to understand how collaborative processes work and whether government could be an equal partner while often being the party accountable for the decisions reached and the outcomes achieved. With this in mind, we identified cases of collaborative natural resource planning that varied based on whether governments led the effort, encouraged the effort without leading it, or followed an effort that was led by other parties. We then systematically examined the influence of governmental actors and institutions on both the processes and outcomes of these endeavors. In each case, we elaborated on how governmental actors and institutions affected the way issues were defined, the resources available for collaboration, and the organizational processes and structures established. We also considered the environmental and social outcomes realized, and the extent to which these outcomes resulted from government influence and intervention.

We have structured this book in several parts. In the opening chapter, we discuss trends in public administration, public policy, and environmental management leading to increased interest in and emphasis on collaboration. We also identify key themes and issues raised in the scholarly literature, which we use to frame the chapters that follow. In Parts I, II, and III, we describe six cases of collaborative environmental management. We have grouped these cases into three broad types of governmental roles: following, encouraging, and leading. These cases span a wide variety of natural resources, including watersheds, farmland, animal habitats, rivers, forests, and estuaries. In Part IV, we synthesize findings across the cases to explain the ways that government as actor and as institution affects collaborative efforts.

The structure of this volume can be likened to improvisational jazz. As with jazz, early on we articulate the dominant themes that will be featured throughout the performance. The middle portion of the work provides variations on these themes, with each chapter including subthemes and riffs along the way. In concluding the piece, the dominant themes are revisited and replayed, though synthesized in a new way. This metaphor is not limited to the chapters, but also applies to the process through which the book was written. As with improvisation, each author both took the lead and followed others, generated and expressed new ideas, reconceptualized themes using input from collaborators, and built creatively on shared ideas. Thus the dynamics among jazz musicians and the concept of improvisational jazz serve as metaphors for the process of writing this book as well as for the product that has emerged. We hope that students, researchers, practitioners, and other interested readers will find this collaborative effort interesting and thought provoking.

Reading this book in its entirety will give the fullest picture of governmental roles in collaborative environmental management. We also intended, however, to provide lively cases that could stand meaningfully on their own. To this end, each case chapter focuses on a particular question concerning the practice of collaborative environmental management and its relation to government. This arrangement, we believe, makes the book accessible and relevant to individuals, members of nongovernmental organizations, policy-makers, and resource managers who are interested in developing a richer understanding of collaborative environmental management. It also is well-suited for classroom use, where an instructor with limited course time might assign the first and the last two chapters, along with a subset of the case study chapters.

T.K., T.S., J.C.,
K.S.K., C.M., C.T.

ACKNOWLEDGMENTS

This book was made possible through the contributions and assistance of numerous individuals, organizations, and institutions. We thank the many organizations that provided research funding for the case study chapters, including the C. William Swank Program in Rural-Urban Policy at the Ohio State University, the Center for Public Policy and Administration at the University of Massachusetts–Amherst, Denison University, the Edna Bailey Sussman Fund, the National· Science Foundation, the Ohio Agricultural Research and Development Center's Research Enhancement Competitive Grant Program, the Ohio State University School of Natural Resources, the University of Colorado–Denver, and Yale University. Many of the case studies are based on data collected from interviews and surveys. We are grateful to the many individuals who generously took the time to participate in these research activities. This project also benefited from excellent research assistance provided by Jennifer Balkcom, Rachel Brakeman, Travis Masters, Alice Napoleon, Sara Nikolic, Lori Schwarz, Josh Stephens, and Jessica Rajotte Wozniak.

We owe a debt of gratitude to Don Reisman at Resources for the Future for providing valuable guidance and for helping us move the project from inception through to completion. Our text benefited from the exceptional assistance of editorial staff at Resources for the Future. We are grateful to the Center for Environmental Solutions at Duke University for providing support that facilitated the comparative case analysis and to the Massachusetts Institute of Technology, North Carolina State University, the Ohio State University, and the University of Oregon for administrative support that aided in the completion of the volume. This book benefited from the insightful feedback we received on the manuscript from five anonymous reviewers and from Sara Nikolic. We also are thankful to Tom Beierle for the helpful comments he provided as a discussant on a panel at the 2001 Association of Public Policy Analysis and Management research conference, where we presented several of our cases, and for suggesting the metaphor of improvisational jazz.

ABOUT THE AUTHORS

JOANN CARMIN is assistant professor of environmental policy and planning in the Department of Urban Studies and Planning at Massachusetts Institute of Technology. She worked on portions of this volume while a visiting research scholar in residence at Duke University's Center for Environmental Solutions. She conducts research and has authored numerous publications on the role that nongovernmental organizations and other civil society actors play in environmental policy, planning, and sustainable development initiatives in the United States and Eastern Europe.

TOMAS M. KOONTZ is associate professor of environmental and natural resource policy in the School of Natural Resources at the Ohio State University. His primary research areas include collaborative environmental management, citizen participation, and agency policymaking related to forest and land resources in the United States. He is the author of *Federalism in the Forest: National versus State Natural Resource Policy*, as well as articles in several public policy, public administration, political science, and natural resource journals.

KATRINA SMITH KORFMACHER is community outreach coordinator at the University of Rochester's Environmental Health Sciences Center, where she assists community groups in mobilizing science in collaborative policy processes. Her research explores the interactions between scientists and citizens in areas including environmental health, coastal management, farmland preservation, and ecosystem management. She has published in journals such as *Environmental Management, Policy Sciences, American Behavioral Scientist,* and *Coastal Management.*

CASSANDRA MOSELEY IS director of the Ecosystem Workforce program, Institute for a Sustainable Environment, and courtesy assistant professor of planning, public policy and management at the University of Oregon. Her research focuses on community-based forestry in the American West, especially collaboration, federal land-management institutions, and forest work. She has published in the *Journal of Forestry* and *Society and Natural Resources.*

TODDI A. STEELMAN is associate professor of environmental and natural resource policy in North Carolina State University's Department of Forestry. She conducts research on community and public involvement in environmental and natural resource governance. She is the author of numerous articles and book chapters that address aspects of community and public involvement in watershed remediation, land and open space protection, national forest management, community forestry, climate change, and wildfire.

CRAIG W. THOMAS is associate professor of political science at the University of Massachusetts–Amherst, where he is also on the faculty of the Center for Public Policy and Administration. His research focuses on collaborative environmental management and endangered species policy. He is the author of *Bureaucratic Landscapes: Interagency Cooperation and the Preservation of Biodiversity,* as well as numerous articles in public policy, public administration, and political science journals.

CHAPTER 1

GOVERNMENTAL ROLES
IN COLLABORATIVE
ENVIRONMENTAL MANAGEMENT

Like many parts of the country, California faces increasing environmental challenges, including those related to urbanization. Explosive suburban growth during the 1980s and 1990s, much of it spreading out from the urban cores of Los Angeles and San Diego, left a wake of development that decimated many natural plant and animal communities. A significant collaborative effort emerged in the 1990s to save what remained of one such natural community: coastal sage scrub.

Coastal sage scrub is composed of several species of sage plants, shrubs, and seasonal wildflowers. It is not something most people want to save, because it is too dense and prickly to walk in without a well-cleared path; it contains no charismatic species whose names are readily known; and it dries and turns brown in the summer. Yet coastal sage scrub provides habitat for species whose populations had been declining because of development pressures, such as the coastal California gnatcatcher, the San Diego cactus wren, and the orange-throated whiptail lizard. Most landowners, developers, and local government officials were little concerned with coastal sage scrub until the early 1990s, when environmentalists and federal officials began to argue that some wildlife species that relied on coastal sage scrub, particularly the gnatcatcher, should be listed under the federal

Endangered Species Act (ESA). If these species were listed, development might come to a halt on some of the most expensive undeveloped real estate in the country.

The ESA is one of many command-and-control environmental policies created in the 1970s. It tells people what they cannot do, not what they should do, to protect the environment. Although the ESA provides some incentives for collaboration among the public, private, and nonprofit sectors through federal matching grants passed through states to local communities, it does not require collaboration. On the contrary, in many contexts, listing of endangered species has led to considerable conflict and polarization. Moreover, the potential for listing a species as threatened or endangered under the ESA could encourage self-interested individuals to act unilaterally before others do—that is, to alter the habitat of a species that might soon be listed, rather than risk having development opportunities stymied when the ESA's regulatory regime kicks into gear after a species is listed.

Despite the lack of formal incentives, some individuals in the public, private, and nonprofit sectors established a formal collaborative process in the early 1990s to preserve coastal sage scrub before species were listed. Natural Communities Conservation Planning (NCCP) initially was conceived as a state-sponsored program that depended on voluntary participation by landowners, developers, local governments, and public agencies to protect habitat before species were listed under the ESA. Yet some of the NCCP partners recognized that without a federally listed species, many private landowners would not enroll their lands in the program. Small landowners, in particular, lacked an incentive to participate in a lengthy and costly planning process, preferring instead to develop their land in the short term before species were listed. Large landowners, by contrast, sought a longer-term strategy because they did not want to flood the market with new housing. But it was clear that if NCCP remained a voluntary program, with participation occurring primarily among a few large landowners, collaboration would be limited, less habitat would be saved, and more species likely would be listed in the future. With NCCP failing as a voluntary program because of limited enrollments, state officials asked federal officials to level the playing field by listing the coastal California gnatcatcher under the ESA.

Collaboration could have disappeared at that point, as command-and-control regulations under the ESA were implemented. But the NCCP example is interesting precisely because the stringent regulations of the ESA provided an incentive for landowners to collaborate. State and federal officials worked together to develop a special rule that linked the federal ESA to the state-sponsored NCCP, whereby voluntary participation in NCCP became a means for meeting legal obligations under the ESA. Thus, although the federal government had stepped in to assert regulatory authority, it did so primarily to encourage participation in a collaborative process. Listing provided sufficient incentives to encourage a significantly larger group of landowners, developers, local government officials, and others to develop their own collaborative plans to protect coastal sage scrub in the long run under the auspices of the state-run program.

Federal officials faced several options as the coastal sage scrub crisis unfolded. One option was to maintain the status quo and wait for one or more species to be listed under the ESA, without encouraging any stakeholders to work together. Under this option, the courts likely would have played a predominant role as environmentalists, developers, and others filed lawsuits. These lawsuits would open up a wide range of possible outcomes, including moratoriums on development, which would significantly affect the local economy and the political legitimacy of the ESA itself. A second option for federal officials was to participate in collaborative efforts initiated by other stakeholders, such as developers, environmentalists, or local and state governments. A third option was to play an active role by encouraging collaboration in habitat conservation planning. This might have included providing technical and financial assistance or other resources to aid those developing collaborative plans to preserve coastal sage scrub. A final option was for government officials to play a lead role in the emergent collaborative process, by formally convening meetings, developing decision-making procedures, and otherwise taking charge of the collaboration.

Given the wide distribution of coastal sage scrub within many local jurisdictions and on both public and private lands, federal officials believed that large-scale collaboration likely would produce a more encompassing and consistent plan for preserving coastal sage scrub and the species that depended on it. Moreover, with such a diverse array of stakeholders involved, the likelihood of lawsuits was high if collaboration failed. Therefore, federal officials did not simply rely on the ESA's standard provisions. Nor did they take a lead role or follow others as they developed a collaborative process. Instead, they sought to encourage the emergent collaborative effort—NCCP—by designing federal regulations in a way that assisted the effort and by providing technical and financial support.

This opening story illustrates the complex set of roles government has played in a collaborative effort to preserve coastal sage scrub on public and private land in Southern California.[1] By wielding a regulatory threat under the ESA, on the one hand, and providing various kinds of assistance, on the other, federal officials encouraged broader participation among multiple stakeholders in a collaborative process. In this instance, governmental institutions defined the problem to be one of conserving the habitat of a federally listed species and promoted collaboration through regulations that made it possible to provide financial resources. At the same time, government representatives were individual actors who provided technical assistance. This distinction between governmental institutions and actors is important in clarifying the multiple roles government plays in collaboration. Governmental institutions and actors can encourage collaborative environmental management in some instances. In other situations, governments can initiate a collaborative endeavor or can follow the lead of nongovernmental actors. In some cases, governmental institutions establish a legal basis for action in policies that determine the composition of a group, while governmental actors may work as nonspecialist team members, seeking to accomplish collaborative goals and objectives, or may fill the roles of experts and technical advisors.

The central purpose of this book is to analyze how government influences collaborative environmental management through its dual role as actor and as institution. In the search to create better policy, it is vital to understand different governmental roles and how they influence both the process and outcomes of collaboration. The rise of collaborative environmental management is the result of years of policy change, as well as policy experimentation and learning. Understanding governmental roles in collaborative environmental management therefore requires looking at the genesis of public participation in policymaking in the United States, the transition to collaborative approaches to governance, and the influence these trends have had on environmental decision making and management.

FOUNDATIONS FOR COLLABORATION

The movement toward collaboration has roots stretching back to the late 1940s, when U.S. federal agencies began efforts to seek out and incorporate the views and preferences of the public in policy decisions. Before that time, public involvement in policymaking processes occurred on an ad hoc basis at the discretion of each governmental agency. With the institutionalization of the New Deal programs and the rise of larger bureaucratic agencies, however, concerns arose over the public's opportunity to influence decision making. Congress passed the Administrative Procedure Act (APA) in 1946 to set a minimum standard for public involvement in administrative decision-making processes (ACIR 1980). The APA required all federal agencies to publish draft rules in the *Federal Register*, provide public notice and comment periods during the rulemaking process, offer opportunities for group representation during trial-type hearings, and hold public hearings when appropriate (ACIR 1980; Kerwin 1999). Participation in rulemaking has varied widely, however, in part because the process is obscure to most citizens, which allows well-organized interests, particularly corporations, to dominate during the notice and comment period (Golden 1998).

In the 1960s, the United States, along with many other countries, experienced a "participation explosion" (Almond and Verba 1963, 4). As part of this movement, calls for citizen participation in federal policymaking were heeded in the urban poverty programs of the Great Society. Citizens' right to be involved in policy formation was affirmed in the 1960s, and in contrast to the 1940s, a more explicitly participatory approach for the public was adopted. Congress passed the Economic Opportunity Act in 1964, which created the Office of Economic Opportunity (OEO). Two years later, the Demonstration Cities and Metropolitan Development Act (Model Cities) was passed. The OEO legislation provided that programs be "developed, conducted, and administered with maximum feasible participation of residents of the areas and members of the groups served"; Model Cities encouraged "widespread participation" of traditionally underrepresented groups. In contrast to the earlier participation laws, the intent of these initiatives was to accord citizens partnership status and real decision-making power (Stenberg 1972, *192*). But rarely was the participatory ideal of the public working hand in hand with agency bureaucrats realized during these early phases of citizen involvement. Instead, antipathy, alienation, and confrontation characterized citizen involvement in many of the OEO and Housing and Urban Development (HUD) programs (Stenberg 1972; Wengert 1971).

At the same time that public participation efforts were increasing, skepticism was rising over government's ability to deliver community services. Concerns about effective and efficient service provision led to pressures for devolution of authority to state and local organizations in the 1960s and 1970s. As governmental agencies and nongovernmental organizations emerged to deal with social problems at the local level, efforts at devolution laid the foundation for the development of interorganizational and intergovernmental relationships to facilitate service coordination and integration. Community Action, community mental health programs that created centers, model cities, comprehensive health planning, and service integration, set the stage for collaboration in the years to come (Agranoff and Pattakos 1979; Alter and Hage 1993). Building on these nascent structures, the 1980s movement to deinstitutionalize the mentally ill led to community-based care and created the need for interagency coordinating committees (Alter and Hage 1993). Contracting, client orientation, the use of market mechanisms, and other new public management ideas were taken from the private sector and applied to the public sector to improve efficiency (Osborne and Gaebler 1992). These changes transformed the role of government from the sole provider of services to one of many participants working in loose coalitions with private and nonprofit providers. As such, government increasingly has come to be viewed as an equal player in a world of interdependent activity (Mandell 1990, 1999; Kickert et al. 1997).

The consequence of public participation legislation combined with devolution, decentralization, and privatization in the United States has been increased emphasis on collaborative approaches to policy and public management. Under these types of arrangements, *government*, as a formal institution of the state, ceases to hold sole power through command-and-control mechanisms, thereby shifting to *governance*, a process that takes place through the collective action of a variety of participants, all of whom retain some control over decision making or implementation (Milward and Provan 2000). As more "nongovernmental governance" emerges (Milward and Provan 2000, 359), some public policy, public management, and public administration scholars have argued that government no longer is the governing agent over society (Rhodes 1996). The movement away from government and toward governance established a foundation for collaboration along two critical dimensions. One is the rise of interorganizational and network arrangements, which reduced the role of government in public policy, public administration, and public management. The other is the provision for public participation, which increased the role of nongovernmental actors in these processes.

THE EMERGENCE OF COLLABORATIVE ENVIRONMENTAL MANAGEMENT

Similar to the general patterns present in U.S. policy and public decision making, regulatory change and devolution contributed to increased collab-

oration in environmental management. A key piece of legislation contributing to this shift was the National Environmental Policy Act (NEPA).
The NEPA dictated that all federal agencies undertaking any "actions significantly affecting the quality of the human environment" were required to
prepare detailed statements regarding the "environmental impacts of proposed action." The call for public participation in the environmental
impact statement (EIS) process usually was restricted to involvement in
public hearings and scoping processes during the early stages and to solici-
tation of public comments when the draft EIS was released (Westman
1985). According to regulations set forth by the Council on Environmental
Quality, the draft EIS was made accessible to the public for a minimum of
45 days. Agencies were required to respond to each public comment
received (Westman 1985). In addition to the NEPA, the Federal Water Pollution Control Act Amendments of 1972 established the basic structure for
regulating discharges of pollutants into the waters of the United States,
while also providing for public participation in the development, revision,
and enforcement of any regulation (Rosenbaum 1978). Following in the
footsteps of these initial laws, a flurry of environmental and natural
resource statutes with these new provisions for public participation were
passed in the 1970s.[2]

Many programs developed in this era were criticized on several fronts.
First, this so-called participatory legislation did little to allow the public to
substantively influence environmental policymaking. The formalized procedures used to gather input did not lend themselves to spurring policy
change. Second, the scope of citizen involvement was not representative of
society at large (Ethridge 1987). Privileged, directly affected, and well-organized groups were disproportionately involved. Third, in many cases, the
programs were not effectively implemented. Three years after their creation,
the participatory provisions of the Federal Water Pollution Control Act
were critiqued by the Commission on Water Quality as lacking goals,
explicit objectives, and funding, which hampered the ability of the U.S.
Environmental Protection Agency (EPA) to implement or enforce the mandate (Rosenbaum 1978). These results were not unique, as Rosenbaum
(1978, *122*) noted: "The EPA can claim not only the prototype program,
but unfortunately, prototype results." Thus, while the ideals for public
involvement remained lofty, the reality was much less inspiring.

Efforts to promote public participation in federal decision-making
processes declined in the late 1970s and remained low through the mid-
1980s. At the same time, the United States experienced an expansion in

local environmental activity. By the early 1990s, growth in grassroots concern about the environment led to new demands on agencies for alternative means to solving environmental programs, including greater involvement of diverse stakeholder groups in decision-making processes. In response to these pressures, federal agencies began promoting collaborative approaches to environmental management. For example, the EPA embarked on its Community Based Environmental Program in 1994, and the Forest Service moved to integrate collaborative planning into forest management (Carr et al. 1998; Wondolleck and Yaffee 2000). More broadly, 18 federal agencies, including the Natural Resources Conservation Service, National Oceanic and Atmospheric Administration, Department of Energy, Bureau of Land Management, and Fish and Wildlife Service, adopted ecosystem management approaches that included collaboration as a central tenet (Morrissey et al. 1994). In 2000, both the secretaries of agriculture and interior announced a unified policy for land and resource management that focused on watersheds. The policy, Watershed Approach to Land and Resource Management, called for agencies to work with state and local governments, citizens, and other interest groups to coordinate efforts to protect and manage natural resources (USDA and U.S. DOC 2000).

A number of states, as well, have embraced collaborative approaches for addressing environmental issues, in many instances actively promoting the creation and development of collaborative partnerships. State programs have provided technical, educational, financial, and facilitation assistance to support watershed protection. In Ohio, for example, state agencies have given grants to watershed partnerships to develop watershed action plans, and they have created the Ohio Watershed Network to provide technical assistance to scores of watershed groups across the state (Ohio Watershed Network n.d.). The Oregon Plan for Salmon and Watersheds emphasizes community-based action and coordination among multiple stakeholders (Malone 2000). In Florida, the Office of Ecosystem Management spearheads efforts to involve stakeholders in environmental management decisions (Malone 2000). In West Virginia, a state program was created to fund collaborative watershed associations and provide assistance in the form of arranging meetings, providing facilitators, and furnishing technical assistance (Collins et al. 1998).

The ideals for involving the public remain, but it is clear that they have not been fully achieved. To understand the transition from command-and-control to collaborative approaches to environmental management at federal, state, and local levels, it is useful to examine the evolution of policy and management practices within three specific policy arenas: public land management, private land regulation, and water pollution control.

Public Land Management

Public land management in the United States is perhaps the best example of changing environmental management strategies and a transition toward collaboration. Federal land management initially was vested in several agencies at the turn of the twentieth century. Since that time, Congress passed legislation to broaden public involvement in the management of public lands and placed greater pressure on agencies to decentralize their management efforts. Federal policy shifted from land disposal in the eighteenth and nineteenth centuries to expert-led conservation and preservation during the Progressive Era, then to regulations enforced by courts after 1970, and more recently to collaborative endeavors. Each new phase has not abolished the old so much as added a new layer to management approaches.

Two hundred years ago, as the fledgling United States sought to expand its borders after achieving independence, the federal government acquired vast amounts of land. The Louisiana Purchase of 1803 added 560 million acres of land, the Florida Purchase 16 years later added nearly 50 million acres, and the 1840s saw the acquisition of more than 520 million acres from the Oregon Compromise and Mexican Treaty (Cubbage et al. 1993, 285). As the country expanded its borders, policymakers sought to move ownership into private hands. The Homestead Act of 1862, for example, provided a process for citizens to gain title to 160 acres by settling the land and cultivating it for at least five years. The governmental role in managing public lands was to privatize them. Government management focused on selling and giving away these lands to encourage economic development through farming, grazing, and the building of transportation networks such as canals and railroads.

With growing concern about corporate monopoly, resource exploitation, and corruption, Congress passed the General Revision Act in 1891, which allowed the federal government to retain public lands for natural resource values. The Weeks Act of 1911 empowered the federal government to acquire land from private owners for the development of dams and waterways and inclusion in national forests. In that era, the federal government began to assert more authority in regulating public land management.

A new model of public land management emerged in the early twentieth century, riding the crest of the Progressive reform movement. Stressing expert-based management within a structured agency hierarchy, Gifford Pinchot championed a cadre of professional agency employees applying natural science to maximize efficient and wise use of resources (Hays 1959). His efforts led to the creation of the Forest Service. As its leader, Pinchot emphasized efficient use of national forest lands for meeting human demands, rather than ecological preservation. At the same time, preservationists such as John Muir worked to have federal lands set aside in national parks, where they could be preserved for people to enjoy. The dual emphasis on conservation and preservation continued throughout much of the twentieth century, with national forest land management based on the notions of agency experts directing practices to achieve efficient use of natural resources and long-term conservation. In parallel fashion, other federal public lands, such as Bureau of Land Management (BLM) holdings, gradually came to be managed under the same centralized, scientific model by the middle of the twentieth century (Cubbage et al. 1993; Hirt 1994; Mullner et al. 2001). Under this approach, bureaucratic experts increasingly had authority to make management decisions, based largely on natural science knowledge.

Before World War II, many resources were in abundant supply, and public land management agencies were primarily custodial. After the war, however, natural resources, especially timber from private lands, began to run short, and the Forest Service and BLM continued to apply principles of scientific forestry to timber extraction on federal lands (Hirt 1994; Klyza 1996). But even as rapid economic growth fueled rising demand for commodities such as timber and minerals, the public was increasingly interested in using public lands for noncommodity purposes such as recreation and the enjoyment of scenic beauty (Hays 1987). With a wider array of stakeholders expressing interest in public land issues, federal managers faced growing requirements to provide opportunities for public input into management decisions (Davis 2001).

Until the 1970s, Congress had left the Forest Service to implement expert-driven conservation based on general principles and provisions. The Forest Service, however, used this broad authority to pursue intensive timber management just as environmental awareness and the demand for noncommodity uses of the national forests were increasing. After controversies and court cases over timber management in the Monongahela and Bitterroot National Forests, Congress responded with the National Forest

Management Act (NFMA) of 1976, which provided some specific guidelines about how the agency should balance timber management with ecological protection and other land management objectives. The NFMA, along with the NEPA and ESA, created a new body of positive law directing the Forest Service to incorporate environmental provisions. Perhaps most significantly, the NEPA and NFMA expanded the opportunity for the public to affect Forest Service decision making by inviting citizens to comment on proposed forest management plans and environmental analyses of those plans, as well as creating avenues for appealing agency decisions.

Timber harvests declined as these laws took effect and with the recession of the early 1980s. But during the Ronald Reagan and George H. Bush administrations, timber harvests from the Forest Service and BLM rose to record levels. In response, environmental groups that opposed harvest decisions began to use administrative appeals and the courts to ensure that their perspectives were heard or to greatly constrain the actions of the Forest Service and other public land management agencies (Culhane 1981; Hoberg 1997). Environmentalists won major victories in courts in the late 1980s and early 1990s, but the battles among timber interests, environmentalists, and the federal land management agencies over public land management created enormous conflict and administrative deadlock.

Legislation leveled the playing field between timber interests and environmentalists by giving environmentalists a way to be involved in the decision process. But administrative deadlock became unacceptable to some groups, and at the local level, collaborative groups began to emerge to find ways to move beyond conflict (Snow 2001; Brunner et al. 2002). In this new collaborative approach, environmental management shifted to combine multiple stakeholder interests, perspectives, preferences, and knowledge in arriving at collaborative decisions about public land management (Mullner et al. 2001).

Following the lead of these localized community-based collaborations, the Clinton administration began encouraging federal land management agencies in the early 1990s to participate in these collaborative efforts. By the late 1990s, Congress was providing authority and direction to federal agencies to collaborate with each other and with the public. Beginning with the Forest Service's 1998 appropriation, Congress directed the Forest Service and, more recently, the BLM to use collaboration when developing stewardship contracts—mechanisms to implement ecosystem restoration while benefiting rural communities. In 2000, the Secure Rural Schools and Community Self-Determination Act mandated that the Forest Service and

BLM use a collaborative process to set priorities and approve restoration projects using funds from the so-called county payments law. These two recent laws followed a decade of ground-level collaboration and encouragement from agency officials to collaborate with communities and other stakeholders to develop agreements about how to best manage public lands. In part, the drive toward collaborative environmental management was a response to the expanded involvement that had brought deadlock in the courts. Collaboration was seen as a strategy to avoid such impasses. Collaboration continues to vary among agencies, with the least sued (e.g., the National Park Service) being the least responsive to calls for collaboration (Thomas 2003b). Despite such variation, the move toward collaboration has been consolidated as a new generation of resource managers, trained in new ways of thinking, has risen in the ranks of these agencies (see Chapter 2). Although the agency-directed approach has not disappeared, collaborative environmental management of public lands has become more prominent.

Private Land Management

Unlike federal public land management, private land management has been marked by decentralization in the hands of private landowners. Regulatory authority rests predominantly with state and local agencies, with federal agencies playing a more limited role as both a regulator and a provider of funding to encourage particular types of management behavior by private landowners. The primacy of property rights in the United States limits government's role in the regulation and management of private lands, although laws such as the ESA have placed major constraints on how some private lands are managed. Local, state, and federal programs also have encouraged collaboration in the management of private lands, primarily through financial incentives.

Government's role in private land management has varied over time. Taking a laissez-faire approach in the eighteenth and nineteenth centuries, the federal government shifted in the twentieth century to increasingly shape private land management through command-and-control regulations and technical and financial assistance. By the end of the twentieth century, collaborative approaches became much more common as public officials realized the limits of command-and-control regulations in addressing some environmental problems.

During the nineteenth century, federal regulation of private land was virtually nonexistent. Federal policy focused on privatizing the public domain, not regulating private landowners or encouraging good stewardship practices. Instead, state and local laws regulated land use. In addition, common-law notions of nuisance limited landowners' actions in some cases. A nuisance is an intentional or unintentional act that interferes with the ability of others to enjoy the reasonable use of their lands or with the health, safety, or welfare of the community as a whole. Before the implementation of federal environmental legislation in the 1970s, court interpretations of nuisance under common law were the most important federal limitation of behavior on private lands.

Hunting statutes provided the first significant federal regulation of management practices on private land. During the nineteenth century, state governments typically owned wildlife, which meant that state laws governed wildlife use and management on private lands. The state ownership doctrine was challenged repeatedly in court during the nineteenth century, but it was not seriously eroded until the twentieth century. The Lacey Act (1900) was arguably the first serious challenge to the state ownership doctrine. It prohibited the interstate transportation of any game killed in violation of state law and allowed states to prohibit the importation of game killed lawfully in other states. This was followed by the Migratory Bird Act (1913), which declared all migratory game and insect-eating birds to be under federal protection and regulation. Many more laws asserting federal supremacy over wildlife policy followed, culminating with the Endangered Species Act in 1973, which provided for species management on both public and private lands. The ESA placed far-reaching constraints on private land use with provisions limiting habitat modification. Although the ESA later afforded important incentives for collaboration, it initially appeared to be just another in a long line of regulatory prohibitions telling private landowners and those using private lands what they could not do.

In addition to regulations, the federal government developed programs to provide technical and financial assistance to landowners to help them become better stewards of the land. After the Dust Bowl of the 1930s, the Soil Conservation Service, now called the Natural Resources Conservation Service (NRCS), became the primary organization for delivering such technical assistance to farmers and ranchers. The NRCS does not have regulatory authority as the EPA does. Instead, it collaborates with private landowners and local governments, such as resource conservation districts, to implement stewardship practices. Unlike regulatory agencies, technical assistance agencies long have relied on collaboration as a means for achieving programmatic goals.

State governments also shape management practices on private lands through regulation and technical and financial assistance. Some states, such as California, have promulgated more stringent regulations than the federal government. Other states, such as Ohio and Colorado, seek to influence local land use through financial incentives. Ohio uses incentives to encourage collaboration in the preparation of plans to preserve agricultural land (see Chapter 5). In Colorado, a quasistate agency provides funding for open space protection as long as proposals meet requirements that include collaboration in the creation and implementation of proposed projects (Steelman 2000). Many western state governments have enacted comprehensive forest practice statutes to regulate private lands (Cubbage et al. 1993). State governments also delegate zoning authority to local governments because local governments do not have sovereign status in the United States.

Hence the exercise of local land-use control must be based on state authorization. Private landowners who seek to challenge local zoning ordinances must press their cases against state governments in court. In such cases, courts must decide whether the land-use law constitutes a regulation or a taking under the Fifth Amendment. If the law is deemed to prevent harm to the public, then courts typically consider it to be a regulation, and thus a permissible use of policy power to regulate private land under common law. On the other hand, if a court finds that land-use law provides a public benefit, rather than prevents harm, then it becomes a taking that requires just compensation. Thus far, there have been few takings cases that have limited land-use laws, but several states have developed takings statutes. Although these cases and statutes have had limited effects to date in terms of rolling back land-use restrictions, they have nevertheless concerned local, state, and federal officials, who must now think more carefully about the limits of their regulatory authority on private lands.

Within this context, collaborative environmental management has become increasingly attractive to public officials and private landowners. Federal statutes such as the ESA provide an incentive for multiple stakeholders to collaborate at the local level to avoid more stringent and inflexible regulations imposed from above (see Chapter 4). Many government and nongovernment officials have recognized the limits of command-and-control regulations in other situations (see Chapter 3). Not only have command-and-control regulations not effectively addressed some environmental problems, especially those requiring site-specific knowledge or adoption of rapidly changing technology, but their very existence is potentially threatened by takings legislation and court decisions (John 1994). Moreover, the popularity of such regulations has been undermined by horror stories in the press about their effects on jobs and the economy. With regard to endangered species, for example, former Interior Secretary Bruce Babbitt referred to such horror stories as "environmental train wrecks," which might ultimately lead Congress to weaken the Endangered Species Act itself. Therefore, Babbitt developed new incentives to encourage private landowners to develop collaborative habitat conservation plans that would protect species before such "train wrecks" occurred. For public officials facing the limits of regulations, and for private landowners seeking more discretion on how to manage their lands, collaboration seemed increasingly promising in the 1990s.

Water Pollution Control

For most of U.S. history, controlling water pollution was left to states and localities. In a nation viewed as having boundless natural resources, little interest in expending federal resources to curb pollution existed. Economic growth and development took precedence over pollution reduction, and states and localities were not eager to set controls that would discourage industries from locating in their jurisdictions. Beginning in the 1970s, water pollution control gradually was centralized at the federal level. In more recent years, greater authority has devolved back to states and localities to address their water pollution problems, thereby creating more opportunities for participation in decision making at the local level.

The earliest water law in the United States was based on common-law principles such as riparian rights, the nuisance doctrine, public trust, and the prohibition against government taking private property without compensation (Rose 1983). Under these principles, in the eastern United States, rights to water arose from owning riparian land, so disputes about water were seen as disagreements between property owners based on their expectation of "reasonable use" of the water flowing by their property (Rose 1983, 307). The nuisance doctrine could be invoked when water pollution caused a "substantial and unreasonable interference with the use and enjoyment of one's property" (Rose 1983, 315). That is, a downstream property owner could sue an upstream discharger for damages suffered as a result of pollution.

Relying on common law to address water quality issues had obvious logistical problems. Because the effects on any one downstream user were generally smaller than the benefits that accrued to the discharger, the affected parties did not have the incentives, nor often the resources, to file suit. Also, it was often more efficient to treat wastes in large-scale plants than for each discharger to treat its own wastes. Addressing pollution through individual cases did not imply a standard level of water quality among regions, nor was there any provision for transmedia pollution. Therefore, some kind of regional water quality authority was needed to manage water resources (Kneese and Schultze 1975).

Water law developed to reflect the public interest in clean water. Over time, local, state, and finally the federal government became involved in protecting water quality. The first federal law addressing water pollution was the 1899 Rivers and Harbors Act (33 USC 402–413), which declared it illegal to discharge refuse into navigable waters without a permit from the secretary of the army (Patrick 1992).

After World War II, public interest in cleaner water grew. The postwar economic boom contributed to substantial increases in pollution, while at the same time creating additional leisure time and opportunities for people to engage in outdoor recreational activities. As a result, citizens began calling attention to environmental problems and demanding a greater governmental role in solving them (Davis 1998). At this time, the federal government's primary role was to provide technical assistance and funding to states, which generally retained a laissez-faire approach to regulating pollution. For example, the Water Pollution Control Act of 1948 (33 USC 466) and its amendments gave primary responsibility for water pollution control to the states, sponsored research on water quality, and authorized federal construction grants for municipal waste treatment facilities. It was not until the Water Quality Act of 1965 (PL 89–234), however, that interstate water quality standards were established. This attempt at federal water quality protection was viewed widely as ineffective (Patrick 1992; Freeman 2000; Lamb 1980; Kneese and Schultze 1975).

A new governmental role was evident in significant amendments to the Water Pollution Control Act in 1972 and 1977, which became commonly known as the Clean Water Act (Freeman 1990). In addition to including public involvement provisions, the central feature of the Clean Water Act's water quality protection strategy was effluent control through the National Pollution Discharge Elimination System (NPDES). Under this system, all point sources of pollution into navigable waters must have effluent permits. Point sources are "discrete, identifiable" sources of pollution, such as "industrial or municipal discharges" (Lamb 1980, 83). An effluent permit lists the pollutants to be discharged, along with average and maximum daily limits for each, a compliance schedule, monitoring and reporting provisions, and an expiration date no more than five years after issuance (Evans 1994; Rose 1983). The NPDES is overseen by the EPA, but most states have qualified to administer their own NPDES permit programs (Evans 1994; Freeman 1990). Thus water quality protection historically has focused on control of point sources through permits established by state and federal agencies. Assigning permits based on individual point-source emissions, rather than establishing ambient water quality, encourages polluters to act independently rather than to collaborate. Because polluters are held responsible only for their own effluent discharges, not the cumulative and collective degradation of the water body, they have no incentive to work together.

In recent years, the cumulative importance of nonpoint sources of pollution has been increasingly recognized (Patrick 1992). Nonpoint sources are those that cannot be traced to a single source; these include agricultural, urban, and road pollutant runoff (Evans 1994). The 1987 Clean Water Act Amendments, in Section 319, required states to prepare nonpoint-source management programs (Evans 1994; Patrick 1992). Although significant steps were made toward controlling nonpoint-source pollution and conducting comprehensive basinwide planning, these efforts were technically and politically more difficult than point-source control (Freeman 1990).

Several things account for this difficulty. First, agricultural and other land-use practices, particularly plowing and fertilizing, are major contributors to nonpoint-source pollution. The EPA historically has not been involved in directly regulating agricultural practices. Local governments are responsible for regulating changes in land use, including conversion of forested or agricultural land to development. Such conversion is a major cause of nonpoint-source pollution (Barker 1990). Atmospheric inputs of pollution, especially nitrogen, are increasingly recognized as a cause of eutrophication, but the Clean Water Act does not regulate airborne pollutants (Tripp and Oppenheimer 1988). Thus the act does not provide for the effective control of three significant sources of water pollution that were regulated by separate agencies: agriculture, development, and atmospheric deposition. Subsequent environmental policy changes have been aimed at facilitating more comprehensive management of water resources, with collaboration as one means to do so.

One area in which particular attempts have been made to integrate management efforts is the coastal zone. The federal Coastal Zone Management Act of 1972 encouraged states to develop comprehensive coastal management plans (Archer and Knecht 1987). The states' coastal program authority is limited to the coastal zone, so these management programs seldom have influence over activities in the upper watersheds, even though such activities may be significant sources of estuarine pollution. This challenge is compounded when the watershed includes land in two or more states. Within a single state, multiple agencies dealing with issues such as water quality, fisheries, habitat, and transportation may have jurisdiction within the coastal zone (Lawrence 1988; Beatley et al. 2002; Cicin-Sain and Knecht 2000). Thus even in coastal areas included under relatively comprehensive coastal zone management programs, many different regulatory frameworks apply to the various activities and impacts within the watershed.

These challenges have led to increasing efforts to implement collaborative watershed management. Several programs have sought to encourage comprehensive, collaborative planning and actions for water resources. For example, the Great Lakes Remedial Action Planning process prescribes using an "ecosystem approach" to restore beneficial uses to 43 "areas of concern," with substantive public and industry participation across multiple jurisdictions (MacKenzie 1996). The National Estuary Program provides for state and federal partnering to involve managers, scientists, and stakeholders in creating comprehensive plans to protect critically threatened estuaries (see Chapter 6). Across the nation, the federal EPA and state agencies increasingly are focusing on improving ambient water quality by encouraging stakeholder participation and community involvement in watershed planning (see Chapter 7).

CHARACTERISTICS OF COLLABORATIVE ENVIRONMENTAL MANAGEMENT

Across a wide range of environmental arenas, the paradigm of expertise-based, scientific management of public lands is evolving to include collaborative environmental management. Even where government officials have regulatory authority over private land, they are now working in more collaborative ways in many parts of the country. Further, the transboundary challenges associated with diffuse water pollution have begun to eclipse traditional command-and-control models of pollution control as more collaborative approaches to regulation, especially with respect to water resources, emerge in numerous jurisdictions.

Whether these efforts are called community-based environmental management (Kenney and Lord 1999), collaborative conservation (Brick et al. 2001), community-based initiatives (Brunner et al. 2002), grassroots ecosystem management (Weber 2003), participatory natural resource management (Vira and Jeffrey 2001), partnering (Leach et al. 2002), co-management (Singleton 2000), or ecosystem management (Cortner and Moote 1999), a common theme is collaboration among or between different stakeholder groups as a means for airing diverse viewpoints and generating information that will address increasingly complex environmental problems. Rather than government solely regulating the actions of private parties or managing publicly owned resources, collaborative environmental management implies that government shares decision-making power and authority with other stakeholders.

Collaboration can be led or encouraged by governmental actors and institutions or by citizens and nongovernmental groups. Across these configurations, collaborative environmental management can take many different forms. For instance, government participation in collaborative efforts may or may not include legally binding outcomes, depending on the purposes of the group. With habitat conservation planning under the ESA (see Chapter 4), collaborative groups develop plans to manage land-use activities in a specified area; these plans are formally adopted by the U.S. Fish and Wildlife Service, which issues regulatory permits that allow activities covered by these plans. In other cases, such as Ohio's Farmland Preservation Task Forces (see Chapter 5) and the Darby Partnership watershed effort (see Chapter 3), a collaborative group does not possess binding legal authority, but the group nevertheless strives to effect changes in both environmental and social conditions.

Collaborative environmental management addresses some of the gaps and problems found in traditional approaches to regulation. A number of scholars, however, have raised concerns about the performance and appropriateness of such efforts. For example, the environmental outcomes of collaboration may be less protective of natural resources than under traditional efforts, especially if consensus decision making leads to a "lowest common denominator" decision (Coglianese 1999). This can put government officials in the awkward position of having to either enforce a policy they believe is flawed or overturn a collaborative decision (Rhoads et al. 1999). Some fear that collaborative decision making may provide federal regulatory agencies with an excuse to abdicate their power over environmental protection (Kenney 1999; Coggins 1998). This could lead to government policymaking being co-opted by special interests (McCloskey 1996). Moreover, collaboration emphasizing local stakeholders may not adequately represent broader interests in matters of national scope (Coggins 1998; McCloskey 1996). Even within a local community, groups such as the poor or minorities are often left out of a collaborative process.

Nevertheless, a wide variety of people, from policymakers and scholars to community members and grassroots activists, promote collaborative environmental management as a means to transcend political boundaries, manage environmental conflicts, and address complex problems that have not been solved by traditional means (Kenney and Lord 1999; Weber 2003; Vira and Jeffrey 2001; Leach et al. 2002; Singleton 2000; Brick et al. 2001; Cortner and Moote 1999). Furthermore, many recommend collaboration as a way to formulate more locally relevant policies and include diverse interests and values in decision making. In a wide range of settings, governmental agencies have come to recognize the importance of integrating community knowledge, skills, values, and views into environmental decision making and management. The resultant proliferation of collaborative approaches raises the issue of how to think about government's role in collaboration and how its influence imprints such efforts.

In this volume, collaborative environmental management is explored as an application of the general concept of collaboration. Collaboration is a process in which diverse stakeholders work together to resolve a conflict or develop and advance a shared vision (Gray 1989). In collaborative efforts, stakeholders come together to gain a more comprehensive understanding of problems and implement strategies to address important issues. Whereas traditional participation has connoted involvement in scoping issues, commenting on plans, or attending public meetings, collaboration strives for more integrated involvement of diverse groups of stakeholders in the initiation, creation, implementation, and evaluation of alternatives that they have identified. Moreover, collaboration promotes equal decision making among all stakeholders, at least in theory (Gray 1989). Throughout the remainder of this text, we use the term *collaborative environmental management* to refer to collaboration in the management of environmental issues. We take an inclusive approach and therefore regard the initiation, planning, implementation or generation, and evaluation of alternatives as integral aspects of environmental management.

GOVERNMENTAL INFLUENCES ON COLLABORATIVE PROCESSES AND OUTCOMES

Collaborative environmental management is based on diverse groups, including public, private, and nonprofit stakeholders, working together to address environmental issues. Given that the traditional role of government is as expert, manager, or enforcer, collaboration implies significant changes in the way that governmental agencies and actors engage in environmental management. To some, it may be paradoxical to imagine a governmental role in collaborative environmental management as anything other than "getting in the way" or "getting out of the way." After all, collaborative environmental management often is described as a grassroots, bottom-up endeavor—the antithesis of government-directed management and regulation. But governments rarely leave the picture entirely; in fact, they often play a central role in the creation or development of a collaborative effort.

In recent years, numerous case studies and a few broad survey analyses have described a wide variety of collaborative environmental management efforts across the country, examining group activities, barriers to success, and accomplishments (Kenney and Lord 1999; Weber 2003; Vira and Jeffrey 2001; Leach et al. 2002; Singleton 2000; Brick et al. 2001; Cortner and Moote 1999). Although such research provides a large and growing mass of data, little progress has been made in understanding the role of key players, particularly governments, in collaborative environmental management. Where research has considered the role of government, it has focused on how agencies and institutional constraints pose barriers to collaboration (e.g., Grumbine 1994; Cortner and Moote 1999; Meidinger 1997). Analysts have largely neglected the diversity of roles—some more positive than others—that government can play in collaborative environmental management. As a result, a number of important questions remain unanswered about the extent to which government is able and willing to share power in environmental management, the means through which government actions and efforts facilitate or hinder collaboration, and the extent to which collaboration leads to better environmental outcomes. It is unclear whether collaborative environmental management has fostered achievement of the aspirations embodied in previous attempts to involve the public or delegate authority to nongovernmental actors in decision making.

Government as Institution and as Actor

In order to understand governmental roles, it is important to distinguish between government as institution and as actor, and to consider key factors that influence collaborative processes and outcomes. Institutions are described differently by different scholars (Hall and Taylor 1996; Crawford and Ostrom 1995; Peters 1999). Building on historical institutionalist and rational choice definitions, we define institutions to be structures, rules, laws, norms, and sociocultural processes that shape human actions (Thelen and Steinmo 1992; Hall 1986; Peters 1999). For our purposes, governmental institutions are the structures, processes, rules, and norms of the administrative state. Structures, rules, and laws formalize the constraints and incentives facing participants by prohibiting, requiring, or permitting specified actions (Ostrom et al. 1994; Crawford and Ostrom 1995). Although norms and sociocultural processes often are informal or implicit, they too shape behavior by establishing parameters for what forms of action are acceptable (March and Olsen 1989; Peters 1999).

Governmental actors are the flesh-and-blood employees, elected officials, and other people in government who take action within the context of institutions. They are not simply individuals who carry out the formal rules or embody the social norms of the agencies within which they work. Actors also have the ability to shape those norms and rules and to act outside of them. Institutions do not entirely constrain actors, although rational choice and historical institutionalism differ in how much autonomy they attribute to actors (Smith 1992; Hall and Taylor 1996). Typical governmental actors include civil servants, political appointees, and elected officials at the federal, state, and local levels. As participants, governmental actors bring their individual perspectives, personalities, skills, and needs to collaborative groups and endeavors. Governmental actors can choose to take action in certain collaborative processes, including challenging the rules and norms of their organizations to enhance or reduce collaboration.

Governmental actors and institutions, together or separately, constitute governmental roles in a particular collaborative effort. The relative influence of governmental actors and institutions is likely to vary from one collaborative case to another. In some cases, governmental actors might critically affect collaboration; in others, institutions may dominate; in yet others, both could be crucial; and in some cases, neither may make a substantial impact. Governmental actors and institutions are also interdependent, in that actors shape institutions and institutions shape actors. Thus governmental roles in a particular case may be quite complex, particularly if the actors are seeking to change institutions in ways that promote or constrain collaboration.

Factors Influencing Collaborative Processes and Outcomes

To understand how governmental actors and institutions influence collaborative environmental management, we must carefully examine the factors that are thought to affect processes and outcomes. Previous research examining collaboration has identified a number of critical factors. These can be grouped into three broad categories: issue definition, resources available for collaboration, and group structure and decision-making processes.

Issue Definition. Issue definition refers to how an issue is framed, what set of solutions is seen as feasible, and the scale of the issue. Scholars have long noted that the way a problem is presented and understood lays a foundation for who is likely to become involved, what forces will come into play, and which solutions will be given serious consideration (Schattschneider 1960). Framing a particular problem one way, such as "there is too much pollution in the river," rather than another, such as "pollution control along the river is not being properly implemented," establishes a basis for the range of action and solutions that are relevant and appropriate (Snow and Benford 1988). The way that a problem is defined and framed can affect potential stakeholders' interest level and willingness to participate, as well as the way that a collaborative group approaches environmental management (Moseley and KenCairn 2001).

Issue definition also includes the biophysical scale of the effort, which is intertwined with the definition of the problem and the range of possible solutions. One collaborative endeavor might have the goal of changing who participates in federal land management; another may tackle the challenge of remedying water quality in a degraded watershed. The biological and physical characteristics of the landscape that are linked to problem definition can affect collaborations in a number of ways. For example, whether pollution is concentrated or diffuse can greatly affect the likelihood that collaborative partnerships will emerge (Lubell et al. 1998). If pollution is diffuse, the ability of concerned parties to recognize the problem and organize around it may be more limited than if the problem is concentrated in one geographic locale. Another important biophysical element is geographic size. Thomas (1999) describes how collaborative efforts operating on a large bioregional scale fell apart as potential participants faced a half-day's drive to attend meetings.

Resources for Collaboration. Resources for collaboration are the second set of factors that shape collaborative processes and outcomes. A number of researchers have argued that group resources are critical in determining what collaborative partnerships can achieve (MacKenzie 1996; Yaffee et al. 1996). In a comparative case study of two collaborative groups working on similar water quality issues, Steelman and Carmin (2002) argue that strategies, activities, and success were tied closely to group resources. Three types of resources commonly discussed in writings on collaboration are human, technical, and financial.

Human resources refer to the personnel and the skills, abilities, experience, and level of effort they bring to collaboration. As in other endeavors involving human interactions, people and personalities matter in collaborative environmental management. Collaborative partnerships often hinge on the ability of leaders to facilitate group processes to build trust, reciprocity, and a supportive environment for members (Kellogg 1998; Moseley 1999; Thomas 1999; Steelman and Carmin 2002). In addition, volunteer and paid staff members are crucial to such efforts (Wondolleck and Yaffee 2000).

Technical resources consist of information and knowledge about the natural resource and its management. Both scientific and local time-and-place data are important resources that can affect interactions among public and private stakeholders. For example, because the Applegate River Watershed Council was led by a geologist, the collaboration could easily engage and work with government scientists on technical problem solving. In contrast, other nearby watershed councils lacking internal technical capacity relied more heavily on government technical advice and had more difficulty in developing viable restoration programs (see Moseley 1999). Technical consultations and expertise can be contracted from entities external to the collaborative group or may be found among actors within the group itself (Steelman and Carmin 2002).

Financial resources refer to funds obtained from members, fund-raising activities, and grants from governmental and nongovernmental sources. Funding has been described as one of the most important resources shaping group activities (Yaffee et al. 1996). In some instances, funding comes from individual and organizational donors that place requirements on how the funds may be used; in other instances, the issues addressed and the type of expenditures incurred are at the discretion of the collaborative group. The amount of funds available and the way they are disbursed to the collaboration will influence what types of projects can be undertaken and the extent to which group efforts can be directed toward environmental rather than fund-raising activities.

Group Structure and Decision-Making Processes. Group structure refers to the types of organizational or administrative arrangements that have been established, including hierarchy, authority, reporting relations, and division of labor. Collaborative groups develop a variety of structures, ranging from loose federations to groups with tightly controlled membership, and from ad hoc committees with minimal administrative capacity to formal organizations with full-time staff working within a well-defined administrative framework. Structure and the leadership roles that are established are important because they can facilitate or impede relationships among organizations and actors. Tightly controlled groups, for example, may need approval from their membership before working with other groups and agencies; informal groups may have a desire to collaborate but may not have sufficient structural capacity to promote an ongoing relationship.

Collaborative groups can structure and coordinate activities through a number of means, primary among them convening group meetings. Some groups choose to structure workloads by creating subgroups (e.g., standing or ad hoc subcommittees) assigned to particular tasks, whereas others conduct activities primarily through general meetings (Koontz and Korfmacher 2000). Although delegation has many positive qualities, it also may allow important actions to be taken without full consideration by the broader group (Bonnell 2001). Some collaborative structures may be limited in the types of decision-making processes that can be delegated. For instance, the Forest Service often is criticized for its traditional chain-of-command bureaucracy, which constrains the ability to engage in collaborative activity. In contrast, agencies with a looser organizational structure, such as the BLM, are more flexible in the decisions they can delegate within a collaborative activity (Thomas 1999).

Organizational decision-making processes are used to select participants, coordinate activities, and aggregate individual preferences into group decisions. Selecting who constitutes a group is an important task. When inviting citizens to interact with public officials, selection methods may affect the degree to which a group represents the broader community's interests, as well as the degree to which public officials will be responsive to the group's policy recommendations (Pierce and Doerksen 1976).

Collaborative groups in action must aggregate individual input into collective decisions about setting goals, choosing strategies, obtaining and allocating resources, and developing plans and policy recommendations. Many collaborative environmental management scholars, including Wondolleck and Yaffee (2000), have stressed the importance of consensus decision rules in helping find successful solutions and build social capital. But group decisions requiring consensus can lead to policy recommendations on which a group can readily agree, rather than bold, innovative approaches that may be difficult for the group to develop but could lead to more effective outcomes (Coglianese 1999; Blomquist and Schlager 1999). In practice, groups may use a wide range of aggregation rules, including consensus, modified consensus, majority voting, and supermajority voting (typically where two-thirds or three-quarters of voters must support the proposal). Group participants may also "agree to disagree," which provides a respectful means to avoid bringing contentious issues to a vote. In some cases, decisions by collaborations are binding; in other cases, they are not. Collaborative groups sometimes serve as advisory councils, rather than as true decision-making bodies. In still other instances, citizens have no substantive input or power sharing, with their involvement being nothing more than symbolic efforts designed to give the appearance of collaboration (Arnstein 1969).

Collaborative Outcomes

Investigating the role of government and the influence of these actors and institutions on collaborative environmental management requires appropriate measures of outcomes.[3] In this book, our measures include both environmental and social outcomes. Environmental outcomes include such things as planning documents, restoration projects, pollution reduction, and environmental education. Social outcomes refer to social capital and civic engagement, including increased trust among stakeholders, improved relationships between formerly adversarial parties, and strengthened community capacity to engage in self-governance and community problem solving.

Collaboration may enhance environmental outcomes because it provides a means for diverse stakeholders to coordinate their behavior and support collective actions to address environmental concerns (Wondolleck and Yaffee 2000; Kenney and Lord 1999). As John (1994) and others have emphasized, legal strategies such as command-and-control regulation and permitting are not well suited to problems of waste runoff, soil erosion, and other forms of natural resource degradation involving many dispersed decision makers. Instead, for multiple decision makers conducting myriad activities across a landscape, collaboration allows the possibility of integrating multiple viewpoints and knowledge sources to protect and enhance environmental quality (Weber 1998). In instances in which environmental solutions require local, voluntary implementation, support from local stakeholders is essential for effective and efficient results (Brunner et al. 2002). Collaboration may be valuable in providing time- and place-specific information to foster better environmental management.

Despite widespread agreement about the potential of collaboration, knowledge is limited about the degree to which collaborative environmental management fosters improved ecological conditions in practice. Because of long time horizons, multiple scales, and complex interactions among ecosystem components, measuring causal relationships in environmental quality represents perhaps the greatest challenge in evaluating collaborative environmental management (Brunner 2000; Conley and Moote 2003).[4] In many instances, groups do not monitor the environmental quality effects or outputs of their activities, focusing instead on tangible environmental management outcomes. Given this limited knowledge, collaborations typically focus on tangible products such as the formation or implementation of plans, projects, standards, and activities associated with environmental improvement, rather than on ecological measures of environmental quality.

In addition to enhancing environmental conditions, collaborative environmental management may alter and improve government relationships with nongovernmental organizations and citizens, as well as with other agencies. Social outcomes involve benefits both to participants and to broader populations through increased abilities to solve problems and the experience of working cooperatively. Collaborative environmental management may encourage faith in government and its efficacy in problem solving (Cortner and Moote 1999; McGinnis et al. 1999) while, at the same time, building local capacity to engage constructively in self-governance. Moreover, it may help build trust and foster improved relationships between formerly adversarial parties (Beierle 1999; Buckle and Thomas-Buckle 1986).

Networks and legitimacy are two additional social outcomes that can arise from collaboration. The repeated meetings, discussions, and activities involved in collaboration may foster the development of social networks. The presence of networks of people dealing with related issues can be a crucial asset, enhancing group efficacy (Lynn 1987; Moseley 1999) as well as a group's ability to garner support throughout the broader community (Press 1998). Legitimacy results when a collaborative group is seen as an appropriate and credible actor (Gray 1989). Legitimacy affects the ability of a group to mobilize resources to implement plans and policies; groups out of step with the broader community may face difficulty in gaining support for their activities. Because relations and perceptions endure, networks and legitimacy often are social outcomes of a given collaboration, and once established, they can serve as a basis for future collaborations.

Rigorous evaluation of the social outcomes of collaboration is challenging. Participants in collaborations typically focus on practical activities and do not expend resources to monitor or measure social processes and relations. Those groups that attempt to monitor social outcomes find that these, too, can be difficult to measure because of conflicting meanings and interpretations of concepts such as trust, self-reliance, and cooperation (Beierle 1999).

FOCUS AND ORGANIZATION OF THE BOOK

With more governmental actors and institutions at the federal, state, and local levels becoming engaged in collaborative environmental management, a better understanding is needed of the roles they play in such efforts. Previous research suggests that issue definition, resources, and group structure and decision-making processes can influence the nature of a collaborative endeavor. Little consideration has been given, however, to the influence that governmental actors and institutions have on these factors. The chapters that follow focus on how governmental actors and institutions affect these three sets of factors and, consequently, the direct and indirect influences that government has on both the processes and the outcomes of collaboration.

Chapters 2 through 7 present case studies illustrating different governmental roles in collaborative environmental management. Because governments at all levels, federal, state, and local, can play myriad roles, we did not seek to catalog all of the possible permutations. The case studies were purposely selected to represent a discrete range of roles, grouped as government-followed, government-encouraged, and government-led collaborative efforts. To facilitate comparison, all of the cases focus on the planning dimension of environmental management, and each considers how government as actor and as institution influences problem definition, resources for collaboration, structure and processes of collaboration, and outcomes from collaboration (see the Methodological Appendix for a more detailed discussion of the case selection and research methods). We rely on systematic approaches to case selection and case analysis to enhance the validity of inferences from data to theory (Geddes 1990; Yin 1994; King et al. 1995). Along the way, each case also addresses a different conceptual question about governmental roles in collaborative environmental management.

Part I of this volume includes two cases of government-followed collaboration, in which governmental institutions set the stage for collaboration, citizens and nonprofit organizations initiated the collaborative efforts, and governmental actors participated to varying degrees in the collaboration. Chapter 2 uses the Applegate Partnership in southwest Oregon to illustrate how government as actor and as institution influences collaboration even when government is following the lead of others. The case study suggests how perceived failures in government policymaking can lead citizens to seek collaboration as a remedy in public forest management. It also examines the types of challenges governmental actors face when they participate in collaborations that seek to change the governmental institutions in which they are embedded.

Chapter 3 discusses the Darby Partnership, in which a nonprofit organization initiated a collaborative process to change an unacceptable status quo, filling a collaborative void left by existing governmental institutions. Although governmental stakeholders participated in the process, questions arose about how much could be achieved when governmental actors were only participants without any institutional influence. This chapter addresses questions regarding the potential benefits and limitations of collaboration that is led by nongovernmental actors with minimal formal commitment from government.

Part II describes two cases of government-encouraged collaboration. Governmental institutions instigated collaboration in these cases, both directly and indirectly. Chapter 4 discusses habitat conservation planning under the ESA. Here the federal government serves as both institution and actor. As institution, the act, its implementing regulations, and court cases have created a baseline set of expectations regarding environmental management on private land, and for local and state agencies. Within this context, federal officials act as participants in habitat conservation planning efforts by providing various forms of assistance to encourage collaborative efforts. Such efforts typically are initiated by nonfederal actors as a means to avoid the more negative consequences of strict command-and-control regulations for species protection under the ESA. This chapter delves into issues related to how government officials wield command-and-control rules in combination with financial and technical assistance to encourage collaboration.

Chapter 5 demonstrates how a state governmental institution—a capacity-building grant in Ohio's Farmland Preservation Planning Program—can affect collaborative land-use planning efforts at the county level, and how local governmental actors play key roles in collaborative processes and outcomes. It also assesses whether grant funding from institutional sources can buy collaboration.

Part III examines examples of government-led initiation of collaboration. Here governmental actors and institutions both played dominant roles in the collaborative efforts. In Chapter 6, government played an active role by defining the issues, providing resources, and establishing group structure and processes for a collaborative federal-state initiative under the National Estuary Program in North Carolina. This chapter also considers whether science-based collaborative planning can overcome the divergent agendas of different governmental agencies, interest groups, and members of the public.

Chapter 7 illustrates the most active governmental role in collaborative environmental management in this book, with governmental actors taking the lead in developing a collaborative group to create water quality standards for the Animas River. This chapter also reflects on whether or not government-led, community-based environmental management is an oxymoron.

Part IV provides a synthesis and discussion of lessons drawn from the case chapters. Chapter 8 recaps the diversity of findings from each case, moving from government-followed to government-encouraged to government-led efforts. It also compares variations in governmental roles in and influence on issue definition, resources, and group structure and decision making across the cases. This analysis suggests that government, whether it follows, encourages, or leads, leaves a heavy imprint on collaborative efforts. Because governmental actors and institutions featured prominently in most facets of collaboration, these patterns raise questions about how far we have come from the failed versions of public involvement models developed in the 1960s and 1970s, whether government is sharing power, and the extent to which collaborative efforts are achieving integrated and effective approaches to environmental management. These issues are addressed further in Chapter 9, which considers the implications of the findings from the case analyses and discusses the choices and challenges faced by governmental institutions and actors as they seek to realize the potential of collaborative environmental management.

PART I

GOVERNMENT AS FOLLOWER

CHAPTER 2

CITIZEN-INITIATED COLLABORATION

The Applegate Partnership

The government, as both actor and institution, played a significant role in shaping the Applegate Partnership and its accomplishments. Yet these roles were anything but straightforward or simple. Viewed from one angle, governmental participants sat at the table as equal players working alongside others to reach agreements and create change. Although central participants, governmental actors were not conveners or directors, as in the case of the Animas River Stakeholder Group (Chapter 7), nor did they primarily provide funding, as in the case of the Ohio Farmland Preservation Planning Program (Chapter 5). The Applegate Partnership made every effort to make federal personnel equal participants. Nevertheless, the governmental institutions of federal land management still dominated the partnership's efforts. Governmental actors were embedded in federal land management agencies that created particular roles and rules for governmental participants. The larger institutions of federal land management were what the partnership at once had to work within and sought to change. A crisis in these institutions created the impetus for the partnership and, at times, impeded its progress even when the group had reached agreement. This chapter examines the challenges governmental actors face when they participate in collaborations that seek to change the governmental institutions in which they are embedded.

FORMATION OF THE APPLEGATE PARTNERSHIP

The Applegate Partnership first came together in 1992 in the Applegate Valley in southwest Oregon. The Applegate Valley is a 500,000-acre watershed in the Klamath-Siskiyou Mountains, one of the most ecologically diverse regions in the American West (Davis et al. 1997). The watershed has steep mountains and narrow valleys, first settled by Europeans looking for gold in the 1850s and 1860s. Before 1900, considerable land in the valley was given to railroad companies and placed in forest reserves. Because of railroad bankruptcy and corruption, Congress reversed the railroad land grant and restored the lands to the public domain in 1916 (Richardson 1980). Today the Bureau of Land Management (BLM) and the Forest Service manage 70 percent of the land in the watershed.

Large-scale federal timber harvest began in the late 1960s, and local protests against aerial spraying of herbicides associated with clear-cutting quickly followed. Environmental activism against the federal timber program continued throughout the 1970s and 1980s, as it did across the Pacific Northwest, while federal agencies increased harvest at the behest of the White House and Congress. With abundant federal timber, forest products processing industries grew in nearby Medford, Grants Pass, and White City. Because of the requirement that the federal government share its timber revenue with county governments, federal timber harvest supplied county governments in this region with half of their revenue, which enabled county governments to provide services with only limited taxation (Moseley 1999; Jackson County Government 1992).

Tensions built through the late 1980s here and across the Pacific Northwest, as environmentalists actively opposed timber sales and forest plans through appeals and litigation. Environmentalists made use of provisions in the National Environmental Policy Act, the National Forest Management Act, and the Endangered Species Act to force the Forest Service and the BLM to document the impacts of intensive forest management and protect populations of vertebrate species such as the spotted owl and marbled murrelet. As environmentalists won battle after battle in court, the federal government's management plans and timber harvest levels were ruled to be in violation of environmental laws. Timber industry proponents countered that environmentalists were threatening the jobs of forest and mill workers. In 1991, the situation grew to crisis proportions. The U.S. 9th Circuit Court enjoined the Forest Service and the BLM to halt all timber harvest in the territory of the northern spotted owl—federal land in the western portions of Oregon, Washington, and northern California—because the Forest Service and the BLM had not developed management plans that would protect the northern spotted owl and other old-growth-dependent species, as required under the Endangered Species Act and the National Forest Management Act (Sher 1993; Yaffee 1994). Public meetings threatened to erupt into violence as frightened forest and mill workers and angry county commissioners confronted protesting environmentalists.

Seeking a way to reduce conflict and manage the forests to restore ecological conditions, Applegate Valley resident Jack Shipley, a longtime environmental activist, began talking with people from neighborhood environmental groups, timber companies, federal land management agencies, and county governments in 1992. After months of shuttle diplomacy, in which Shipley, other residents, and interest group representatives built support for diverse people to come together to develop a new way to manage land in the Applegate Valley, the Applegate Partnership began with a meeting in the fall of that year. By the third meeting, participants had agreed to a vision statement and a structure:

> The Applegate Partnership is a community-based project involving industry, conservation groups, natural resource agencies, and residents cooperating to encourage and facilitate the use of natural resource principles that promote ecosystem health and diversity. Through community involvement and education, this Partnership supports management of all land within the watershed in a manner that sustains natural resources and that will, in turn, contribute to economic and community stability within the Applegate Valley. (Applegate Partnership n.d.)

Early meeting participants created a board of nine members and nine alternates to represent a broad cross section of interests and values. The initial board included two federal land managers, two environmentalists, two timber company employees, a community organizer, and a soil and water conservation district employee. Participants in the early meetings picked board members by consensus, choosing people whom they thought would be able to bridge traditional interest group boundaries. Many were experienced social and environmental activists. The partnership did not have any staff, instead relying on the donated time and resources of volunteer participants and their organizations and agencies.

Because of the extreme political tension around them, participants met in unpublicized meetings for five months to get to know each other and develop a sense of what they were trying to accomplish. After these first months, the group went public, opening the partnership to participation by anyone who was interested and to scrutiny by traditional interest groups across the region involved in the spotted owl crisis.

Partnership participants had a strong sense that open participation was key to their efforts, and they worked hard to be inclusive. The partnership held weekly meetings, alternating between day meetings, which were convenient for people whose participation was related to their jobs, and evening meetings, which were more convenient for people who could not leave work to attend a meeting. Although the partnership had a formal board, membership on the board reflected a commitment to participate more than a right to do so. Participation was open, and the group agreed that all who attended a meeting could sit at the table, regardless of who they were, what they believed, or where they lived, as long as they were willing to consider active management on public lands. Like the Darby Partnership (Chapter 3), the Applegate Partnership eschewed procedural rules and formality. There was no board chair, and initially professional facilitators volunteered their time to facilitate the group. Later, facilitation rotated informally among frequent participants.

Board members and other regular participants represented particular perspectives more than they represented specific organizations or interest-based constituencies (Moseley and KenCairn 2001). Although there was some organizational and interest group representation, the partnership encouraged participants to represent perspectives rather than take positions. The group believed that a key to innovation was bringing people and ideas together in new ways, and members described a philosophy of "leaving positions at the door and bringing only values and interests." Rather than negotiate from extremes toward the middle, the group tried to focus on problem solving and collectively identifying alternatives. Because many participants, especially community residents, did not formally represent others, discussions were often preliminary, and then participants would use social and professional networks to test ideas, identify areas of improvement, and garner support outside the meetings.

In addition to weekly meetings, partnership participants went on frequent field trips. They visited potential project areas and sought examples of management activities from which they might learn. The group found that walking together in the woods helped them discover common ground. Members discovered that they could agree on particular actions on the ground (for example, particular trees to be cut or specific roads to be repaired) more readily than on principles while sitting in a meeting room.

Through meetings and field trips, participants sought to develop a new way to manage the lands of the Applegate Valley. They created management processes that were open, inclusive, and transparent, and included a diversity of participants early in planning and decision-making processes. They sought ways to restore and maintain ecological processes and ensure that the by-products of these efforts would provide maximum ecological benefit.

With these goals in mind, the partnership used the meetings and field trips to develop specific projects that moved them toward more comprehensive land management. They saw early projects as experiments in which they could try new techniques and discover what worked and what did not. They sought to combine local knowledge and values with the technical expertise of the Forest Service and the BLM. One such early project was known as Partnership One. To come to an agreement about which treatments to use, participants visited the project area together and marked trees to be cut or left. The marks were shifted around as ideas changed about how the forest should be managed. Through a series of field trips and meetings, the group reached agreement for this first experiment.

Over time, through the meetings, collaborations, and outreach to community residents who were not active participants, Applegate Partnership participants and other community residents developed social capital—collaborative norms, habits, and skills and social networks—to move beyond federal land management to address collaboratively a wide variety of issues, ranging from private land restoration to county-level land-use planning to agricultural and small-business development. Applegate Valley residents replicated the approach of bringing together diverse people to reach agreement about issues that had heretofore been decided upon by forces beyond their community—or neglected entirely. They were able to do this in part by building dense networks of friendship and acquaintanceship among participants, informal community leaders, and formal political and administrative leaders (Moseley 1999).

GOVERNMENT AS INDIVIDUAL PARTICIPANT

At partnership meetings or on field trips, perhaps the most obvious role of government was that of participant. Federal land management personnel participated in the partnership from the beginning. Even before the first meeting, the partnership founders spoke with government personnel informally to get input about what a collaborative effort might look like and should seek to accomplish. Forest Service and BLM staff initially served as partnership board members, and after the Clinton administration required that they resign from the board because of concerns over the Federal Advisory Committee Act (FACA), they continued to participate actively in meetings and field trips. Some personnel attended meetings regularly; others attended only meetings or field trips related to projects on which they were working. Several more supported the partnership through their work by prioritizing projects that met partnership objectives, even though their meeting attendance was rare.

In early meetings, government employees worked along with other participants to define both the geographic scale and substantive scope of the collaboration. They also provided valuable human resources, such as familiarity with federal land management rules and requirements, knowledge of legal and administrative processes, and technical and scientific expertise. A couple of frequent governmental participants altered their career paths to participate actively in the partnership, providing dedicated time and skills. Another government employee occasionally provided his skills as a trained facilitator along with several other nongovernmental facilitators.

As actors, they did not bring financial resources in cash. They did, however, contribute significant amounts of time. In addition, they made in-kind contributions, such as making meeting space available and providing access to a photocopier to duplicate meeting minutes.

The Applegate Partnership created its own decision-making procedures and coordination mechanisms. Participants, including Forest Service and BLM personnel, designed the group to be egalitarian and democratic, to ensure that all people would have an equal voice. Decision making was by informal consensus. Theoretically, a formal vote of board members could occur as a last resort, but this never happened. On the rare occasion when the partnership considered making a group formal recommendation to a federal land management agency, agency personnel did not participate in the decision-making process.

The group also avoided formal symbols of leaders and followers, such as board or committee chairs. Much of the language and self-image of the group emphasized the notion of equality of participation, such as the group's motto, "Practice trust, them is us." Similarly, participants often talked about all coming together to work through a problem and find a solution. The problems to be solved were concerns not only of industry or environmentalists, but also of agency personnel.

Informal, broad leadership developed in the group, with different people taking on different types of group maintenance roles. One or two people typically made grand suggestions that stimulated innovation; others were skilled at turning these ideas into something workable. Another was good at smoothing ruffled feathers, and others excelled at holding alliances together. Partnership regulars, including government personnel, adopted these roles based on their personal skills and inclinations.

In such a culture, federal government personnel were, in many respects, participants like any others, be they community residents, industry executives, or environmentalists. People from all of these perspectives attended meetings, shared in facilitation, and contributed the time and resources that they or their organizations could bring to bear. As with other participants, the federal officials came to the table with different concerns, levels of commitment, and skills that reflected their varied personalities and life and professional experiences.

GOVERNMENT AS ACTORS EMBEDDED IN INSTITUTIONS

The group made every effort to establish federal land managers as equal players. At the same time, however, federal land managers had formal decision-making authority over federal lands, which they could not legally delegate to the group. The district rangers and other decision makers could listen to people's opinions and recommendations, but decisions over federal land management remained formally in their hands. In addition, the Forest Service and the BLM had strong Progressivist cultures in which trained federal staff were assumed to be experts, possessing scientific expertise and administrative and legal understanding of federal land management, and thus were best suited to make land management decisions for the public good. Finally, the federal land managers had considerable organizational capacity behind them, which other participants did not. The combination of decision-making authority and different types of knowledge put federal land managers in somewhat different positions than other partnership participants. Federal participants were the ones who had to be persuaded to act in agreed-upon ways. In that way, they had a sort of de facto veto power that other participants did not.

This is not to suggest, however, that federal personnel held all the power in the group. Other participants brought skills, relationships, and power to the table. Specifically, nonfederal participants brought a compelling vision, selective political pressure, and viable collaborative alternatives (Moseley 1999).

The partnership offered a compelling vision that held the promise of change after more than a decade of highly stressful and conflict-laden processes. Working together, founders argued, would create solutions that were better than could be created individually and would allow people, including agency personnel, to maintain control of land management. Parts of the vision were repeated often in meetings and informal discussions, particularly when participants got discouraged or questioned the utility of putting so much energy into the partnership. This vision and all that it implied led some government personnel to make a commitment to the partnership's vision, values, and goals, and then work within their agencies to foster change.

Not all governmental participants were readily or consistently responsive to the demands of the partnership, either because they differed philosophically or because they felt pulled by other priorities. In these instances, the partnership along with the larger Applegate community applied both indirect and direct pressure. The partnership drew on extensive sets of social networks to argue credibly that the agencies would either "pay now" by creating inclusive, responsive processes from the beginning or "pay later" through costly and time-consuming legal appeals and civil protests. They pressured agency line officers (decision makers) directly through frequent visits to their offices and phone calls to encourage them to sit down with stakeholders and work through a particular conflict, devising solutions that would meet the needs of citizens and the agency. If a federal staff member was particularly unresponsive, the partnership contacted higher-level agency officials in hopes that they might exert pressure down the chain of command.

Ultimately more important than the ability to offer a compelling vision or apply political pressure was the nongovernmental participants' ability to offer viable alternatives to previous political processes. Limits to change often were institutional rather than due to a lack of adequate incentives for agency personnel. For example, budgeting structures and organizational culture made it difficult for agency staff to collaborate internally or to move away from a focus on timber targets. Instead of merely asking the agency to "just fix it," the partnership argued that they should sit down together and solve both nonagency and agency problems. The partnership developed a culture of good-faith participation in which agencies and communities actively listened and engaged in problem solving rather than taking positions or assigning blame. Agencies informally gave some of their decision-making power to participating citizens by responding to community concerns. In exchange, citizens were expected to help develop viable options that enabled agencies to address community complaints and agency needs simultaneously.

In sum, viewed from the perspective of government as actors, federal land managers were relatively equal participants in the collaborative process. They did not convene or fund the group; instead, they participated as others did in defining the issues and developing group structure and process. Like other participants, federal land managers brought their personal skills to the table, along with as much of their organizations' capacity as they could muster. Yet some governmental participants held formal decision-making authority, which other participants did not, and other governmental participants had more technical and scientific knowledge than did nongovernmental participants. Nongovernmental participants were able to counter these advantages, however, by providing vision, political pressure, and viable alternatives that both encouraged and pressured governmental participants to implement the partnership's objectives.

GOVERNMENT AS INSTITUTIONS

If government personnel were important players at a nearly equal table, it was also the case that federal institutions loomed large in the partnership. Federal institutions and reactions to them largely defined the context in which the partnership worked, in three key ways. First, the institutions of federal land management agencies, and the laws and political processes that governed them, led directly to the partnership's founding. Second, the partnership sought to change institutional dynamics of agency policymaking. And third, larger institutional processes and politics at times inhibited the partnership's work and even threatened its existence.

The Applegate Partnership was founded in response to the injunction preventing timber harvest in spotted owl habitat. The federal land management agencies, environmental organizations, and the timber industry were locked in a battle that had ground federal forest management to a halt. Although laws had been on the books for two decades requiring the Forest Service and the BLM to manage for vertebrate species on public lands, federal land management had considerable difficulty shifting away from the rules and norms that kept the agencies focused on timber production.

Environmentalists successfully used federal laws such as the National Forest Management Act and Endangered Species Act and the courts to force change in the Forest Service and the BLM. Through litigation, environmentalists' actions and agency and industry reactions created political crisis and bureaucratic stalemate. It was within this context that the Applegate Partnership was founded. Early participants sought to move beyond the deadlock and restart federal land management by initiating participatory processes that would create economic opportunity by restoring naturally functioning ecosystems. Thus, although both nongovernmental and governmental participants came together to agree upon a geographic scale and substantive set of issues, it was done in the context of this larger institutional crisis, which created the impetus for the collaboration and focused attention on public land management that would resolve the crisis at the local level.

Partnership participants agreed to work within existing laws. Even so, the group sought to change federal management processes to involve citizens earlier in planning processes, provide a broader array of information to the public, consider ecological and social systems rather than manage for single purposes in isolation, and think about management across ownership boundaries, among other new approaches. Partnership participants quickly discovered that making these sorts of changes required not only agreement among participants, but also institutional shifts in agencies that had been expert driven and fragmented, and generally communicated formally with the public and only late in the planning process. Participants in the Applegate Partnership expended considerable time and effort in seeking these institutional changes in the Forest Service and the BLM.

They had some successes getting local federal land management units to adopt these new ideas, such as with the Forest Service's Partnership One and the BLM's Thompson Creek projects. With Partnership One, agency and nongovernmental partnership participants collectively developed a restoration-oriented timber sale through a series of field trips and meetings. With the BLM's Thompson Creek projects, the Ashland Resource Area BLM expended considerable energy early on outreach to partnership participants and community residents. The Ashland Resource Area developed a process to incorporate what was learned in one phase about the effectiveness of particular prescriptions and treatments into the next phase.

The agencies did not always follow collaborative approaches, however. For example, after the Thompson Creek projects were well under way, managers of another BLM management unit in the Applegate Valley presented a timber sale to the partnership and community residents only after it had been developed, largely following old-style planning processes. Local grassroots environmental activists not involved in the partnership vehemently opposed the timber sale. Although Applegate Partnership participants initially attempted to broker a resolution to the disagreements between the BLM and community residents, over time the conflict was played out in ways that harked back to the formal adversarial processes, such as through public comment and appeals. Moreover, trust, never very high between the environmental activists from the local subwatershed and the BLM, diminished further.

In another example, a Forest Service innovator developed a long-term management project for one of the Applegate Valley's key subwatersheds. The project was to last for several years. The innovator pulled together a team of cross-disciplinary Forest Service staff to participate in the project. It entailed analysis and planning across ownership boundaries and considerable resident participation, and it was to involve implementation of a long list of restoration projects. Eventually, however, the Forest Service and BLM land managers became impatient with the project's complexity and slow process and canceled it, to the considerable frustration of local residents who had been involved in the project over the course of several years. Ultimately, the project did not fit well with the institutional norms of the Forest Service, which favored projects that could be done with segmented staff and budgets, emphasized routine over creativity, could show concrete, measurable progress, and could be easily supported up the chain of command.

These examples suggest the constant struggle that governmental and nongovernmental partnership participants faced in trying to change the institutional habits of the federal land management agencies. At times they succeeded in creating a collaborative, participatory environment in which a diversity of knowledge and opinions were incorporated into planning processes. But other times more traditional institutional processes prevailed.

Sometimes the Applegate Partnership found itself at the mercy of institutional processes and politics beyond the partnership and the Applegate Valley. Shortly after the adoption of President Clinton's Northwest Forest Plan, external actors, both industry and environmentalists, threatened by the diminished power that the Northwest Forest Plan and collaborative forest management might mean for them, used federal rules and laws to try to block partnership efforts. Timber industry members sought to use the Federal Advisory Committee Act (FACA) to argue that the collaborative, public-private process the administration had used to develop the plan was illegal because it involved inappropriate advice from nongovernment personnel. Concerned that the plan could be scuttled, the White House required that government personnel pull back from collaborations, including the Applegate Partnership. The partnership was a particular lightning rod, because during the development of the Northwest Forest Plan, Secretary of the Interior Bruce Babbitt visited the partnership, and the president held up the partnership as an example of the type of efforts he hoped would emerge from the plan. The White House forced government personnel to resign from the partnership board, and for a while, they were not sure whether they were even allowed to attend meetings.

Over time, FACA was clarified, and government personnel resumed active participation in the partnership, though not as board members. Board membership was not an important symbol of participation, and thus federal membership continued largely as before. In addition, the Forest Service and the BLM created a joint staff position to act as a liaison between the partnership and the agencies. At the time, the FACA crisis caused substantial upheaval in the partnership, and many feared that it would not survive. Ultimately it did, and participants became more determined to succeed, but the FACA crisis is one example of how governmental institutions, in this case laws, can combine with interest-based politics to affect a collaboration.

A second example of political institutions affecting a collaboration was the legal appeal of the partnership's first on-the-ground collaborative project, Partnership One. In this project, agency, industry, environmental, and community participants sought to create an agreed-upon restoration activity that would produce timber as a by-product. The group, including environmental participants, hoped that by focusing on restoration and low-impact timber harvest methods, and by using a collaborative process, the agency would be able to avoid environmental appeals that would try to halt the project. After the participants had agreed on the goals and prescriptions of the project, Partnership One was shepherded through the formal environmental review processes. But a regional environmental organization appealed the project on technical grounds, largely because it opposed community-based collaborative processes. The Pacific Northwest Regional Office of the Forest Service upheld the appeal, requiring the local ranger district to rewrite the environmental assessment. Although the partnership had reached agreement about the project, this did not exempt them from the rules of environmental appeals processes or the larger culture of adversarial environmentalism, which was still largely in play when the partnership was founded.

Thus, in many ways, governmental institutions affected the Applegate Partnership fundamentally. A crisis of the federal land management agencies led to the partnership's founding and defined the group's initial focus. The partnership sought at once to change these institutions, especially the organizational norms and habits of the Forest Service and the BLM, while working within existing laws. These efforts yielded mixed results, sometimes leading to changed management approaches and other times to retrenchment. The partnership and the agencies implemented several management projects that had involved considerable collaborative input and were based on the ecological, social, and economic principles that the partnership had developed as part of its vision. At the same time, however, the agencies frequently followed older institutional habits. As a result, federal land management in the Applegate Valley came to be driven at once by traditional conservationist institutions and by new collaborative approaches, creating a complex and sometimes contradictory management environment. Although collaboration was a popular concept with the Clinton administration, and many local agency personnel were open to the idea, more deeply embedded bureaucratic habits and norms dominated agency actions at times. Moreover, people outside the partnership who felt threatened by the institutional changes and loss of power that collaboration implied sought to scuttle the partnership.

CONCLUSIONS

As a set of institutions, the government had a large impact on the issue definition of the collaborative effort. It was a crisis in federal land management that led to the group's founding, and it was federal land management institutions—laws, organizational norms and procedures, management practices, and interest group politics—that the group had to work within and sought to change. These institutional realities led the group to focus primarily on federal land management, especially initially. When the partnership faced major roadblocks, such as the FACA crisis and the appeal of Partnership One, partnership participants broadened the way that the group framed the problems to address restoration on private lands in the Applegate Valley.

As participants, the government brought human resources—people with varied skills, abilities, and experience—and technical expertise about land management to the collaboration. These government resources had varying effects on the partnership's efforts, depending on the particular circumstances that brought them to the table. Sometimes agency technical expertise helped the group understand ecological processes and develop innovative plans for management. At other times this technical expertise could get in the way, such as when it was backed with an attitude that experts know best and others have little to contribute, or when it reflected old ways of managing national forests.

The government both as participant and as institution affected the group's structure and decision-making processes. Although beliefs about open, inclusive, informal structures were broadly and deeply held by participants, federal involvement also required that meetings be open and participation be informal. The prohibition against federal personnel as board members reinforced the group's belief in a weak role for formal structures.

The government both as institution and as actor interacted with partnership participants in diverse ways to affect social and environmental outcomes. Governmental actors were nearly equal participants in a community-based collaborative process whose goal was, in large part, to create more inclusive public land management. Because the group was focused primarily on public land, government personnel were participants on whom the group depended for its ecological success. With federal involvement, the Applegate Partnership began to create ecosystem-based management on public land in the valley. Federal personnel tried to listen to input, incorporate new ideas, and change management practices.

Although government personnel participated actively in trying to make this happen, in the end, governmental institutions were as important to the outcomes of the group. The partnership created space within the thick institutional milieu of federal land management for collaborative approaches and ecosystem-based management. But alongside this collaborative environmental management effort, the institutions of expert-driven management and adversarial environmentalism remained, constantly shaping its focus and limiting its activities.

CHAPTER 3

NONPROFIT FACILITATION

The Darby Partnership

A s in the case of the Applegate Partnership (Chapter 2), nongovern-mental actors initiated the Darby Creek Partnership. In this case, the local chapter of a national nonprofit organization, The Nature Conservancy, founded the Darby Creek Partnership to pursue its interests in biodiversity conservation. This chapter looks at the potential benefits and limitations of collaboration led by nongovernmental actors with minimal institutional commitment from government. Government's failure to coordinate management of the Darby Creek watershed created a void that The Nature Conservancy sought to fill by fostering collaboration. Although the Darby Creek Partnership had no formal authority and limited financial resources, it did create a flexible, open structure and coordinating process that governmental actors alone could not have achieved. The role of government in this case is primarily as an actor with limited influence over the resources of the collaborative effort. In the end, The Nature Conservancy's facilitation of the partnership helped government collaborate with itself, as well as with nongovernmental actors.

FORMATION OF THE DARBY PARTNERSHIP

The Big and Little Darby Creeks drain land in six counties west of Columbus, Ohio. Before settlement by Europeans, the 560-square-mile watershed was a mixture of prairie and forest, with extensive forested wetlands surrounding the creeks (TNC 1996a; Allan 1991). Today 98 percent of the watershed is privately owned and 80 percent is in pasture or cropland. Significant acreage has been converted to residential development in recent years. The Darby Creeks constitute one of the top five warm freshwater habitats in the Midwest, with 103 species of fish and 38 species of mussels, 2 of which are listed as federally endangered (TNC 1996a, 1996b; U.S. EPA 1996).

The extraordinary diversity of this stream system has drawn the attention of conservationists and environmental managers. The existence of such a diverse aquatic community in the midst of agricultural lands prompted the Natural Resources Conservation Service (NRCS) to include the Darby watershed as one of its 70 Hydrologic Unit Areas (HUA) in 1991 (Lohstroh 1992; USDA 1998a). The purpose of this program was to preserve the creeks by reducing agricultural sediment loading and protecting the riparian corridor. This designation made available additional NRCS funding to encourage agricultural best-management practices and to partner with other agencies in the watershed (Lohstroh 1992). Other agencies had ongoing efforts around the creeks as well. For example, the Ohio Environmental Protection Agency was working to improve wastewater treatment facilities in the watershed. Local, county, and regional planners were beginning to turn their attention to controlling the westward spread of development, but these efforts were not well coordinated with each other.

Nongovernmental organizations also were becoming active in the watershed. The Nature Conservancy (TNC) had embarked on a program to protect 75 of the world's "Last Great Places" and conducted ecological studies to identify areas as outstanding examples of endangered ecosystems (Endicott 1993). It selected the Darby watershed as one of the first dozen areas to be named a "Last Great Place" in 1991 because of the biodiversity of the Darby system, particularly the aquatic endangered species and some upland prairie oak habitats, and because of the perceived threats from development and agricultural practices (Weeks 1997; Zwinger 1994). TNC's primary goal in the Darby watershed was "to maintain and, if possible, enhance the mussel and fish populations" (TNC 1996a, 8).

TNC is known for buying land for conservation purposes, but because of the size of the Darby watershed, this approach alone was not feasible

(Zwinger 1994; TNC 1996a; Lohstroh 1992; Allan 1991). The potential did exist, however, to partner with agencies, private landowners, and other interested parties to pursue their common goals of protecting the watershed. Although this was a new approach for TNC at that time, the organization saw a partnership as the most effective way to achieve the goal of protecting the Darby's biological diversity.

The simultaneous interest of governmental agencies and TNC led to the formation of the Darby Partners in 1991 (the group became known as the Darby Partnership around 1995). Although several governmental agencies had been interested in protecting the Darby, none possessed the political will or authority to convene a collaborative group, and there were concerns that leadership by any one of the involved governmental agencies might alienate other agencies or stakeholders. The NRCS staff recognized the need for involvement by a broader range of actors than its HUA project included but lacked higher-level political support to take a leadership role. In addition, the NRCS history of working primarily with farmers might have damaged the collaborative effort's credibility in the environmental community. The Nature Conservancy stepped into this void to facilitate a partnership in which a wide range of interests was represented.

ISSUE DEFINITION AND THE DARBY PARTNERSHIP

The Darby Partnership's mission is "to be a proactive resource for the citizens of the watershed who want to protect the Darbys" (USDA 1998a, 5). In contrast to the NRCS's HUA program, which primarily addressed agricultural land-use issues, the partnership took a comprehensive approach, including agricultural practices, wastewater treatment, residential and industrial development, and citizen education. The partnership chose a broad focus in response to the limited focus of existing programs such as the HUA and the lack of coordination among the various governmental efforts in the watershed.

Because of the attention and ongoing efforts in the Darby watershed initiated by the HUA, the partnership initially focused primarily on agricultural practices. Other development concerns also were brought before the partnership, including expansion of an industrial facility and a major highway construction project, both of which affected the headwaters of Big Darby Creek. In later years, the partnership focused more on rapid residential development as Columbus expanded westward into the Darby watershed. Related to this shift were discussions of floodplain regulations, regional planning, stormwater controls, and the 1999 proposal of the U.S. Fish and Wildlife Service (FWS) to establish a wildlife refuge in the area.

Although the partnership was created to fill a void in what existing government programs were addressing, the geographic scale of the partnership's efforts was borrowed from the HUA. Both the HUA and the partnership focused on the watershed of the creeks. The decision to focus on the watershed also suited TNC's interest in the aquatic diversity of the system, since land-use practices were the main threat to the biota of the creeks.

Interestingly, in the late 1990s, another government initiative called into question the geographic boundary of the partnership. In 1999, the FWS proposed the creation of a Little Darby Wildlife Refuge. This proposal was opposed strenuously by the local agricultural community. Because the proposed refuge intersected only a small part of the Little Darby watershed, some argued that the issue was not within the partnership's purview. Others maintained that this issue should be discussed by the partnership, because before the proposal was formalized, the partnership was the only inclusive, neutral forum in which opposing sides could address the significance of the refuge proposal for agriculture, development, and the environment in the region. Additionally, because TNC had publicly supported the wildlife refuge, some members of the public assumed that the Darby Partnership supported the proposal. This perception made some partners very uncomfortable. After two contentious meetings that focused on the refuge issue, the partnership devoted its agenda to other issues, leaving that debate to the public process coordinated by the FWS.

The debates over whether to address the refuge issue highlight the partnership's flexibility. For example, the partnership was able to adopt a watershed boundary, something that governmental efforts around the Darby Creeks had not accomplished, with the exception of the limited HUA planning process. The group seriously considered, but eventually rejected, further expanding its boundaries to encompass the area targeted by the Little Darby Wildlife Refuge proposal. Similarly, the partnership was able to address new issues as they evolved in importance, rather than remain limited to a narrow set of mandated issues, such as agriculture, as was the HUA. Had the group been created by a governmental agency for a designated purpose, it is unlikely that it would have had such flexibility. The flexibility to redefine the issues could in one sense be seen as a liability, as the partnership was not obligated to address potentially volatile problems and produce consensus outcomes. On the other hand, the partnership had

Table 3-1. Darby Partnership Membership and Participation (1999)

	Listed members	Core members
Local officials	32	7
County officials or staff	18	4
State agencies	13	8
Federal agencies	12	9
Nongovernmental organizations	12	7
Universities/extension offices	10	5
Other	6	3
Total	103	43

Note: Listed members include everyone on the partnership mailing list; core members were identified through interviews and survey responses.

the advantage of being able to pick issues where progress could be made and relationships maintained.

RESOURCES FOR COLLABORATION

One way in which government involvement affected the Darby Partnership was through government agencies' contributions to human resources. The initial list of partners consisted of more than 40 organizations, including the relevant state and federal agencies, the six counties' Soil and Water Conservation Districts, several major local industries, environmental or conservation groups, and the Operation Future Association, a newly formed farmers' group. Additional members subsequently were added, including local elected officials from cities, towns, and townships in the watershed and representatives with local land-use planning interests. Overall, the Darby Partnership included representation from a wide range of governmental bodies, especially at the state and federal levels (Table 3-1).[1]

Significant membership attrition in the Darby Partnership occurred after the end of the HUA, when several governmental agencies redirected their resources and staff time elsewhere. When the government-directed HUA process was finished, some governmental actors dropped out of TNC's effort because they no longer could justify their time. Although this diminished the partnership's human resources, a core group of partners continued their involvement. This pattern of a core group was noted by interviewees and evidenced by the fact that respondents to a 1999 membership survey had been involved with the partnership for an average of 5.6 years (Korfmacher 2000). Most of these core members were government representatives, which indicates that although government was unable or unwilling to take the lead in forming and maintaining the partnership institution, governmental actors were willing participants in the TNC-facilitated collaborative effort.

Among governmental actors, federal and state officials were the most numerous and active, even after the HUA-related attrition. Although a growing number of planning staff at the county and regional level became involved in the late 1990s, local and county-level elected officials were less involved. In fact, lack of involvement by local governments, especially rural township trustees responsible for regulating land-use decisions in much of the watershed, was cited in interviews and survey responses as a key challenge facing the partnership. Overall, active participation was strongest by state and federal agencies and nongovernmental organizations with professional staffs.

One prominent reason for continued participation by some governmental actors was that it was personally rewarding, even if it was not an official priority of their agency. Because the partnership did not take positions or actions, agency staff could share ideas openly without being censored by their superiors.[2] In fact, several partners emphasized that although they sat on the partnership as part of their jobs, they made it a priority to attend even when they were not required to. As one partner who works for a Soil and Water Conservation District said, "I'm there because I love the Darby—I'm a watershed resident."

In contrast, local government officials did not participate or contribute as consistently to the partnership. They may have perceived that the costs of attending meetings outweighed potential benefits from involvement. The benefits of potential collaboration and information sharing, though important to state agencies, may have been less relevant to local officials. In addition, partnership meetings were held during the day. Many officials in small towns in the Darby watershed were volunteers and held full-time jobs that prevented them from attending daytime meetings.

Governments' financial resource contributions were indirect rather than direct. In fact, governments did not contribute any financial resources directly to the partnership. Governmental actors directed significant financial and technical resources to Darby-related programs, however, many of which were attributed to or associated with the partnership, such as the Darby Days educational activities. Several grants were written jointly by partners who probably would not have worked together if not for the partnership institution. Governmental actors also contributed technical resources directly to the partnership, primarily in the form of presentations made by government employees during partnership meetings.

Human, technical, and financial resources stemming from governmental sources affected activities and accomplishments that were indirectly attributed to the partnership, but the resources that supported the direct activities of the partnership were provided by TNC. The primary human resource TNC contributed was through staffing the partnership. TNC agreed to facilitate and provide administrative support because, as one interviewee said, "nobody else wanted to do it." TNC also organized the meetings, sent out agendas, and made available a number of technical resources.[3] Financially, TNC subsidized all the direct costs of the partnership, estimated at several hundred dollars per year for mailings, facility rentals, and refreshments for quarterly meetings. TNC also contributed funding, much of which was obtained from grant sources, to projects related to the partnership, such as a survey of freshwater mussels in the Darby Creeks.

While TNC staff devoted significant time to the partnership, it was all part of the organization's efforts to protect the Darby. At the same time, the benefits of the partnership to TNC were significant. The partnership provided TNC with an opportunity to share its technical resources, increase agency awareness of issues facing the watershed, and help initiate projects to advance protection of the Darby. For example, TNC's Darby steward was a key participant in the Stream Team, an interagency task force that wrote a manual to help landowners solve common drainage and erosion problems in environmentally sensitive ways.

Facilitating the partnership also conferred greater credibility on TNC. TNC staff often attended local planning board meetings and spoke in opposition to development plans. Although these staff members never claimed that their position was that of the partnership, several observers suggested that TNC's role in the partnership enhanced the legitimacy of their positions. Thus TNC's efforts to improve land-use management in the watershed were bolstered by its role in the partnership.

Given that the partnership did not make decisions or run programs, contribution to the direct maintenance of the partnership was arguably less important than the continued indirect efforts of individual governmental agencies associated with the partnership. Therefore, despite the lack of significant technical or financial resources contributed by governments directly to the partnership, government was an important actor.

GROUP STRUCTURE AND DECISION-MAKING PROCESSES

The partnership was designed to be an informal, flexible, collaborative effort. The group typically met just four times per year, for about three hours per meeting, and attendance rates varied. The partnership did not take public positions on issues. Rather, it sought to influence decisions, actions, programs, and positions of its members through information sharing, networking, and discussion at its quarterly meetings. Therefore, one of the main direct activities of the partnership was to organize discussions and information sharing about timely topics such as major land-development proposals, newly available scientific data, and opportunities for joint public education programs. Meeting agendas were open, with the facilitator, generally TNC's Darby project director or other TNC staff member, simply allocating time for presentations to those requesting it and then facilitating any relevant discussion.

Governmental actors were influential in establishing the structural characteristics of the partnership. They argued that having minimal structure and formality would encourage more diverse participation than would a more formal organization. In addition, the partnership decided from the outset that to take positions on issues would be inappropriate and potentially threatening to some of its members (TNC 1996a, *11*). Particular consideration was given to the position of agency staff who could not speak on behalf of, nor make commitments for, their agencies. Governmental actors were given the opportunity to behave more like independent participants than institutional actors on behalf of their agencies. Several agency members stated that if the partnership were to take public positions on issues, their agencies would not have allowed them to participate.

Whereas governmental actors played a role in shaping the structure of the partnership, the lack of any governmental mandate resulted in limited influence from government as an institution. In particular, the partnership had no authority to make or implement public policy decisions. Because of this lack of authority, the partnership provided a discussion space for partners to explore opportunities without making binding commitments, and it promoted widespread governmental actor participation.

OUTCOMES OF THE PARTNERSHIP

Partners reported numerous ways in which the partnership advanced protection of the Darby watershed. Defining these accomplishments is more com-

Table 3-2. Partnership Objectives and Accomplishments

Objective	Importance Mean (N = 44)	How fully accomplished Mean (N = 43)
Improve development practices and land-use controls	4.3	2.6
Educate the public about ongoing management issues	4.2	3.0
Educate partners about ongoing management issues	4.1	3.8
Share scientific information relevant to Darby protection	4.1	3.6
Coordinate Darby watershed management efforts	4.0	3.5
Gather and incorporate public input into management	3.8	2.8
Change environmental regulations to better protect the watershed	3.6	2.6

Note: Scores ranged from 1 to 5, where 1 = not important or not accomplished and 5 = strongly important or fully accomplished.

plicated than simply looking at how well the objectives of the partnership were achieved, as the partnership had no official or commonly held objectives. In addition, it is difficult to separate changes in management of the Darby watershed that were inspired by the partnership from those that would have come about without the partnership. For example, increases in agricultural best-management practices during this period are frequently attributed to the Darby Partnership; however, this effort was heavily supported by the NRCS through the HUA program independent of the partnership (Napier 1998a, 1998b; Vosick and Cash 1996). Although the partnership may have enhanced this program through greater participation and awareness, the HUA programs and funding would have existed without the partnership. Despite these complications, partners gave many specific examples of how the partnership influenced their thinking as well as their actions related to the Darby.

To explore the various partners' perceptions of the partnership's goals and accomplishments, a list of perceived partnership objectives was constructed based on key informant interviews. Survey respondents rated the importance of each objective on the list and indicated their perception of how well each was achieved (Table 3-2). Interestingly, the two objectives respondents rated as most important, improving land-use controls and educating the public, were among those rated as least fully achieved. This divergence is attributable to the fact that those responsible for land-use decisions—landowners, developers, and local government officials—were not well represented on the partnership.

The three most fully achieved objectives relate to the coordinating function of the partnership: educating the partners about management issues, sharing scientific information, and coordinating protection efforts. These results indicate that the partnership is perceived as providing a positive venue for coordination. They do not, however, reveal what effect, if any, such coordination had on actual management of the watershed.

To better understand how the coordination accomplishments may have facilitated watershed protection, interviews probed the specific effects of the partnership on individual members and the organizations they represent. Partners gave diverse responses about outcomes associated with partnership efforts. Although a few partners said that participation did not affect their work in the Darby, most reported that the knowledge they gained from the partnership positively influenced their agency's or organization's efforts to protect the watershed.[4] Some common themes emerged from the responses:

- Participation in the partnership increased agencies' and organizations' focus on Darby-related issues.
- What participants learned through the partnership influenced their agencies and organizations beyond their Darby watershed work.
- Partnership activities affected the behavior of landowners.
- The partnership provided opportunities and contacts for joint projects that otherwise would not have happened.
- The partnership lent legitimacy to efforts to protect the watershed.

Respondents gave numerous examples of new ways of doing things that resulted from contacts, information, and opportunities provided by the partnership. One county government engineer credited the partnership with heightening his awareness of how sediment damages aquatic ecosystems, which led him to change his county's approach to controlling agricultural ditches. Another respondent told of creating planning and development policy aimed at protecting the Darby as a direct result of the partnership. Still another noted, "We used to be big into clearing and snagging creeks to help farmers with drainage. We realized through the Darby Partnership this may not be the best thing for the creek." Another wrote of obtaining many educational program ideas while participating in the partners meetings, and that many of the partners had been teachers or leaders of his organization's educational programs.

Several respondents reported that participating in the partnership exposed them to a new approach to environmental protection that their organization then replicated elsewhere. Responses ranged from the philosophical to the very practical. One respondent noted, "There has been an increasing shift to a watershed emphasis in our surface water programs. Hopefully we are taking a cue on how to interact with our constituents based on the success of the Darby Partnership." Another said, "[Our agency] expanded our expertise .... This was a positive experience for our office and has expanded our work into other watersheds. We always use the Darby as an example of how to do collaborative planning and watershed approach to problem solving." Thus as a pioneering ecosystem management effort in central Ohio, the partnership seems to have had positive effects beyond the Darby through its members' ongoing work.

Many respondents credited the partnership with fostering greater environmental sensitivity among partners and the public. Some members reported that the partnership increased farmers' environmental appreciation and willingness to adopt conservation measures (Mihaly 1994).

An important social outcome that emerged from the informal structure of the partnership was networking among those who attended meetings, at which state and federal agencies tended to be the best represented. Agency staff credited the partnership with enhancing communication and coordination among governmental agencies and programs that had common goals but lacked other opportunities to interact with each other. Several agencies collaborated in organizing the Darby Days, a weekend of recreation, education, and cleanup activities on the creeks. In addition, a significant new network attributed to the partnership was the Operation Future Association (OFA). Funded by an outside grant submitted through TNC, the OFA was a farmers' environmental organization. Its director was housed in TNC's offices and organized programs to encourage environmentally sensitive agricultural practices. Although it was not officially tied to the partnership, its existence was a direct result of the partnership's efforts to bring farmers and environmentalists together in protecting the Darby. Thus the partnership network facilitated the securing of additional financial resources for members, even though these were outside the use of the partnership itself.

A further social outcome stemming from the activities and membership composition of the partnership was that it was regarded as a credible and legitimate entity. One factor that promoted legitimacy was the perception that the partnership was a neutral forum. Some agricultural representatives, in particular, were skeptical of becoming involved in government programs. Because they generally perceived TNC to be an unbiased party, they were more comfortable participating in the partnership. The Ohio Chapter of TNC was described in meetings and literature as a conservation, as opposed to environmental, group, and it was seen as sincere in its efforts to work with farmers to protect the creeks. In the late 1990s, this reputation was shaken when TNC took a public position in support of the Little Darby Wildlife Refuge. Many observers linked TNC's position with the partnership, causing those who were opposed to the refuge to question their participation. Although a few agricultural representatives stopped attending, the partnership retained participation of the major governmental and nongovernmental interests in the watershed. Several agency partners also noted that not having governmental actors lead the meetings was an important means of increasing legitimacy, to avoid perceptions that the partnership's decisions were biased toward government agendas and interests.

The partnership also gained legitimacy through the perception that it was a representative forum. This meant having input from both environmental and agricultural perspectives, since these perspectives were often in conflict. This input tended to be from relevant environmental and agricultural agencies, however, rather than from grassroots stakeholders. The partnership was considered to be a groundbreaking effort with respect to enhancing communication among governmental agencies and organizations that represented different interests in the watershed, but it was not a grassroots organization in the sense of directly involving lay citizens.

The partnership played an important role in sparking and supporting diverse efforts to protect the Darby despite having no strong central source of funding for projects, no authority to implement or create standards, and no concrete goals. Simply by providing a neutral forum for discussion, the partnership exposed members to ideas, information, and potential collaborators they otherwise would not have encountered. This in turn influenced the actions of member agencies and organizations in the Darby watershed and beyond. The examples cited above are probably just a subset of the ripple effects the partnership had in the watershed. One partner said that a land developer's involvement in the partnership "led to an environmentally friendly development, which served as an example for county zoning," and wondered, "What else has happened like this that we'll never know about?"

Despite such achievements, the partnership has not accomplished the objective most members feel is most important: improving land-use management to better protect the watershed. Given the prominent role of governmental actors and staff of nongovernmental organizations in the partnership, it is not surprising that it was most successful in affecting the decisions of governmental agencies, OFA farmers, and county officials who participated in the partnership. Conversely, the partnership had the least success in accomplishing objectives that required the action of parties not strongly represented in the group—local governments, developers, and landowners—such as influencing land-use decisions. Given the ever-increasing threat of development in the watershed, the lack of participation by those who control land use was a significant challenge to the partnership.

CONCLUSIONS

The Darby Partnership is collaboration in a very minimal form. It lacks tangible resources such as dedicated funding for studies or pilot projects and the services of technical experts, which many researchers cite as important to the success of collaborative efforts (Wondolleck and Yaffee 2000; Cortner and Moote 1999; MacKenzie 1996). It also has no authority to make or implement regulations. Nevertheless, process-oriented issues such as broad participation by diverse stakeholders, leadership, and providing a forum for sharing ideas can contribute to success. This case therefore raises an important question: What are the potential benefits and limitations when collaboration is led by nongovernmental actors with minimal formal commitment from government?

Despite the lack of direct financial, human, and technical resources, the partnership's activities led to significant accomplishments in the protection of the Darby. New relationships were established between and among governmental agencies and nongovernmental organizations, and they continue to cooperate in watershed management efforts, both within the partnership and beyond. Many partners attributed increased technical and financial resources directed by their agencies to watershed protection to the awareness and coordination facilitated by the partnership.

Most of these social and environmental outcomes resulted from the governmental actors in the effort facilitated by TNC. The partnership provided a neutral meeting ground for government representatives and other interest groups, mobilizing network resources that likely would not have existed with a more formal structure. Although it had virtually no dedicated staff or financial or technical resources, the partnership's extensive, diverse participation conferred legitimacy, especially among federal and state agencies. Whereas many analyses of collaboration focus on tangible resources such as money and technical staff, the accomplishments of the partnership emphasize the importance of process and organizational dynamics, particularly the roles of group structure, networks, and legitimacy in shaping achievements. Thus despite the weak institutional role of government in the organization of the partnership, government representatives were critical actors. The effects of governmental actors' participation were manifested not through direct actions of the partnership, but in the changes in behavior participating staff fostered in their individual agencies.

The informal structure of the partnership, combined with facilitation by a nonprofit organization, encouraged collaboration among a variety of governmental agencies and nongovernmental actors. No governmental agency, however, was willing or able to take on a leadership role in structuring the partnership at the time the effort began. Even if an agency had stepped forward, there were concerns that it might have dominated the agenda and alienated nongovernmental constituencies who were suspicious of it. In addition, a government-led effort would have been accountable to its mandate, such as showing tangible outcomes, disbursing funds, or making recommendations. Instead, The Nature Conservancy created a safe haven for a wide range of governmental actors, who did not have to make commitments or take positions that might threaten their agencies. The partnership's flexibility allowed partners to focus on areas of agreement where productive joint projects could be pursued and to respond to changes in opportunities and constraints over time. The Nature Conservancy's facilitation of the partnership helped government collaborate with itself, as well as with nongovernmental actors, in ways that might not have been possible if government had taken a leading role.

PART II

GOVERNMENT AS ENCOURAGER

CHAPTER 4

ENCOURAGEMENT THROUGH "CARROTS" AND "STICKS"

Habitat Conservation Planning and
the Endangered Species Act

This chapter and the next one explore the role of government as an institution at a programmatic level in collaborative efforts. In this chapter, a governmental institution, the Endangered Species Act (ESA), plays an important role in encouraging collaboration. Rather than simply being one of many laws that can stymie public agencies and private actors in court, thereby creating problems in local communities, the ESA authorized a proactive program for habitat conservation planning that created a venue for collaboration among a wide range of stakeholders. Public and private actors participate in this federal program to avoid the ESA's more stringent command-and-control rules. The ESA does not require collaboration as a condition for participating in this program; instead, government officials offer incentives to encourage collaboration. This chapter uses the case of habitat conservation planning to assess how governmental actors can use their influence through command-and-control rules, in combination with other incentives, to encourage collaboration.

THE ENDANGERED SPECIES ACT AND
HABITAT CONSERVATION PLANNING

The Endangered Species Act is a landmark piece of federal legislation designed to prevent species loss. When the ESA became law in 1973, policymakers tended to believe that particular types of human activities, such as hunting, were the primary causes of extinction. Their understanding was partially accurate, because hunting had decimated some well-known species, such as the passenger pigeon, bison, and gray whale, and because they thought largely in terms of charismatic species, such as marine mammals and the bald eagle. Yet scientists and environmental activists saw a bigger picture. Many more species—particularly less charismatic ones that most Americans knew little or nothing about—were nearing extinction or headed in that direction, and the primary cause of their decline was not hunting. It was, and still is, loss of habitat.

Throughout the world, the leading cause of the decline and extinction of species is habitat transformation, including fragmentation, degradation, and loss. Therefore, reversing the decline of most species requires preserving habitat (Noss et al. 1997; Noss and Cooperrider 1994; Morrison et al. 1992). Yet this is often difficult to do, for at least two reasons. First, humans continue to transform species' habitats because doing so is productive economically. In the United States, some of the leading causes of habitat transformation today include logging, farming, and suburban sprawl. If habitat cannot be purchased to limit these human activities, then political will is required to regulate them.

A second reason is that the habitats of many species cross multiple public jurisdictions and private parcels. Thus coordination among public and private actors to create effective habitat preserve systems is an important component of conservation efforts (Thomas 2003b). Effective coordination requires knowledge about the location of species, the relative quality of remaining habitat patches, and appropriate planning tools for balancing human uses with habitat conservation. With this knowledge, conservation planners can design habitat preserve systems in principle, but collaboration is needed in practice to plan and implement preserve systems that cover multiple ownerships and jurisdictions.

The ESA provides the statutory framework within which habitat conservation planning occurs. As in the case of forest management in the Applegate Partnership (Chapter 2), governmental institutions play an important role in endangered species protection through rules that primarily constrain economic activities while indirectly encouraging collaborative planning processes. Without the ESA, habitat conservation planning would be much more limited in scope on public land, and perhaps not exist at all on private land. Nonprofit organizations such as The Nature Conservancy still would acquire or manage habitat for conservation purposes, as would some local, state, and federal agencies. But most private actors would not sacrifice economic gain, and most public agencies would not sacrifice their primary missions, for habitat conservation. The ESA provides the regulatory authority to prohibit human transformation of species' habitats on public and private property. The ESA does not, however, mandate collaboration as a means for compliance; instead, public officials encourage collaboration through a wide variety of techniques during the habitat conservation planning process. Thus government as institution and government as actor interact to create a powerful set of incentives for stakeholders to collaborate as a means for compliance.

GOVERNMENT AS INSTITUTION

Section 9 of the ESA prohibits all persons and organizations, other than federal agencies, from taking fish or wildlife species listed as endangered by the U.S. Fish and Wildlife Service (FWS).[1] *Take* is defined broadly in Section 3 to include "harass, harm, pursue, hunt, shoot, wound, kill, trap, capture, or collect, or to attempt to engage in any such conduct."[2] On its surface, this language appears to target only human activities that affect individual members of a species, not those that affect its habitat. Yet the FWS subsequently expanded the ESA's definition of *take* through a rule that defined *harm* to include "habitat modification or degradation where it actually kills or injures wildlife by significantly impairing essential behavioral patterns, including breeding, feeding or sheltering" (50 CFR 17.3). Because of this rule, human activities that modify the habitat of a listed species are included under the Section 9 prohibition on take. This rule opened the door for environmental activists, who could now successfully sue a private landowner for altering habitat through logging, farming, or grading land for housing developments, among other activities. Environmental activists also could sue a local government or state agency for permitting these activities to occur. The Supreme Court, in a pivotal ruling, upheld this rule in 1995.[3]

Although the Section 9 prohibition on take applies only to fish and wildlife species listed as endangered, Section 4 of the ESA authorizes the

FWS to issue specific rules for species listed as threatened.[4] Subsection 4(d) instructs the FWS to promulgate rules deemed "necessary and advisable" to provide for the conservation of threatened species. These special rules can extend the prohibition on take and the rule on harm to threatened species. As of November 2003, 388 animal species were listed as endangered and 128 as threatened in the United States (U.S. FWS 2003). (Plant species also are listed in both categories, but they are not covered by the Section 9 prohibition on take.)

If this were the end of the regulatory story, there would be little incentive for collaborative environmental management. It simply would be a traditional enforcement story about command-and-control rules, albeit one played out primarily through the courts rather than through the discretion of agency personnel. Collaborative environmental management arose because Congress amended the ESA in 1982 to encourage those subject to the prohibition on take to develop habitat conservation plans (HCPs) that would protect species and their habitats proactively. Specifically, new language in Section 10(a) authorized the FWS to issue permits for take that is "incidental to, and not the purpose of, the carrying out of an otherwise lawful activity." To receive an incidental take permit, applicants must submit an HCP to the FWS that specifies how sufficient habitat will be preserved to maintain the long-term viability of the species. In other words, rather than protecting habitat through reaction by blocking bulldozers, chain saws, and plows at numerous sites, Congress placed incentives in Section 10 for private actors and local and state governments to develop proactive plans to protect habitat in exchange for allowing some human uses to continue. Federal agencies do not have a direct incentive to participate in HCPs, because they are not covered by the Section 9 prohibition on take and thus do not need incidental take permits. Nevertheless, some federal agencies and officials occasionally do participate in HCPs.

Some environmental activists since have argued that HCPs allow resource users and developers to evade the ESA's strict prohibition on take. Although undoubtedly true, this critique overlooks some important points regarding the actual impact of the strict prohibition on take. Federal officials never have been able to monitor habitat modification at every site, which means that evasions routinely occur. Moreover, given the extent of habitat degradation that was occurring, some scientists have argued that it makes more sense to think in terms of triage, preserving the best habitat patches through proactive planning rather than struggling to preserve all remaining patches through the strict prohibition on take. If the strict prohibition on take cannot protect each site in practice, then attempting to do so may produce haphazard outcomes in which some of the best habitat patches are lost while other patches with less conservation value are saved. Moreover, the saved patches might not result in an interconnected preserve system that would increase the conservation value of each patch. Hence the new Section 10 language on HCPs did not simply reflect a compromise between species protection and economic development; it also reflected a scientific logic regarding the importance of foresight in conservation planning.

To receive an incidental take permit, applicants must submit an HCP that meets several basic conditions (U.S. FWS and NMFS 1996, *III-10*). The HCP must include the following:

- detailed information on the likely impacts resulting from the proposed take;
- measures applicants will undertake to monitor, minimize, and mitigate such impacts;
- available funding to undertake such measures;
- procedures to deal with unforeseen circumstances;
- alternative actions applicants considered that would not result in take, and the reasons why they will not pursue these alternatives; and
- any additional measures the FWS requires as necessary or appropriate for purposes of the plan.

How applicants meet these conditions is left largely to them, subject to FWS approval. This discretion empowers applicants to determine the institutional design of their HCP. They need not collaborate in preparing or implementing an HCP, but they often can benefit from doing so wherever habitat sprawls across private parcels and public jurisdictions.

The first incidental take permit was issued in 1983 for an HCP that covered 3,500 acres on San Bruno Mountain south of San Francisco. The second permit was issued in 1986 for an HCP that covered 70,000 acres in the Coachella Valley near Palm Springs. Since then, the pace of HCP planning, permitting, and implementation accelerated markedly, peaking in 1995, when more than 80 permits were issued. As of November 2003, the FWS had issued incidental take permits for 435 HCPs (U.S. FWS 2003). Although the first two HCPs were collaborative, this has not been true of all HCPs, which vary widely on many dimensions (Thomas 2003a; Karkkainen 2003). Some are small, covering only a few acres. Others are large, covering tens of thousands—even millions—of acres. Typically, larger

HCPs are more collaborative, because they involve more stakeholders, but this is not always the case.

HCPs have become an attractive alternative for complying with the Section 9 prohibition on take, because incidental take permits provide increased certainty in the minds of private landowners and local and state officials regarding what land uses will be possible in the future. Without this permit, the ESA's regulatory hammer looms, poised to foreclose any and all activities on nonfederal land. This increased certainty provides the fundamental incentive for nonfederal actors to participate in HCPs. In the words of one FWS official, who participated in several early collaborative HCPs:

> [W]hen you're putting these planning efforts together, and when you have a listed species, then you are looking at people and saying "To get a permit [for incidental take] you gotta come up with a plan that protects the species, and that means you're gonna have to give up some of your property or [purchase] some property somewhere else. In other words, you're giving up some of your assets, hopefully to get permission to earn more." I strongly believe ... that you're not gonna get very many people that will do this sort of thing voluntarily. (Thomas 2003b, *218–19*)

Thus HCPs tend to occur where the Section 9 prohibition on take is enforced aggressively (Yaffee et al. 1998, *I-1*). Government as institution, therefore, provides the background conditions for collaboration, because the ESA and its implementing regulations provide the basic incentives to prepare and implement an HCP. Without these incentives, there would be no HCPs, let alone collaborative HCPs.

GOVERNMENT AS ACTOR

While federal institutions provide the background conditions for encouraging HCPs, federal officials play a more direct role in encouraging collaboration within HCPs. Sometimes they are joined by local and state officials, in which case government as actor may involve public officials at all three levels of government. Federal officials encourage collaboration by providing technical and financial assistance to help private actors and public officials at the local and state levels prepare and implement HCPs. They also provide assurances that additional regulatory burdens will not be imposed on those who take proactive steps to conserve habitat. Because these regulatory assurances, in addition to the incidental take permit itself, further enhance certainty about future land uses, they provide a significant incentive to pre-pare HCPs and for federal officials to influence the content of those HCPs.

ISSUE DEFINITION

Federal institutions and actors play different roles in defining the issues for which HCP collaboration occurs. Federal institutions such as the ESA and its implementing regulations frame the problem as preserving species and their habitats, while empowering stakeholders to determine the biophysical and social scales of the HCP. Thus an HCP may cover most or relatively lit-tle of the habitat of a particular species; it may cover many species or only one; and it may include many or relatively few stakeholders. No explicit rules determine the biophysical or social scale of HCPs. FWS officials offer guidance, which carries authority because they must approve HCPs before issuing incidental take permits, but there are no general rules carrying the force of law. Thus federal institutions largely determine the issue framing, while federal officials may shape the biophysical scale of policy alternatives and the social scale of the planning process within each HCP.

One might argue that FWS guidance constitutes an institution if the guidelines are formally written and disseminated. Indeed, written guide-lines encourage public participation for large HCPs, but these guidelines do not require public participation for any HCP or provide standards regard-ing who should participate. Moreover, these guidelines do not carry the force of law. Given the vagueness of these guidelines, and the fact that they are not rules, they should not be considered part of the institutions govern-ing collaboration. As individual actors, FWS officials play a more important role than institutions in this regard when using their discretion in approv-ing HCPs, because they can argue that more public participation should be included in a specific HCP.

FWS officials also can influence the scale of collaboration among permit applicants, some of whom might initially prefer to prepare their own HCPs, regardless of the scope of public participation. An individual appli-cant may not own or manage sufficient habitat to maintain the long-term viability of species covered by the HCP. Hence FWS officials may not grant an incidental take permit for the HCP or might signal to an applicant that they will issue a permit only if the HCP is coordinated with other HCPs. FWS staff used this signaling strategy to encourage collaboration in Natural Communities Conservation Planning (NCCP), a state-run program in California that provided the opening vignette for this book. The FWS issued incidental take permits for numerous HCPs within the 6,000-square-mile NCCP planning area. Because NCCP covered numerous species, jurisdictions, and private parcels, some participants were tempted to prepare their own HCPs independently of the larger state-sponsored program. To encourage participation and collaboration, FWS officials let it be known that anyone choosing to develop a separate HCP would have to demonstrate that it was compatible with NCCP plans. Thus if permit applicants chose not to participate in the larger NCCP planning process, they would still be bound by NCCP plans, so it behooved them to shape those plans by participating (Thomas 2003b).

Federal officials have another important lever for influencing the scale of collaboration. Since 1994, they have offered permit applicants regulatory assurances providing immunity from specific rules in exchange for proactive efforts to conserve habitat. The most prominent such assurance is the No Surprises Policy, which was introduced in 1994 and codified in 1998 (U.S. FWS and NMFS 1998). During the interim period, the policy was so popular among permit applicants that at least 74 HCPs were thought to contain No Surprises assurances (Yaffee et al. 1998, 2–5). When applied, this policy assures permit applicants that no additional land-use restrictions or financial compensation will be required with respect to species covered by an incidental take permit if unforeseen circumstances arise indicating that additional mitigation is needed. Instead, the federal government, not the permit holder, assumes responsibility for implementing additional conservation measures. This broad guarantee increases the leverage of FWS officials in encouraging applicants to broaden the scale of their HCP, because activities covered by the incidental take permit will be immune from further regulation if new findings indicate that species covered by the HCP are in more trouble than initially thought.

This broad guarantee sparked criticism from numerous parties, including scientists who argued that the No Surprises Policy should take into account uncertainty about the actual condition of species and habitat when permits are issued. To reconcile this conflict, federal officials issued revised guidelines in the *Habitat Conservation Planning Handbook* (U.S. FWS and NMFS 2000). According to these new guidelines, "an adaptive management strategy is essential for HCPs that would otherwise pose a significant risk to the species at the time the permit is issued due to significant data or information gaps" (U.S. FWS and NMFS 2000, 35252). Under these guidelines, each HCP planning group should adopt its own adaptive management strategy, which would become part of the HCP and a condition of the permit; thus any adjustments within the stated range of the adaptive management strategy would not constitute a regulatory surprise under the No Surprises Policy. These are only guidelines, but they do provide FWS officials with some leverage to shape the scale of collaboration within HCPs.

RESOURCES FOR COLLABORATION

Human, technical, and financial resources can shape collaborative efforts in important ways. Collaboration in habitat conservation planning depends significantly on governmental actors, as federal officials have great discretion to determine how resources are allocated to specific HCPs.

Human Resources

Permit applicants are the most significant human resource in HCP planning processes. Because the FWS is understaffed relative to its mandated tasks, its officials participate sporadically during HCP planning processes. Permit applicants have a strong incentive to encourage the participation of FWS officials because the FWS must approve their HCP before issuing an incidental take permit. Without this permit, applicants cannot implement the HCP, which means they cannot legally pursue the economic activities that led them to develop the HCP in the first place. Once the permit is issued, FWS officials play a much more limited role, with other actors such as environmental activists usually monitoring HCP implementation. For this reason, permit applicants may invite broad public participation in the planning and implementation phases to allay suspicions, enhance legitimacy, and ward off lawsuits. Federal guidelines encourage public participation, though it is not required.

Some federal officials bring extensive collaborative expertise to HCPs. At the national level, Interior Secretary Bruce Babbitt and his staff were particularly notable in this regard during the Clinton administration, when the No Surprises Policy was developed. Some FWS staff also bring considerable expertise. Gail Kobetich became legendary in California, where 12 of the first 14 HCPs occurred, and where the initial collaboration success stories emerged. He retired in 1998, after 33 years with the FWS, during which time he oversaw the creation and expansion of the FWS Endangered Species Program in California, worked on the first HCP on San Bruno

Mountain, and developed a reputation for collaboration that transcended his position of regulatory authority. In one indication of his reputation for enhancing collaboration, he was "demoted" to a local office in Southern California in the early 1990s to buttress NCCP.

Technical Resources

On one level, technical assistance is simply a bureaucratic matter. As in other policy areas, federal officials provide technical assistance to help permit applicants comply with the law, follow procedures, and complete paperwork. For example, federal officials compiled and distributed the *Habitat Conservation Planning Handbook*, a thick compilation of technical documents that contains all the rules, guidance, and templates that applicants need to prepare and submit an HCP. Although this type of technical assistance enables more people to prepare HCPs, it plays no obvious role in collaborative compliance. Indeed, the handbook itself does not even contain a section on collaboration, though it does recommend that applicants use steering committees for large, regionally based HCPs to "provide a forum for public discourse and reconciling conflicts," among other purposes (U.S. FWS and NMFS 1996, *III-3*).

On another level, however, technical assistance plays a pivotal role in collaborative HCPs by providing evidence and arguments to persuade applicants that collaboration may be in their best interests. Federal officials use technical information about the geographic distribution of habitat, along with technical knowledge about the causal mechanisms of extinction through habitat modification, to educate applicants about the distribution of habitat beyond their property boundaries and the role of others in the collective deterioration of that habitat. In so doing, they educate applicants about the collective-action problem that exists wherever habitat extends across multiple ownerships and jurisdictions, thereby providing a logical foundation for collaboration. In the words of one applicant, who explained how technical assistance from several sources, including federal officials, led her to believe that habitat-wide collaboration was the preferred strategy for conservation planning, "We started hearing the same thing over and over: first of all, you don't look at the species, you look at the habitats; and you do things as comprehensively as you can" (Thomas 2003b, *212*).

Moreover, even if several applicants own or manage sufficient habitat to prepare individual HCPs that the FWS would accept unconditionally, collaboration might still benefit them if they were to pool land and other resources (financial, technical, and human) to create a common preserve system. By collaborating on a common plan, and by contributing to a common pool of high-quality habitat, each applicant might be able to set aside less land for conservation purposes and use fewer personal resources, while producing a collaborative HCP that conserves habitat more effectively than several uncoordinated HCPs. Applicants might also be able to reduce the transaction costs of preparing and implementing an HCP by pooling their administrative efforts.

Technical assistance about the benefits of collaboration expands applicants' understanding of their interdependence with other applicants and the potential gains from joint action. Yet federal officials are not the only source of such technical assistance. Scientists have distilled arcane knowledge about the causal mechanisms of extinction into practical advice for conservation planning (Noss and Cooperrider 1994; Noss et al. 1997). Some environmental groups also provide technical assistance. Although some litigious environmental groups prefer filing lawsuits in federal courts to enforce the ESA's rules, other groups, such as land trusts, favor providing technical and financial assistance for collaborative conservation efforts. The Nature Conservancy, for example, does not litigate, but provides both technical assistance to help others design effective preserve systems and financial assistance to acquire and manage habitat preserves, including core habitat in HCP preserve systems.[5]

Financial Resources

The federal government also provides financial assistance for HCPs, but these funds are limited and not spread equally across all HCPs. The funds tend to go to collaborative HCPs, primarily for institutional reasons, but also because federal officials use these funds to encourage collaboration. Section 6(d) of the ESA authorizes the secretary of interior to provide financial assistance to states, and through them to local communities and individuals, to aid in the development of programs for the conservation of threatened and endangered species. These federal grants must include a contribution from nonfederal partners, either financial or in kind. The financial match must be at least 25 percent of the estimated cost, or 10 percent if two or more states or territories implement a joint project. Thus the institutional rules encourage collaborative rather than single-applicant HCPs, because the funds are passed through state agencies to local actors and the matching requirement is reduced if more states are involved. Indeed, most of the HCPs funded in 2002 were large, regionally based, collaborative HCPs. Yet this funding varies greatly from year to year, depending on federal budget priorities. In 2002, the FWS awarded $68 million in grants to 16 states to support the planning process for 24 HCPs and land-acquisition costs for 17 HCPs (U.S. FWS 2002).

ORGANIZATIONAL STRUCTURE AND DECISION-MAKING PROCESSES

The institutions of government largely empower applicants to determine the organizational structure and decision-making processes of HCPs. Although FWS officials may suggest changes in these areas for specific HCPs, applicants typically are given much discretion. Thus an HCP may be planned and implemented within the structure of an existing organization, or an entirely new organization may be created to plan or implement an HCP. The Coachella Valley HCP, for example, was developed by a multipartner steering committee specifically created for this purpose (CVHCP 1985). Similarly, applicants may use a highly insular decision-making process, with no public participation, or one that is broadly collaborative. They are free to choose decision-making rules, such as consensus, majority rule, or even hierarchy. Although federal institutions do not determine what structures or decision-making processes are appropriate, FWS officials may use their leverage to encourage certain types of structures or processes.

COLLABORATIVE OUTCOMES

Environmental Outcomes

HCPs produce many environmental management outcomes, such as plans, permits, implementation agreements, land acquisitions, and restoration activities. The most obvious outcome of an HCP planning process is the plan itself. For large, collaborative HCPs, these plans can run hundreds of pages, and they are routinely incorporated into other planning processes, such as local zoning plans. These large, collaborative plans specify numerous implementation activities, such as land acquisitions, restoration activities, funding mechanisms, monitoring programs, and enforcement provisions. When the FWS approves a plan, the agency issues an incidental take permit that specifies the conditions of the permit, including implementation of the plan. For collaborative HCPs, an additional document, known as an implementation agreement, also is prepared, which specifies who is responsible for implementing specific provisions in the plan. The signatures on the implementation agreement provide accountability should parts of the plan not be implemented.

Yet despite all of this documented management activity, it is difficult to assess whether any HCP has had a net positive effect on the environment. One reason is that the baseline for comparison is an unknown counterfactual condition: What would have happened under a strict prohibition on take, in which case some development likely would have occurred without an HCP in existence that contained proactive protection measures? Second, most research on HCPs has focused on the planning process, not implementation. Thus the most we can extrapolate from this research is that "appropriate" planning processes will lead to desirable environmental outcomes. A consortium of scientists examined how science was incorporated into 208 HCPs through 1997 (Kareiva et al. 1999). If one assumes that scientists are the best judges of the environmental merits of an HCP, and that HCPs are implemented as written, then their findings provide an indirect indicator of expected environmental outcomes. Third, only one implementation study of an HCP has been completed, and the findings of this study are ambiguous as to whether the HCP improved environmental conditions (Schweik and Thomas 2002; Thomas and Schweik 1999). Fourth, the FWS does not maintain a database of indicators regarding the extent to which HCPs have been implemented, let alone indicators of environmental impacts. Fifth, even if multiple case studies of HCP implementation and indicators of environmental performance existed, it would be difficult to make claims about the environmental impacts of an HCP, because many other factors can cause fluctuations in the population of a species and the condition of its habitat, such as climate change, weather patterns, and human impacts beyond the boundaries of the HCP. In sum, though we know a great deal about the paperwork generated by HCP planning processes, we know very little about the degree to which any of these activities actually improve environmental conditions, which is one of the reasons why HCPs remain so controversial.

Social Outcomes

As with environmental outcomes, little direct evidence exists regarding social outcomes. Again, we can rely on indirect evidence, because a consortium of social scientists has completed a systematic study of public participation during HCP planning (Yaffee et al. 1998). Hence one might argue that variation in public participation explains variation in social capital. Moreover, if we include economic opportunities as a social outcome, then we can assume that the HCP program has affected social outcomes, because the program was created in part to allow some economic activities to occur within the habitat of endangered species.

Direct evidence of social outcomes from the only case study of HCP implementation is mixed (Thomas and Schweik 1999; Schweik and Thomas 2002). On the plus side, participants in the Coachella Valley Fringe-Toed Lizard HCP built a great deal of collaborative capacity in the 1990s, which carried over to a new and larger planning process for a multiple species HCP nearing completion in 2003. On the downside, critics of the first Coachella Valley HCP argued that it preserved only 5 to 10 percent of the lizard's remaining habitat (roughly 2 percent of its original range), leaving most of the valley open to economic development. Participants later acknowledged that because of incomplete technical knowledge during the planning process, the HCP failed to include some critical habitat in the preserve system, which likely would diminish the environmental effectiveness of the HCP. Thus the scientific legitimacy of the HCP was questioned, although the collaborative process itself, which benefited from government technical and financial resources, as well as the existence of ESA rules, created social capital among the participants. This social capital is now an important factor in the new multispecies HCP, which may incorporate habitat for the lizard that was not included in the original HCP.

CONCLUSIONS

The guiding question in this case was, How can government officials use command-and-control rules, in combination with financial and technical assistance, to encourage collaboration? Financial and technical assistance were insufficient incentives for private landowners and local and state officials to prepare and implement an HCP, regardless of whether it was collaborative, because the cost of preparing HCPs is high. Instead, the fundamental incentive came from the lurking threat of enforcement under the ESA's command-and-control rules. The HCP program provided an institutional alternative to the strict prohibition on take. It also empowered participants to determine their own fate by designing their own land-use plans, rather than allowing courts to determine land-use restrictions. Once the FWS approved an HCP, the incidental take permit provided increased certainty in the minds of permit holders regarding future uses of land and natural resources covered by the HCP. The No Surprises Policy further assured applicants and permit holders that an HCP would not require future revision if new information arose indicating that species covered by the plan needed additional protection.

Government officials fostered collaboration within this institutional context primarily through technical and financial assistance. Of these, technical assistance was more important. To the extent that collaboration arose within HCPs, it was largely because FWS officials, along with academic scientists and nonprofit actors, provided technical assistance that educated applicants about the collective-action problems they faced and the benefits of collaborative solutions. Specifically, they used information about the geographic distribution of habitat, along with knowledge about the causal mechanisms of extinction through habitat modification, to educate applicants about the distribution of habitat beyond property boundaries and the collective-action problem that exists wherever habitat extends across multiple ownerships and jurisdictions. Federal institutions could have required collaboration as a rule for participation in the program, but this would have done little more than make people sit at the table together. Meaningful collaboration depends on participants understanding how common problems can be solved through this venue, which is why technical assistance of this sort was crucial.

Once collaboration was under way, financial assistance encouraged and supported it. For institutional reasons, federal funds under Section 6 of the ESA were passed through state agencies to local communities, which increased participation by some actors. The federal matching requirement also was reduced if more states were involved. In addition, federal officials targeted large, collaborative HCPs, rather than small, single-applicant HCPs. Although this funding varied greatly by year and did not cover the entire cost of HCPs, it did provide a supplemental incentive for collaboration. It also increased the likely success of collaborative HCPs by providing significant financial assistance through matching grants passed through states.

Federal institutions have left great discretion to permit applicants to determine the geographic scale and collaborative nature of each HCP. Although an HCP must necessarily occur within the geographic boundaries of the habitat of one or more listed species, federal rules have not required that HCPs cover the entire habitat. Thus some HCPs have been tiny, covering less than five acres. With such small geographic areas, applicants saw less reason for collaboration or public involvement. Technical assistance from FWS officials and other actors educates such applicants about larger collective-action problems of which they might be a part. Where such technical assistance has been unsuccessful, FWS officials have occasionally upped the ante by issuing explicit regulatory threats that HCPs might not be approved if they are not linked with other HCPs in the vicinity (as occurred with NCCP in Southern California). To the extent that these threats are perceived to be plausible, applicants have an additional incentive to collaborate.

CHAPTER 5

ENCOURAGEMENT THROUGH GRANTS

Ohio's Farmland Preservation Task Forces

T he habitat conservation planning case (Chapter 4) highlighted how government as an institution, in the form of the Endangered Species Act, combined with governmental actors to provide regulatory relief to influence collaborative efforts. This chapter examines how, in the absence of regulatory threats, governmental institutions and actors can encourage collaborative environmental management through a grant program. Through a study of 15 counties involved in the Ohio Farmland Preservation Planning Program, we look at the role of the state government as an institution, as well as local governmental actors and institutions, in encouraging collaborative planning. For policymakers considering how to promote collaboration, grants may be especially attractive in that they are less politically charged than regulations. As shown in the analysis that follows, however, government influences far more than just the financial resources available for the collaborative effort.

THE OHIO FARMLAND PRESERVATION PLANNING PROGRAM

Throughout the United States, open space and agricultural land are disappearing. Between 1959 and 1992, land cover in cropland and pasture decreased by 40 million acres (USDA 1998b). Approximately 1 million acres of U.S. agricultural land are being converted to housing, industry, and other uses each year (AFT 1998). Land use, and resulting land cover patterns, increasingly are linked to issues such as food security, recreation, employment opportunities, and community health. In addition, land-use changes can raise many environmental concerns, including rare species protection, wildlife habitat, soil conservation, water quality, and global climate change.

In the eastern United States, where most land is owned privately, efforts to shape land-use patterns face the challenge of coordination among many different stakeholders. Government has limited control over how private lands are used. In addition, local governments, which typically control land-use changes through planning and zoning, may not have the same priorities as state and federal agencies. Therefore, top-down government regulation of land use is neither feasible nor necessarily desirable. Instead, collaborative planning is being used more frequently to address this challenge.

An increasingly popular mechanism for governments to encourage collaboration is to provide funding to applicants and then step aside as the grantees craft collaborative processes tailored to their local circumstances. This raises important questions about what grant giving can achieve, how grantees act with these financial resources, and how governments influence these collaborative processes. In other words, in government-funded efforts to encourage collaborative efforts, what can money buy?

Government grant programs, as institutions, may have a bigger impact on collaboration than conventionally thought. In general, these programs establish goals and then provide funding for collaborative efforts so that they can work to achieve these goals. But government appears to influence much more than goals and financial resources when it works through a grant program. Rather than simply supporting a collaborative effort between governmental and nongovernmental partners, it appears that government places its imprint on all aspects of the process and outcomes.

In the Ohio Farmland Preservation Planning Program (OFPPP), governments played both institutional and actor roles. Most obviously, the state government played an important institutional role in establishing the grant program, including how funding was to be distributed, who was granted authority to oversee it, and what was required of grant recipients. But state governmental institutions were not the only governmental institutions at play here. Local governments (counties and townships) have created existing rules affecting land-use choices, and these formed the backdrop against which the collaborative task forces developed plans and determined which policy recommendations were feasible.

The role of government as actor was played not by state officials, but by a wide range of local government officials who were involved in creating and maintaining task forces and planning activities. In many groups, governmental actors provided critical human, technical, and financial resources. Moreover, governmental actors participating in the task forces were involved in establishing group structures and processes. Thus the importance of local governmental institutions and actors in shaping the task forces indicates that even as one government seeks to spark collaboration through purely institutional means, how that collaboration plays out can depend on governmental institutions and actors at other levels.

Like many grant programs, the OFPPP aimed to transfer funding from state to local governments as a means to achieve policy goals. In this program, the goals were related to land-use planning and farmland preservation, and local communities were given considerable flexibility in carrying out planning processes tied to local contexts.

In June 1998, the Ohio Department of Development's Office of Housing and Community Partnerships (OHCP) announced a matching grant program for rural counties to prepare local farmland preservation plans. The program's objective was to encourage counties to "gather appropriate data from which local goals [could] be established relative to the agricultural industry and farmland." Once they had set their goals, strategies could be devised (Graves 1998).

The program made grants of up to $10,000 available to each of the 81 counties eligible for federal Small Cities Community Development Block Grant funds. Funding was contingent on the counties providing a 1:1 match in dollars or in kind and each establishing a county farmland preservation task force that included a "cross section of interests" (Graves 1998). The state granted the funds to county commissioners, who then were responsible for creating the task forces. The grants came with very few strings attached, requiring only that each task force produce a plan that included soils information, submit its plan to the OHCP by December 31, 1999, and include a "cross section of interests" in creating the plan. Of the 81 eligible counties, 61 participated in the grant program.

Because the program was highly decentralized, task forces operated independently from each other and with little direction from state officials. In practice, many county commissioners delegated responsibility for convening the task force to other governmental actors or to citizens. The task force leaders were free to select members, coordinate procedures, allocate budgets, and handle the division of labor as they saw fit, in conjunction with other task force members. Several counties combined this opportunity with ongoing planning efforts, in effect leveraging significant additional funding for farmland preservation planning. As a result, though each of the participating task forces received the same grant amount of $10,000, collaborative processes and outcomes played out very differently across the counties.

ISSUE DEFINITION

Land-use and land-cover changes in Ohio are not new phenomena. Forests and wetlands were converted to agricultural use in the nineteenth century and first part of the twentieth century. Later in the twentieth century, agricultural use decreased as a result of farm abandonment and metropolitan expansion. As in other states with growing populations, land has been developed as people have migrated into formerly rural areas.

In the past few years, policy debates about preserving farmland often have been combined with discussions about open space and green space. For example, an Ohio statewide voter initiative passed in 2000 created a broad Clean Ohio Fund. The initiative authorized the state to issue up to $400 million in bonds to pay for programs that conserve and preserve natural areas, open spaces, farmlands, and other lands. Framing the scope of an issue broadly is one political strategy for increasing support (Schattschneider 1960).

When government plays the role of grant giver, it gets to define the issue, in terms of problem framing and scale. In the case of the OFPPP, the state defined program objectives as centering on preserving farmland, rather than on open space or green space. This narrow way of framing the issue encouraged task forces to gather information and focus proposed policies on agricultural lands, rather than on land use generally. Moreover, it encouraged task force membership that was weighted heavily toward agricultural interests, rather than a more diverse array of participants.

The grant program also defined the biophysical boundaries when rural counties were designated as the eligible recipients. This set the spatial scale at which the problem was to be tackled—the county. This spatial scale yielded several benefits. First, it was compatible with existing soil data from the Natural Resource Conservation Service and Ohio Department of Natural Resources, which facilitated data gathering to meet the grant requirement that each county plan include soils maps. Second, the county level was conducive to encouraging regular participation from task force members, as all lived only a relatively short drive from the meeting sites. Finally, the county level was a logical scale for interactions between task force members and the government jurisdictions with primary authority over land use related to agriculture: counties and townships (political subdivisions of a county).

Although counties proved to be a workable scale, well suited to the level at which many land-use policies are made, one drawback was that where county farmland was affected by land-use trends in other counties, interests from those counties were not included in the collaboration. For example, watershed boundaries typically do not fall along county lines, yet land uses upstream can affect downstream water and land substantially. Moreover, urbanization and development often are driven by growing urban populations in adjacent counties, and task forces did not analyze such areas in their plans. Another drawback was that in some counties, land-use authority rests with townships; in those places, a county-level planning effort did not match the level of decision-making authority.

Additionally, defining the program around farmland, rather than open space or green space more generally, made it difficult for task forces to garner widespread public support for the issue. In fact, in a number of counties, task force members cited obstacles related to public understanding and recognition that farmland preservation was an important and desirable goal. Although this lack of community concern did not interfere with task forces' ability to create a plan, it did lead some task force members to doubt whether their plans could be implemented. After all, if community members do not view farmland preservation as a big concern, then even the finest plan is not likely to succeed.

Within constraints established by the state, task forces were allowed to tailor their plans to local biophysical and social contexts. This flexibility was appropriate, given several important differences across counties, most notably in geographic location, level of urbanization, and amount of land in farms. These differences are reflected in the set of 15 counties examined in this analysis, which ranged from rural to metropolitan fringe counties located throughout the state, with farmland from 50,000 to 268,000 acres.

Beyond the state grant requirements, important governmental institutions existed at the local level. County-level governmental rules had a substantial impact on the framing of the problem and how it could be addressed. The prevalence of land-use zoning, which is determined by county and township governments, ranged from none to all of the townships in a county. Task force members planning for farmland preservation took the existing level of zoning into account in making policy recommendations. Those without zoning faced a constrained set of alternative solutions. A task force member in one such area said, "We did not use the 'Z' word .... The more rural you get, the more resistant people are to zoning. We had to be very sensitive about this. We had to promise going into these township meetings that we would not mention zoning. If a township trustee became somehow tied to zoning, they would never get reelected." In contrast, in counties with zoning rules already in place, task force members included zoning as a feasible solution for farmland preservation.

Thus the focus of collaboration in the OFPPP was determined largely by the grant program, a governmental institution at the state level. The program provided the funds to establish task forces addressing a particular issue, farmland preservation, at a particular biophysical scale, the county. Governmental institutions at the local level were important as well, particularly the existing set of land-use zoning rules.

RESOURCES FOR COLLABORATION

Grant giving represents an effort to augment resources for collaboration. Although the grant itself is a form of financial resource, the grant requirements, along with the funding provided, can influence other resources, including human and technical resources. In addition, resources are tied to actors and institutions in government jurisdictions other than the state granting agency.

Financial Resources

The funding that is provided through grant programs such as OFPPP is an important resource for promoting collaborative endeavors. In the OFPPP, the $10,000 grants provided resources for task forces to be established, to function, and to produce plans. The 1:1 matching requirement allowed the state government to leverage its investment by ensuring that each task force had additional resources at its disposal. In fact, some task forces expended considerably more than $10,000 of their own funds. But at the same time, the matching requirement discouraged some of the state's rural counties from participating.

Governmental actors often were influential in acquiring funding beyond the $10,000 grant. In some cases, county commissions provided the match in cash; in others, the task force members from governmental agencies such as soil and water conservation districts and county planning offices logged hours as part of an in-kind match. According to one member, county commissioners who did not see farmland preservation as a high priority were less willing to contribute financial resources to the effort. In other cases, task force members who were employees of governmental agencies were entrepreneurial in securing funds from their agencies.

The task forces used government funds to pay for consultants, staff time, materials such as slide shows and brochures, postage, food and mileage for members attending meetings, and the costs of producing and copying plans. Across the 15 cases, task force total expenditures ranged from a low of $400 to a high of more than $30,000.[1]

In some of these counties, state funding was used to pay for existing staff time and planning efforts, for tasks that might have been done anyway. In one county, for example, the farmland preservation funds were directed to the planning commission, which used a portion for a "cost of community services" study and the rest to support its ongoing planning efforts. In another county, grant funds were transferred to a regional planning commission and charged to planning activities that had occurred before the grant was awarded (some information produced from those earlier efforts was included in the farmland preservation plan).

Through the grant program, state government institutions provided a range of influence, relative to other financial sources, across the cases. For some task forces, the state grant program provided nearly all of the fiscal resources; for others, it provided a minority portion. In all cases, financial resources were wholly or predominantly provided by various governments, rather than by private citizens.

Human Resources

The OFPPP did not create a strong human resources presence from the state. Rather, it formally vested authority over the collaborative efforts with county commissioners. Such ceding of power from the state to local officials can increase trust in the collaborative effort, especially in states with strong traditions of local control ("home rule") in land-use matters (see Thomas 1999). At the same time, it does not ensure that a wide cross section of public and private individuals will belong to the groups. Instead, it can serve to foster the engagement of particular sets of human resources—those in existing governmental structures traditionally used by local officials.

In every county, the commissioners delegated leadership to others, resulting in considerable variation in leadership and expertise across the task forces. In more than half (8 of 15) of the counties, government officials working in regional or county land-use planning departments served as task force leaders or coleaders. Ohio State University Extension personnel had a hand in leading six of the task forces, consultants took on leadership roles in four of the task forces, and citizens at large helped lead in four of the task forces. In three task forces, soil and water conservation district public employees served as leaders or coleaders. Overall, local governmental actors provided important leadership roles in most of the task forces.

The state grant did not specify who should serve on the task forces, stipulating only that the resulting task forces must "ensure that a cross section of interests have input into this process" and suggesting the consideration of interests such as "Farm Bureau, Farmers' Union, Grange, environmental organizations, developers, farmers, chamber of commerce, realtors, home builders associations, local government officials, conservation districts, local citizens, non-profit organizations, [and] agricultural business representatives" (Graves 1998). The grants did not specify how many of these might constitute a "cross section." In the 15 counties, task forces ranged in size from 9 to 51 members. So although the grant guidelines did provide task forces with a starting point in selecting participants, the lack of specific requirements meant that the set of participants was not strongly influenced by grant rules. In practice, representation across the task forces ranged from 4 to 12 of the 14 interests listed above.

Most task forces reported that farmers and local government officials were the dominant stakeholders represented on the task forces. In contrast, land developers, real estate interests, and environmental groups were less prevalent. This somewhat narrow range of task force members limited the breadth of expertise brought to bear on the collaborative planning process. One member described his task force as "a bunch of old German farmers sitting around trying to imagine what other groups would think." Several task force members reported difficulties in increasing their legitimacy with broader publics because of this lack of representation. One said that even though his group was supposed to include a cross section of interests, its membership was fairly narrow, and thus the county commissioners viewed it as a special-interest group. This discouraged the commissioners from providing much financial support for the plan.

When the OFPPP defined the problem relatively narrowly, as farmland preservation rather than open space or green space preservation, this affected which interests were invited to the table and which were not. Clearly there was widespread agreement among task force members about the value of farmland and recommendations for how to preserve it. But members recognized that in the broader community, farmland preservation issues did not generate much concern or agreement about appropriate actions. Thus, although a grant program with a relatively narrowly defined problem such as farmland preservation may be well suited to spurring discussions among agricultural interests, it may be less successful in fostering policy change that is implementable and acceptable to the broader community.

In addition to human resources within the collaborative groups, each member brought a set of social relationships that represented networks of human resources outside the groups. The Office of Farmland Preservation sought, to a limited extent, to help build networks across task force members through a farmland preservation conference in March 1999. In this capacity, state governmental actors drew together numerous task force members from across the state.

More important than state-supported networking was the set of social relationships individual members brought with them to the task forces. Important differences across the counties were evident in the level of networks, as some task forces had participants who had been involved in land-use issues previously and were members of well-established networks with planning experience, often involving governmental actors. A task force member in one county said, "We weren't starting from scratch, so the task wasn't so daunting .... There is great agency cooperation in this county, with a track record of working together in the past. That helped us in working together on the task force."

In addition, seven of the task forces were in counties that had county or township comprehensive plans updated since 1995, and four had members currently working with other land-use organizations to develop comprehensive plans. In places where task force members could tap into recent county comprehensive plans, networking with government planners helped them accomplish their goals. As a task force member in one county explained, "The regional planning office had GIS available. We had a good relationship with them and they were able to prepare ... maps for us."

In contrast, other task forces were inexperienced with land use issues and comprehensive planning and had no preexisting networks to support these efforts. Two were in counties without comprehensive land-use plans, and two others were in counties with existing comprehensive plans that were at least 25 years old. Without these human resources to draw on, task forces in these counties devoted significant time and energy to learning about fundamental concepts such as policy tools and farmland preservation benefits. In fact, one such task force plan devoted a substantial section to explaining what comprehensive plans are.

Across the 15 counties, human resources available to the task forces largely were governmental actors. This was facilitated by rules of the grant program, which centered grants on existing governance structures at the county level. By working through the county commissioners, who were already familiar with government planners and soil and water conservation district personnel, the program fostered the use of governmental actors in farmland preservation planning. Where members had experience in prior land-use issues or were skillful at connecting with people—especially government personnel—outside the group, task forces had substantial human resources to employ in their collaborative efforts.

Technical Resources

Technical resources consist of information and knowledge about the natural resource and its management. Both scientific and local time-and-place data are important resources for collaborative groups to draw on in planning. In the OFPPP, grant guidelines had minimal technical requirements—only that the plan include a soils map. As actors, personnel in the Office of Farmland Preservation served as a resource for task forces seeking information, and the March 1999 conference drew participants from task forces across the state to share information. Task forces rarely interacted with each other to share technical information, however. This was partly a function of the grant program, which established 61 independent grants for 61 separate farmland preservation plans, without requirements or incentives for interaction among task forces.

For farmland preservation planning, three key types of information are land use, agricultural economic, and public opinion (Korfmacher and

Koontz 2003). With each task force left to collect information independently, information gathering varied greatly. In some counties, the task force did not access even basic land-use data, such as existing county soils maps, whereas in other counties, the task force developed complex geographic databases and collected rich socioeconomic information.

Task forces drew on a variety of sources of information, both governmental and nongovernmental. Within the task forces, governmental actors as well as citizen members shared in obtaining information. Task forces also drew on resources outside the group, with nine of them turning to private consultants for technical assistance, including financial analyses, technical writing, and land-use analyses. In three of the counties, task forces obtained technical assistance from government officials engaged in broader land-use planning activities.

Much of the technical information used, even that from private consultants, came from governmental sources. The OFPPP grant guidelines listed 19 potential sources of information, 13 of which were governmental (Graves 1998). One listed source that many of the task forces used for agricultural economic data was the U.S. Census of Agriculture. But most used the data without careful consideration of its applicability to the local context; instead of selecting categories of particular importance to their county, they typically just listed categories used in the census. Thus the ready availability of government-generated information contributed to its inclusion in the farmland preservation plans.

GROUP STRUCTURE AND DECISION-MAKING PROCESSES

Group structure and decision-making processes allow a group to select participants, coordinate activities, and make collective decisions. Because the grant rules did not specify any structural or process requirements, each task force was free to create its own arrangements. Thus the state grant program itself did not directly influence structural or process features. Many of the task forces, however, were led by governmental actors, who did affect structure and processes.

An early step that structures a collaborative effort is the selection of participants. Conceptually, selecting participants can be divided into two broad categories: closed or open. Closed selection refers to officials appointing members; open selection denotes people self-selecting or being elected at public meetings (Pierce and Doerksen 1976). Closed selection gives group leaders more influence over group composition than does open selection.

The majority of task forces (10 of 15) used only closed selection. Typically, task force leaders invited particular individuals to join. As one leader explained, "We wanted to include stakeholders in the community, with a balance of rural and agricultural interests on one side, and development interests on the other." Similarly, another leader said, "We brainstormed a list of who the community leaders are in agricultural issues ... and sent invitations to them to join." In cases where governmental actors led the task force, they played an important role in selecting participants.

Five of the task forces used both closed and open selection methods. In these cases, the leaders typically began by creating lists of individuals to invite, and then augmented these lists with announcements and meetings targeting the general public. As one leader said, "We invited people to participate through phone calls, newsletters, ads in the paper. All the meetings were open to the public. We always had an ad in the paper before each meeting."

The OFPPP did not specify how the task forces were to structure their efforts, so the groups coordinated activities and organized themselves in a number of ways. All of the task forces relied on meetings to bring together the whole group. Most task forces held meetings monthly, but attendance varied from nearly all of the task force members, in some counties, to just a small subset of active participants in others. In addition to task force meetings, eight of the groups structured work by creating committees to tackle particular tasks. Across the task forces, decisions about coordinating activities were shared between governmental actors and lay citizens alike.

The process of collaboration requires establishing decision-making procedures to incorporate individual input into group actions. Many proponents of collaboration recommend the use of consensus, whereby a decision requires assent from all group members to be sanctioned by the group. Consensus, they argue, can encourage groups to continue deliberating until a solution acceptable to all is found. This process can lead to the discovery of win–win solutions not previously thought possible. On the other hand, consensus gives any individual a veritable veto power over the decision, which can scuttle promising proposals. Moreover, consensus may result in watered-down compromises rather than innovative solutions.

In deciding how to make collective decisions, task forces were not significantly influenced by governmental institutions. In fact, the grant program was silent on this point. Because the OFPPP did not prescribe any decision-making procedures, task force leaders and members themselves decided how to make collective decisions, developing their own ways to determine what to include in the plan and whether to accept the final version. In several cases, external consultants gave advice on how to manage meetings; in other cases, the methods resulted from the views of task force leaders and members, both governmental actors and lay citizens.

For plan creation decisions, six task forces used consensus; eight used simple majority; and one used supermajority, with 85 percent assenting votes necessary for passage. According to members of the task forces using majority, few if any votes were close. Nevertheless, it was possible for these task forces to adopt something without the 100 percent agreement required for consensus. All but one of the task forces considered the approval of the final version of the plan as a whole, with seven using consensus, six using majority, and one using supermajority. In two of the counties using majority voting, dissenting members refused to sign the final plan, indicating that not all participants supported it.

COLLABORATIVE OUTCOMES

Environmental Outcomes

Because the OFPPP was a planning program, plan contents were an important environmental management outcome. Although the grant guidelines stipulated only that each task force plan include a soils map, they suggested 15 items that a task force should consider for possible inclusion: number and types of farms by commodity; changes in farm numbers and conversion rate of farmland over the last five years; location of existing farm inventory on a map; ages and locations of existing farm owners; identification and locations of important farmland; soil productivity; farm receipts for county (based on commodity); survey to determine the locations and types of investments in agricultural assets; location of agriculture supportive business and trends; identification of farms signed up in agricultural districts; locations of farms with land enrolled in government plans (e.g., wetland reserve, conservation easement); current zoning; identification and analysis of existing and proposed infrastructure; proposed growth areas (residential, commercial, and industrial); distances from municipalities, villages, and major residential or commercial developments and locations of existing protected natural areas, open space, parks, and so on (Graves 1998).

Table 5-1. Plan Contents

County number	Included soils map?	Number of suggested items included in plan[a]	Page count[b]
1	No	1	24
2	Yes	6	83
3	Yes	8	97
4	Yes	7.5	138
5	Yes	12	331
6	Yes	10	56
7	Yes	7	88
8	Yes	9	178
9	Yes	5.5	25
10	No	7.5	80
11	No	9.5	76
12	Yes	6.5	47
13	Yes	3.5	134[c]
14	Yes	7.5	83
15	Yes	1.5	14

[a]Partial item = 0.5.
[b]Double-spaced equivalent.
[c]This document was a more general land-use plan, of which farmland preservation was a small component.

Three of the completed plans did not meet the minimum technical requirement—inclusion of a soils map (see Table 5-1). In addition, the number of suggested content items greatly varied, from 1 to 12. The depth and sophistication of plans ran the gamut as well, with page counts ranging from 14 to 331. Thus the farmland preservation plans, which represent an important environmental management tool, varied significantly across the cases.

Another environmental management outcome from these collaborative efforts, cited by members of several task forces, was increased public education and awareness of farmland preservation issues. As one member explained, "I think that if there are a dozen people in each county that now know more about farmland preservation and can act in their communities, then that is a huge success." This outcome is especially important in counties with low levels of preexisting public concern and knowledge about farmland preservation, where even the most sophisticated farmland preservation plan would not have been likely to influence policy.

Governmental institutions, of both the grant program and the counties within which the task forces operated, had a significant impact on the set of feasible alternative solutions available to task force members carrying out their work. The grant program was for advisory planning, not for policy creation or implementation. Although the role of grant giver, supporting collaborative efforts with no legal authority, may be politically popular, it is not necessarily a reliable means to achieve on-the-ground results. Members of several task forces said their primary goals were to raise public awareness of the need to preserve farmland. They hoped that changes in public opinion might one day lead to policy changes.

Even without policy authority, however, in a handful of cases the task force plans provided input for county comprehensive plans being created or updated. Members of such task forces saw their collaborative efforts as affecting policy indirectly, even without formal authority. It seems that planning exercises, under the right circumstances, may be an effective means to change policy.

In terms of tangible environmental management outcomes, what did the OFPPP accomplish? At a minimum, stakeholders came together and discussed farmland preservation, and plans were written incorporating input from a variety of group members. But the state granting authority did not hold task forces accountable for meeting the original three grant requirements. In addition to the failure of three plans to include a soils map, no standards were in place to determine whether a cross section of interests was represented on the task forces, and several plans were not submitted by the deadline. In the end, the plans varied widely in content, depth, and sophistication.

Social Outcomes

Another measure of outcomes is social benefits. Using this yardstick, the OFPPP can be seen as more widely successful. Members of several task forces reported enhanced civic participation, and in a majority of the task forces, formal or informal networks were created to address future farmland preservation issues, as well as broader land-use issues.

For some of the counties without recent comprehensive land-use plans, the grants spurred discussions and the beginnings of efforts to address farmland preservation. A member in one county where the comprehensive plan had not been updated in more than 25 years described the modest accomplishments of the task force: "People asked, 'Why are we doing this plan?' It's going to just sit on the shelf, they thought. We can be an educational tool—that's why we made the standing committee. Education and

Table 5-2. Civic Participation and Networking Outcomes

County number	Encouraged civic participation?	Formal network that outlasted planning process?	Informal network that outlasted planning process?
1	Yes	No	Yes
2	Maybe	Maybe	Yes
3	Yes	Yes[a]	Yes
4	Yes	Yes	Yes
5	No	No	No
6	Yes	Yes	Yes
7	Maybe	No	Yes
8	Missing data	Maybe	Yes
9	Maybe	No	Yes
10	Yes	No	Maybe
11	Maybe	Yes[a]	Maybe
12	Yes	Yes	Yes
13	Yes	Yes	Yes
14	Yes	Yes[a]	Maybe
15	Yes	No	Maybe

[a]New formal network created with express purpose of facilitating plan implementation.

additional awareness will be the major impact of the plan. I'm hoping that in the future, we will have other reasons to meet and use this group."

The process of bringing together stakeholders to collaborate on problem solving can net social benefits beyond the solution of immediate problems. These benefits may include increased civic engagement and the building of social capital through the establishment of new social networks that may bring people together again in the future.

As shown in Table 5-2, members from most of the task forces indicated that they were encouraged by their experience to engage in future civic participation. In addition, members of seven task forces reported developing new formal social networks. In fact, in three cases, members said their task forces already had created committees aimed at facilitating implementation of the recommendations in their farmland preservation plans. Informal networks were cited by members of 10 task forces. In these cases, members foresaw opportunities for new communications channels when land-use and farmland issues might arise. One task force member explained, "I had one person call me the other day—he has his own business and would normally not be connected at all with other people in the county. But this committee has helped him establish networks. We have social organizations, chamber of commerce—everyone is involved. This is another circle of people in the county that are now communicating with each other."

Governmental Impacts on Outcomes

The environmental and social outcomes of farmland preservation collaboration resulted, to a large degree, from government involvement both as
institutions and as actors. The OFPPP was a governmental institution
designed to be a flexible grant program that would spur local collaborative
efforts without substantial state-level involvement. But the governmental
role as grant giver can affect collaborative outcomes in many ways. Fundamentally, by increasing financial resources, it can encourage new groups to
form around a particular issue or problem and use resources as they see fit
to pursue their collaborative efforts. In some counties, the grant program
led to the first sustained effort to involve community stakeholders in
addressing farmland preservation issues. Here it tended to stimulate educational and network-building outcomes. But in other counties, farmland
preservation planning already had been occurring, and state funding was
used to pay for data gathering and analysis to increase the sophistication of
farmland preservation plans, an environmental outcome.

Grant programs also affect environmental outcomes by how they specify
the biophysical scale and frame the problem. The OFPPP defined rural
counties as the eligible recipients, which set the spatial scale at which the
problem was to be tackled. This clearly affected the spatial focus of farmland preservation plans. Although counties proved to be a workable scale,
well suited to the level at which many land-use policies are made, there
were some drawbacks. One was that where farmland was affected by land-
use trends in other counties, interests from those counties were not
included in the collaboration. Another was that in some counties, land-use
authority rested with townships, and in those places, a county-level planning effort did not match the level of decision-making authority, thus
reducing the likelihood of farmland preservation recommendations being
adopted into public policy. In terms of problem framing, the OFPPP
framed it in relatively narrow terms (farmland preservation, as opposed to
open space preservation), which affected which interests were invited to
participate and, ultimately, the contents of farmland preservation plans
and their likely impact on policy.

Another important institution affecting plan contents was local government zoning regulations. Existing land-use zoning regulations varied across
the counties, and in many places that lacked zoning, plans were less likely
to include land-use regulations as a tool to preserve farmland.

Governmental actors also played a role in determining collaborative outcomes. Local governmental actors led many of the groups and constituted a sizable portion of their membership in most cases. They frequently provided important human, technical, and financial resources that shaped the contents of farmland preservation plans. Moreover, their ties to people outside the task forces often facilitated network building.

CONCLUSIONS

At first glance, it may appear that a flexible grant program such as the OFPPP provides just one type of resource for collaboration: financial. But this governmental institution can affect collaborative efforts in many ways. The OFPPP program had a prominent role in defining the issue, determining both the spatial scale and the way the problem was framed. The program also interacted with existing governmental institutions, most notably the land-use zoning regulations (or lack thereof) at the county level. These regulations affected problem framing by influencing the range of alternative policy solutions viewed as feasible.

The OFPPP also influenced, to some degree, the resources employed by the collaborative groups. By granting local oversight to county commissioners, who were embedded in existing governance structures, human resources tended to be drawn from these structures rather than from grassroots citizenry or nongovernmental associations. In addition, because it did not mandate any requirements for task force membership, the grant program did not ensure a diverse array of human resources for each group; in fact, certain interests were consistently absent across the task forces. Similarly, because it did not prescribe information sharing across counties, the program failed to foster much technical information provision among planning teams. The grant did suggest technical information sources, most of which were governmental. Perhaps the biggest resource impact from the grant program was financial, as the OFPPP provided the lion's share of dollars to many of the task forces.

Governmental actors substantially influenced task force collaborative structures and processes. These were largely determined by task force leaders, who tended to come from the ranks of government planners, university extension staff, and soil and water conservation district employees. This influence was especially notable in member selection, which included closed methods in each task force, with leaders deciding which people to invite to join the group.

Government as institution made significant contributions to the environmental outcomes of task forces. In particular, in some cases the grant money was used to generate richer data collection, analysis, and presentation in the plans. Furthermore, local government zoning affected policy tools recommended in the plans. In terms of policy adoption, the program's focus and scale affected the likelihood that plan recommendations would be embraced by policymakers. Government as actor also affected environmental outcomes. The farmland preservation plans reflected technical, human, and financial resources garnered by governmental actors. In some counties, task force members drew on ties to government planning agencies to obtain maps or other information necessary for extensive analysis of farmland preservation issues.

Government as institution had some effect on social outcomes. The existence of the grant program, with its financial incentive, did spur the creation of task forces in many counties. These task forces engaged in collaborative problem solving and planning, and in many cases, they caused members to view public participation more positively and led to the development of social networks for addressing community issues in the future. The importance of government as actor in affecting social outcomes varied across the cases. In some task forces, governmental actors provided links to people outside the group that came to represent new networks for members.

Despite the myriad impacts of government as institution in the OFPPP, there are many things that flexible grants do not ensure. They do not ensure that all recipients will use rich technical information in developing plans. Nor do they provide uniformity in human or financial resources brought to bear on the effort. For such resources, government as actor can be very important. In particular, local government officials constituted a dominant stakeholder in most task forces, and as such, they shaped the resources that task forces could draw on. The diversity of resource levels available in different task forces reflected the different governmental actors, with unique sets of skills, interests, and ties to other organizations and people, working on the task forces.

Overall, the OFPPP suggests that government grant programs to fund collaborative efforts—even those with few strings attached—do not necessarily reduce the role of government to a minor player. Beyond the enhancement of financial resources, grant programs influence aspects of problem definition. Moreover, when grants are administered by government officials, the subsequent collaborative activities may involve a variety of governmental actors who affect collaborative resources, organizational processes and structure, and ultimately outcomes.

Can money buy collaboration? The short answer is yes. The OFPPP did bring together sets of stakeholders to collaborate for a common purpose: developing farmland preservation plans for their counties. The longer answer is that what government grants can buy depends on the local context. In counties with recent comprehensive land-use planning and rich networks of people dealing with land-use issues, the grant money spurred task forces to create sophisticated farmland preservation plans pulling together data from multiple sources. In counties where land-use planning was a new endeavor, task forces tended to create simpler plans. An important result in these counties was the beginning of network building and discussions that might continue after the grant ended.

An important follow-up question to whether money can buy collaboration is, What kind of collaboration can money buy? In the OFPPP, it is clear that even with minimal grant requirements, government did not exit the stage. Through its roles both as institutions and as actors, government left a substantial imprint on collaborative processes and outcomes.

PART III

GOVERNMENT AS LEADER

CHAPTER 6

SCIENCE-BASED
COLLABORATIVE MANAGEMENT

The Albemarle–Pamlico Estuarine Study

T his chapter and the next examine cases where governmental actors and institutions play dominant roles in collaborative processes. They represent a more proactive role than in the government-encouraged cases (Chapters 4 and 5), with government defining issues, providing the majority of resources, and organizing group structure and decision making largely around governmental personnel. In this chapter, we describe how a federally and state funded regional program established procedures for pursuing ecosystem management through science-based collaborative planning. The many different governmental and nongovernmental actors within the Albemarle–Pamlico Estuarine Study (APES) program had different goals, levels of engagement in the planning process, and roles in the implementation of the resulting plan. To overcome these differences and make progress in the collaborative effort, these actors agreed to base the program on the assumption that conflict about managing the estuary arose from insufficient or differing understandings of the biological system. In the federal and state governmental actors' interpretation of ecosystem management, science was to provide the foundation for resolving conflicts among the many participants. Consequently, this chapter draws attention to an important question: By relying on science, can government overcome conflicting interests and goals of different governmental agencies, interest groups, and members of the public in a collaborative effort? For APES, this strategy backfired in the end, when it became apparent that science could not resolve the key conflicts among stakeholders.

COLLABORATION TO MANAGE AN ESTUARINE ECOSYSTEM

The Albemarle and Pamlico Sounds of eastern North Carolina constitute the second-largest estuarine ecosystem in the continental United States. In the mid-1980s, residents became concerned that increasing development of the estuaries would cause the kinds of ecological crises that had occurred in the Chesapeake Bay. Although the system was still relatively healthy, citizens and managers perceived worsening water quality, problems with fisheries, loss of habitat, and a lack of understanding about how the estuary functioned that made it impossible to design effective management strategies. Concerned citizens and scientists lobbied for the inclusion of this region in the National Estuary Program (NEP), a federal program under the Clean Water Act of 1987, to encourage ecosystem management of the nation's critically threatened estuaries.

Administered by the U.S. Environmental Protection Agency (EPA), the NEP is a governmental institution that establishes a formal framework to characterize and plan for management of critically threatened estuaries across the nation through the establishment of localized estuary programs. The Albemarle–Pamlico Estuarine Study (APES) was one of the first programs established under the NEP. The NEP supplied a framework for the APES program by requiring a 1:3 match of state to federal funding, providing suggestions for assembling an inclusive Management Conference, and recommending a planning process consisting of characterizing the estuary and defining the problem, creating a plan, and implementing the plan. Nonetheless, the actors working within this framework had considerable flexibility in designing the structure of APES. These actors, primarily members of federal and state governmental agencies, as well as marine scientists from North Carolina academic institutions, designed the structure and process of APES to rely heavily on generating new and synthesizing old scientific information in a rigorous, credible way. The result of these choices was to privilege science and scientists throughout the APES planning process.

The National Estuary Program may appear to be a straightforward case of government-initiated collaborative management, but a close study of APES reveals a more complex dynamic. First, substantial community concern already existed about these systems, largely among fishers, environmental groups, and marine scientists. These groups, however, were not organized on an ecosystem scale. By initiating, supporting, and participating in APES, they hoped to influence the government (primarily the state of

North Carolina) to improve management of the system. Second, "government" in this case was far from monolithic. The roles and expectations of local, state, and federal governmental actors in this process were very different and often opposed to one another. Third, the NEP is primarily a planning program. APES was charged with studying the system, gathering public input, and proposing a management plan. The NEP did not include provisions for management; rather, existing state and local agencies were expected to implement the plan.

Although this program officially was initiated and supported by a federal-state partnership, citizen interest was critical in getting this region included in the federal program. The federal government representatives, especially EPA staff, tended to view APES as an opportunity to encourage stronger protection of the estuary by the state. The state of North Carolina's purpose in participating was to improve scientific understanding of the system and assess the effectiveness of existing policies, rather than to assume there were widespread weaknesses in management. Local governments seemed to have little awareness, at least initially, about the potential implications the final plan could have for their land-use planning and so were not very active in the formation of the program. Thus federal, state, and local governmental actors had very different expectations for their participation.

While the NEP guidance documents suggested that "characterization and problem definition" were important early steps in estuary planning, APES focused far more on generating new scientific understanding than did many of the other NEP programs. This reflected a strong focus by the initial APES participants on improving scientific understanding of the estuary. These participants reasoned that better scientific understanding would eliminate conflict and inform appropriate policies. Therefore, the dominant efforts within APES focused on funding new research and involving highly respected scientists in the collaborative process. But governmental and nongovernmental actors within the collaborative effort faced challenges such as disagreements over what science to fund and the inability of scientists to resolve management questions. As a result, the final plan did not resemble a new plan of action based on improved understanding so much as the lowest common denominator of agreement among diverse participants. Nonetheless, the collaborative experience of APES helped initiate new partnerships and programs that have continued to influence estuarine management since the formal end of the APES program.

THE NATIONAL ESTUARY PROGRAM AND ALBEMARLE–PAMLICO ESTUARINE STUDY

The National Estuary Program is one of several federal-state governmental institutions promoting ecosystem management of large bodies of water, including the Chesapeake Bay Program and the Great Lakes Remedial Action Planning programs. These programs were founded on the recognition that the complex problems faced by large ecosystems—including watersheds that span multiple jurisdictions, diverse and intractable land-use conflicts, and great scientific uncertainty—were not adequately addressed by existing regulatory programs.

The National Estuary Program was formed specifically to address problems of critically threatened estuaries. Through a federal-state partnership, the program forms collaborative efforts called Management Conferences in each of the critical estuary regions. Management Conferences involve governmental and nongovernmental managers, scientists, stakeholders, and other actors in a five-year effort to produce a Comprehensive Conservation and Management Plan (CCMP). The EPA provides funding, with a 25 percent state match, during the planning process for research, public outreach activities, and demonstrations of management strategies. NEP Management Conferences do not have authority to implement their CCMPs. Instead, Management Conferences aim to develop a plan with widespread support that will be implemented by existing agencies, state legislatures, local governments, or other organizations.

Within these formal guidelines, NEPs vary greatly with respect to scale, process, rules, and outcomes. There are 28 NEPs in various stages of planning and implementation (U.S. EPA 2003). The APES program was one of the first and geographically largest of the programs. Covering more than 30,000 square miles in northeastern North Carolina and southeastern Virginia, the APES program addressed concerns about water pollution, fisheries, and habitat (APES 1994; Owens 1987).

APES was initiated through a confluence of the ideas of leading marine scientists from universities in North Carolina and a political opportunity that made the program attractive to both federal and state policy actors. The congressional committee overseeing development of the National Estuary Program was the House Merchant Marine and Fisheries Committee, then chaired by Walter Jones, Sr., a Democrat from eastern North Carolina. Representative Jones was interested in ensuring that North Carolina had an opportunity to participate in this program. Meanwhile, marine scientists in North Carolina had been discussing the idea of a comprehensive study of the state's estuaries since the mid-1960s. These scientists believed that knowing more about these estuarine ecosystems could help guide management of the rapid development projected for North Carolina's coastal areas and prevent the ecological disasters they had seen elsewhere in the country.

One of the marine scientists was Dr. John Costlow, then director of the Duke Marine Laboratory. Costlow was a politically active Republican and a former mayor of Beaufort, North Carolina, a small town located in the APES study area. In 1984, Jim Martin, a Republican former university biochemistry professor and congressman, was elected governor of North Carolina. These common political and intellectual pedigrees provided the marine research scientists with an unexpected entree to the state administration. While the size and status alone of the North Carolina estuaries made the area a strong candidate for the new federal estuary program, this combination of the marine scientists' leadership and access to key politicians provided an especially auspicious opportunity for the region. With strong support at both the state and federal levels, APES was designated in the first tier of National Estuary Programs in 1987.

After APES was established formally, the convening partners held a kickoff meeting on Valentine's Day 1987. More than 600 people attended this Saturday meeting, with representatives of governmental agencies, private groups, and many citizens present. EPA staff explained the structure of the program and the resources that would be available. Costlow made a speech challenging the group to make sure that this program did not end up the way so many prior efforts to study the estuary had—as plans "gathering dust on a shelf." Participants later described the mood of people leaving that session as optimistic.

Seven years later, after spending more than $11 million and running several years behind schedule, APES completed its CCMP (APES 1994). There was widespread disappointment with this plan among environmentally oriented stakeholders, particularly over its lack of specific recommendations. Participants also were disappointed by the failure to establish a continuing implementing body to coordinate management efforts. Overall, most of the participants felt that APES had not lived up to its initial promise. No single reason can be given for the perceived failure of this collaborative effort. Part of the explanation, however, certainly lies in conflicting and overly ambitious expectations by the various participants (Korfmacher 1998).

STRUCTURE OF APES

The structure of the APES program had a critical influence on how governmental roles evolved over time. The kickoff meeting in 1987 was organized by the group that became the APES Policy Committee, a seven-member body that included leading marine scientists, a representative of the governor of North Carolina, and federal agency staff members. The Policy Committee had been established in 1986, in anticipation of formal designation under NEP. Most of its decisions were made by consensus of the members, and it was instrumental in determining the structure and membership of the other committees. Based on the decisions of the Policy Committee, the remainder of the Management Conference was established in mid-1987.

The Management Conference included both governmental and nongovernmental actors. It consisted of three standing committees in addition to the Policy Committee: the Technical Advisory Committee (TAC) and two Citizens Advisory Committees (CACs), one for the northeast Albemarle region (ACAC) and the other for the southern Pamlico area (PCAC). In addition, the Management Conference was assisted by a director and a small staff in the office of the secretary of North Carolina Department of Environment and Natural Resources (DENR).[1] The structure of the TAC and CACs, the membership of these committees, the staffing plan, and the placement of the APES program within the administrative hierarchy were the result of Policy Committee decisions.

The Policy Committee was the official decision-making body for the program and its liaison with the convening partners—the governor of North Carolina and the EPA. This committee was envisioned as a group of academic and policy leaders, including the secretary of the DENR, several federal agency representatives, and the directors of the National Oceanic and Atmospheric Administration Beaufort Laboratory, the Duke University Marine Laboratory, and the University of North Carolina Institute of Marine Sciences. In interviews, several federal agency representatives and scientists said that they viewed APES as an opportunity not only to better understand the estuarine system, but also to encourage the state to protect these resources more effectively. Perhaps because of this orientation, on several occasions the sole representative of the state on the Policy Committee, the secretary of the DENR, was at odds with the other members of the committee. Although the chairs of the CACs and a representative of Virginia were added in later years, the Policy Committee remained a small group with relatively low turnover throughout the program.

The TAC was composed primarily of representatives of the state and federal agencies responsible for environmental management of the study area. The TAC's role was to provide scientific and technical advice to the Policy Committee, to manage the program's daily operations, to evaluate technical proposals and reports, and to provide input into the ongoing planning process. The TAC had several subcommittees, including the Technical Review Subcommittee, which was composed of members with strong scientific credentials and was responsible for reviewing research proposals and reports.

Although the TAC nominally included a diverse range of expertise and representatives from nearly all environmentally relevant state agencies, actual participation varied among agencies and over time. Some governmental members did research, some contributed actively to developing program documents and recommendations, and some participated as observers only. For example, while the Virginia representatives attended meetings fairly regularly, several of them noted that their purpose in attending was to prevent any recommendations that would negatively affect Virginia, rather than to advance a particular agenda or contribute to implementation. Several agency heads attended APES meetings initially but later sent designated representatives of lower rank. Even in the first year of the program, attendance by TAC members, especially state agency representatives, was disappointingly low, according to some APES participants. The Division of Marine Fisheries remained actively involved through participation on the TAC and in ongoing research, but the other two agencies critical to the management of estuarine resources, the Division of Coastal Management and the Division of Environmental Management, were involved only sporadically.

Citizens representing a variety of interests were involved through the two CACs and engaged in the APES process in two ways: as committee members and in outreach efforts to broader publics. The two regional committees, ACAC and PCAC, had been formed to minimize driving time to meetings and keep the structure relatively simple, but it also resulted in a divided citizen voice, as the two committees forwarded their recommendations separately and did not always agree.

Initially, the Policy Committee planned to appoint 15 members to each CAC, all but 4 of whom would represent specific interests. But after the

Republican administration pointed out that this would result in domination by Democrats, 15 additional citizens were added to each CAC. In the end, 30 members were appointed to each CAC. These included 19 citizens and 11 designated according to various interest groups: two local government officials, an educator, a coastal engineer–surveyor, and representatives of tourism industries, developers, recreational hunting and fishing, commercial fishing, agriculture, industry, and environmental groups. The CACs met regularly to discuss ongoing planning issues, make recommendations on research funding, and comment on the production of program documents. Although the CACs initially made recommendations to the TAC, midway through the program they successfully petitioned to appoint representatives who would report directly to the Policy Committee.

Participation on the committees was designed to be representative. But respondents to a mail survey mentioned three groups that were not adequately included on the CACs: women, socioeconomic minorities, and the elderly. In addition, numerous respondents commented on insufficient representation by groups that were nominally on the CACs, such as local government, agriculture, industry, and fishing. This reflects the fact that although they were included formally, actual attendance by these groups was weak over the nine-year planning period.

Whereas industrial, commercial fishing, and agricultural interests were perceived as underrepresented, many APES participants commented that the CACs were dominated by environmentalists. Several explanations were given for this observation. First, many of those appointed to serve as interest group representatives, as well as many of citizens, were active in local environmental groups. Although this dual representation did not mean that these individuals did not adequately represent the opinions of the groups they were officially appointed to serve, it did contribute to the overall impression that the CACs were dominated by environmentalists. Second, environmentalists tended to take on the leadership roles on the CACs. Several leading environmental representatives held staff positions with environmental groups, so attending meetings was part of their jobs. This made it easier for them to take on leadership roles than it was for lay citizens. Finally, there tended to be lower turnover rates among environmental representatives than among other participants. As a result, by the last years of APES, the CACs were dominated by a core of longtime members, many of whom had strong environmental affiliations. Thus, although the government-dominated Policy Committee designated diverse CACs, each committee's character was determined more by specific appointments than by formal structure.

In addition to citizen membership on committees, APES sponsored a variety of activities intended to educate and involve the broader public. These included producing public awareness materials, organizing workshops, and promoting environmental education. Annual public meetings were held to report on the progress of the program and to present research reports. Near the end of the program, several public hearings took place to solicit comments on drafts of the CCMP. Throughout the APES planning process, however, the CACs provided the majority of public input.

The program was supported by a small staff housed in the office of the secretary of DENR. Housing the staff in a line agency within DENR was discussed, but it was recognized that to maintain its legitimacy, APES could not be directly affiliated with the state agencies whose programs it would be assessing.

All four committees in the Management Conference met regularly and operated under parliamentary procedures; motions were approved or rejected by majority voting. Final program decisions were made by the Policy Committee, with input from the other committees and staff. Committee members often sent representatives to meetings they could not attend, but these substitutes could not vote. Decisions made by the APES Management Conference informed a nonbinding planning process. The APES committees made decisions about funding allocations, planning processes, and plan recommendations, but these recommendations were not binding on any of the participants, including governmental actors.

THE APES PLANNING PROCESS

The NEP guidelines generally described four phases for ecosystem planning and management that guided regional collaborative efforts: planning initiation (building a management framework); characterization and problem definition; creation of a CCMP; and implementation of the CCMP (U.S. EPA 1989). After designing the Management Conference, the next task in the APES program was to begin characterizing the Albemarle–Pamlico system and defining the problems it faced. The roles of governmental actors in APES evolved throughout these phases, particularly in relation to the scientific community and citizen participants.

Characterization and Problem Definition

The intended role of science in the NEP was to provide a "description of the quality of the estuary, defining its problems and linking problems to causes" and to "transfer scientific and management information" (U.S. EPA 1989, 2, 23). The APES planning process incorporated science by compiling existing information on the system, funding new research, and basing its CCMP recommendations on available technical knowledge. The program began by describing its overall priorities and research needs in a five-year work plan (APES 1987). Between 1987 and 1992, APES sponsored research on the estuarine system through a competitive peer-review process. Each year, the Management Conference developed a request for proposals (RFP) based on the work plan and new information. Researchers developed proposals that were reviewed externally and prioritized by all three committees; the Policy Committee made the final selections.

Some participants from each committee complained that the program did not adequately prioritize its research agenda, so that although many issues were addressed, no management questions were resolved. This was attributed primarily to the fact that research priorities were established by the consensus of the entire Management Conference, whose members had widely varying priorities. Of the 74 priority areas for research identified in the 1987 Work Plan, the program funded studies directly related to only a quarter of these topics (APES 1987). Thus the attempt to be inclusive and make decisions by consensus may have undercut the program's goals with respect to funding useful applied science.

Although the CACs' recommendations for research funding were solicited, the Policy Committee did not always adopt them. The Policy Committee pointed out that in many years, there simply was not enough money to fund all the recommended studies, and that in some other cases, the citizens sometimes recommended proposals that were technically unsound. Nonetheless, rejection of CAC recommendations undercut citizens' support for the program. Many CAC members thought the research funding process was unfair, calling it "scientific cronyism" because they felt that the research community had co-opted the process and that their priorities for research were ignored.

Several of the citizens who felt that their input was ignored cited a single funding decision as evidence for this claim. This was a 1990 decision not to fund a proposal on trawling impacts. Understanding more about the impacts of shrimp and crab trawling was of critical interest to many CAC members, who believed that trawling was causing severe environmental harm to benthic (bottom-dwelling) animals and fisheries. In 1990, the CACs advocated that APES request a proposal to study the effects of shrimp trawling on the benthic community, noting that this was their highest priority. One proposal was submitted in response to this RFP item. Based partly on the strength of the CACs' recommendation, the TAC also recommended this study for funding. The Policy Committee, however, faced with a tight budget, chose not to fund this study. Realizing how important this study was to the CACs, the Division of Marine Fisheries (DMF) director visited both CACs soon after this decision was made to explain that there were technical concerns about the study that had been proposed and that DMF planned to study the issue using separate state funding. Nonetheless, the firm impression that this case made on many CAC members was that their technical recommendations were ignored.

Despite this perception by CAC members, TAC and Policy Committee members emphasized that CAC input was very important in their deliberations and decisions. Some TAC members even complained that the citizens' influence was too strong and that citizens did not always have the program's overall goals in mind. One TAC member said that the CAC research priority recommendations were parochial, focused only on their own geographic areas rather than on the most pressing problems in the system.

As part of this phase of planning, the NEP required that APES produce a status and trends report characterizing the estuary. Production of this report was contracted to North Carolina Sea Grant, because that program had access to a wide range of expertise with respect to the state's estuaries. More than 40 researchers contributed to four work groups that compiled the report between April and December 1989. In addition, a technically trained member of the CACs participated in each work group. The result was a 341-page report describing various environmental indicators and management efforts related to the environmental concerns identified by APES, noting insufficiencies in data and the frequent lack of causal explanations.

Many Management Conference members were disappointed by the first draft, feeling that the report as written was not useful because it stopped short of stating conclusions or making recommendations. Environmental representatives on the CACs and some Policy Committee members were especially disturbed that the report seemed to downplay their concerns about the ecosystem's health. On the other hand, the draft report's editors and many Management Conference members felt that it gave a very sound description of the system. One TAC member believed that environmentalists' objections arose only because "the technical assessments did not bear out their religious notions ... [and] did not fit the environmental party line." Thus the purpose of this report and the extent to which it was appropriate to extrapolate from uncertain and incomplete research findings became very controversial.

The controversy over the report was resolved through a yearlong process of adding judgments to each section, gathering input through seven public hearings, and changing the tone to emphasize management issues. While several changes were made to the structure and substantive content of the document, many members believed that it was the changes in tone that were the most critical to improving its acceptability. After these revisions, the Policy Committee approved a final version of the Status and Trends Report in June 1991. Nevertheless, bitterness remained among many members of the Management Conference about the process of adding judgments to the report. As one TAC member said, "The Policy Committee just changed the findings to meet the environmental group dogma, rather than the scientific evidence ... I gave [them] a speech on the trial of Galileo. The Policy Committee wanted the technical people to recant the witness of their own eyes." Meanwhile, many CAC members had become convinced that the Management Conference's reluctance to make management recommendations in the Status and Trends Report did not bode well for the program's ability to write an effective CCMP.

During the characterization stage, 20 percent of the APES budget was dedicated to funding public involvement projects. One important public involvement project focused on the CACs themselves. Eager to move the program from studies into action, in 1990 the CACs participated in five joint workshops to develop goals and actions as a starting point for the CCMP. The North Carolina Coastal Federation received an APES contract to bring in a facilitator from the Chesapeake Bay Program and document the recommendations from these workshops. Despite fears by some TAC and Policy Committee members that the resulting document would be perceived as a consensus product of the entire Management Conference, it was eventually published as an APES report (Armingeon 1990). The *Blueprint for Action* set forth a proposed framework for the development of the CCMP, a list of goals and objectives, and a list of recommended actions to achieve these goals.

Part of the federal government's mandate for the NEP was that a program be inclusive of a wide range of stakeholders and characterize an estuary using the best available science, but the fact that APES actors interpreted the mandate by focusing on improved scientific understanding of the system reduced the influence of citizens in the program. The process of characterization gave power to technical experts, from both universities and agencies, and reduced the relevance of local government, citizens, nongovernmental organizations, and agency managers. Reinvolving these stakeholders was an uphill battle as the program sought to relate the scientific findings to management questions and to write the CCMP.

Creation of a Management Plan

In accordance with the five-year schedule dictated by the EPA, the goal of APES was to produce a CCMP in 1992. A change in political leadership in North Carolina and some strong public criticism delayed the plan, however. The second public draft of the CCMP was published in December 1992, just after Democrat Jim Hunt won the November elections for governor of North Carolina. Because of substantial opposition to the first and second drafts of the CCMP, sometimes called the Martin Plan, the Hunt administration decided in early 1993 to undertake extensive revisions (APES 1994, 8). The governor and EPA administrator did not sign the final CCMP, referred to by many participants as the Hunt Plan, until November 1994.

Several concerns were raised about the first public draft of the CCMP. One specific recommendation that drew criticism from the public was the requirement of a 20-foot undisturbed buffer strip around all perennial streams, rivers, and tidal water bodies (APES 1992). At least half of the public comment concerned the buffer strip recommendation. Although APES participants strongly supported the use of buffer strips, agricultural and forestry interests had two objections to the recommendation. First, they felt that a standard buffer strip was inappropriate given varying environmental conditions in the region. Second, the mandatory buffer strip recommendation was perceived as government interference with private property by farmers who were accustomed to voluntary best-management-practices programs, not mandatory regulations. In the third public draft and final CCMP, the buffer strip requirement was modified greatly to avoid a backlash against the entire CCMP.

Other significant objections to the first drafts of the CCMP came from local governments. Indeed, one Policy Committee member suggested that "the study's 'Achilles Heel' could be the lack of consensus in local government regarding the CCMP." Local governments were concerned that there had been inadequate consideration of the economic impacts of the CCMP recommendations, and they feared that the Albemarle–Pamlico Estuarine Council, the body proposed to oversee implementation of the recommendations, would promote new regulations that would restrict economic growth, and that local governments would be responsible for implementing these regulations.

Meanwhile, a number of economic developers and local officials in the Albemarle–Pamlico region organized a campaign to get county commissioners to adopt resolutions asking Governor Hunt not to sign the CCMP. APES staff characterized this campaign as "bringing ignorance to power," as a few individuals were able to convince numerous local officials that the Albemarle–Pamlico Estuarine Council represented another layer of bureaucracy that would impose new regulations and stifle economic growth. In fact, the implementation body described in the CCMP had no authority whatsoever. Regardless of whether it was founded on misunderstandings, the objection by the local governments was especially serious because it threatened to affect the governor's willingness to sign the final CCMP.

To address these concerns, the Policy Committee decided to add more local government representatives to the Albemarle–Pamlico Estuarine Council and to rename it the Coordinating Council to emphasize its non-regulatory nature. Although the final solution to this controversy was acceptable to most Management Conference members, the process by which it was resolved made a negative impression on many participants. Many members were angry that the local government officials, who had turned down repeated opportunities to participate in APES, had so much clout at the end of the process and wound up having a significant impact on its outcomes.

The two major objections to the draft CCMP, regarding buffer strips and implementation institutions, came from groups (agriculture and local government, respectively) that, although nominally represented on the CACs, had not actively participated in APES. Several reasons for their lack of participation have been suggested by members, including that they were put off by the domination of environmentalists on the CACs, and that they calculated early on that opposing the final plan would be more effective in protecting their interests than participating throughout a process they perceived to be dominated by environmentalists. Regardless of the reason, these groups were in fact quite successful in advancing their positions by opposing the final plans and appealing directly to the new political administration, rather than participating in the planning process.

When Governor Hunt first took office, opposition to the CCMP was so strong that he doubted whether a CCMP that he would sign could be developed at all. To help increase public support, the program hired a public-relations specialist, held special meetings for different groups of stakeholders (Waters 1993), and hired two part-time staff members devoted to communicating with local officials about APES. At the same time, Hunt's newly appointed secretary of the DENR asked state environmental managers who had not been participating regularly in APES to help make the plan more "implementable." The original CCMP recommendations were seen as too specific to incorporate into ongoing agency programs. The Hunt administration thought it was more likely that general CCMP recommendations could be used to support implementation of new regulations as opportunities arose over time. This was especially critical, because the 1992 elections brought a Republican majority to the state assembly, which was expected to be suspicious of new environmental regulations. Therefore, state agency managers were asked to help revise recommendations to fit in better with their existing programs and agencies' future plans.

The mandate from the Hunt administration shifted the role of state agency actors. Some had been participating in APES to create a new system of estuarine management, while others had essentially abandoned this process. The Hunt administration directive involved many of these state agency actors in recrafting APES recommendations to align them with existing governmental agencies.

In addition to the substantive changes in the CCMP, the document was thoroughly revised and streamlined to be more "user-friendly." The tone was changed to clarify that the recommendations were not regulatory mandates. For example, the pervasive use of *should* in the second public draft was changed to *would*.

Taken together, these changes gave many members of the Management Conference a strong sense that the CCMP had been "watered down" between the second and third public drafts. This observation invokes the warning cited in the first chapter of this book that consensus decision making can result in "lowest common denominator" recommendations (Coglianese 1999). Although some APES participants acknowledged that this was necessary in the face of interest group opposition, many regretted having to delete or soften the few concrete recommendations they had made. The environmental groups represented on the CACs especially were critical of the revisions. On the other hand, state agency actors generally agreed that it was more useful to have a document that had the consensus support of interest groups than to insist on specific recommendations that created insurmountable opposition to the plan.

The process of translating scientific information into management recommendations revealed conflicts between governmental and nongovernmental actors that had remained hidden during the characterization stage. Governmental actors who had not been actively involved became much more involved as APES began to make recommendations that had the potential to affect their programs and activities. This was particularly clear with local governmental actors who had not been significantly involved in APES until the program recommended the establishment of a continuing Coordinating Council, which they feared would impede their autonomy.

Implementation

The final plan was signed by Governor Hunt in November 1994 in a ceremony in Washington, North Carolina.[2] According to the governor, the signing ceremony for the CCMP was "a celebration of people working together and making things work—not of big government but of people collaborating on a voluntary basis." But some APES participants who commented on the finalization of the CCMP had different reactions. Some felt that that the CCMP was "watered down" and were disappointed in its delayed release. Nevertheless, many were hopeful that the document they had worked so hard to produce would finally be implemented.

The final CCMP called for the creation of seven Regional Councils (one for each river basin in the region) and a central Coordinating Council to oversee the implementation of the APES recommendations. As with the Management Conference, these groups had neither authority nor a designated source of financial support. Although there were delays in their formation, they have continued to meet annually. North Carolina's implementation efforts are supported by approximately $300,000 per year in federal funds. This funding was denied one year because of the EPA's judgment that North Carolina was not making sufficient progress in implementation, but since that time, the EPA has been satisfied by the program's efforts. While most implementation of APES recommendations occurs through existing state agencies and programs, the modest funding from the federal government supports several staff, the Regional Councils, demonstration projects, and other activities focusing specifically on the Albemarle–Pamlico system. This federal funding is substantially less than what was available for the APES program before 1994.

Although the dedicated infrastructure for the National Estuary Program within the DENR is minimal, various state agencies have carried out many of the APES CCMP recommendations. The Division of Environmental Management moved to a basinwide planning and permitting scheme for water pollution, and the state's entire fisheries regulatory system has been overhauled. In several cases, APES also provided the basis for cooperation among management agencies in the region. One example is the joint use of the geographic information systems (GIS) initially funded by APES. The North Carolina Division of Coastal Management and Division of Environmental Management continued to use this GIS capacity for cooperative coastal water quality planning after the APES planning process ended.

APES also provided a forum in which citizens, interest groups, and scientists learned about the estuarine system, the management institutions, and how they could influence decision making in the future. This experience continued to influence these groups' participation in coastal policy after the APES planning process. Particularly significant were the contributions of APES to the growth and experience of local environmental groups in the region. Such ripple effects that have improved management of North Carolina's estuaries may be considered "invisible successes" of APES (Korfmacher 1998). Although it may be argued that these changes would have occurred regardless of APES, it is clear that the program brought an unprecedented amount of attention and funding to estuarine management issues.

GOVERNMENTAL IMPACT

When APES was established, it appeared well poised to conduct collaborative planning. The end of the program, however, saw widespread disappointment with its direct accomplishments. Much of this disappointment can be traced to the complexities of the governmental roles in this program. More generally, governmental roles affected the APES issue definition, resources, and group structure and decision-making processes.

Issue Definition

The National Estuary Program encouraged looking at ecosystems that crossed state lines. The NEP designation included the Albemarle and Pamlico Sounds and their watersheds. This study area was so large that individual citizens and local government officials may have had trouble identifying with the scale. Because such a small section of the study area was in Virginia, North Carolina was the dominant state actor in the process. NEP, as a governmental institution, greatly influenced the geographic and biophysical scale of APES.

The scope of the program also was wide, as opposed to being framed more narrowly on a few key issues. This is probably because APES resulted from an opportunity for federal funding, not an immediate perception of crisis in specific parts of the system. In addition, many scientists, politicians, and managers felt that the system was not understood well enough to specifically identify the most critical problems. Finally, the federal program encouraged an ecosystem perspective, which included all aspects of the estuary. Therefore, it is not surprising that the program identified a wide range of issues, including fisheries, habitat, water quality, and human actions. By spreading resources among all of these problems, however, the program was not able to address any of them thoroughly. Thus the general guidance of the NEP institution, with the cooperation of governmental actors and nongovernmental scientists, favored addressing a broad range of issues through the APES program.

It appears that different actors entered the process with different definitions and ways of framing the problem facing the Albemarle–Pamlico system. Although the NEP was designed on a federal model for ecosystem institutions that emphasized increasing state and local management of ecosystems, many of the EPA staff saw APES as an opportunity to encourage North Carolina to strengthen its protection of the estuary. Thus federal actors looked at APES as a way to influence other aspects of ecosystem protection in North Carolina. The state's administration perceived that the main problem was lack of knowledge—about how the system functions, whether it was changing, and how existing management was working. Several state agency staff members recognized that North Carolina's environmental protection laws were quite strong but that implementation was insufficient. Local government's response varied, but local officials did not perceive an immediate reward or direct local impact of spending time studying and making recommendations about such a large area. Meanwhile, environmentalists believed that the estuarine system was in imminent danger because of lax protection.

Because of the orientation of state agency actors and the scientists who helped initiate the program, APES ended up focusing primarily on information gathering. It funded numerous studies to improve understanding of the physical system in hopes of leading to better management. Representatives of environmental groups and many private citizens on the CACs were frustrated by this approach throughout the program because it postponed action. Thus, although the intent of the NEP institution was to promote proactive ecosystem planning, various governmental actors had different agendas including, according to several observers, state actors' desire to postpone more aggressive management actions.

The APES program was based on general guidance and resources provided by the NEP combined with scientific and governmental actors' insistence that the estuary was insufficiently understood. If actors within APES had acknowledged that action in the face of uncertainty is essential to sound ecosystem management, the APES resources could have been allocated differently to address the estuaries' problems. For example, if the citizens involved had been the primary drivers of the program, as in the Applegate Partnership (Chapter 2), they might well have maintained a local orientation, focusing on bays or river segments with which individual communities identified. It is likely that they would have funded more demonstration and priority action projects to test the effects of new management strategies, rather than the more basic research that APES funded. They might have focused on a few issues that were of great concern to local communities at that time, such as the impacts of trawling. Although such approaches may not have been more successful than APES was, it is clear that the structure established by the Policy Committee and its decision to focus on increasing scientific understanding significantly constrained the approach of APES to ecosystem management.

Resources for Collaboration

The human resources available to APES depended directly on participation by governmental actors and indirectly on choices made about how to involve different nongovernmental participants. State and federal governmental agencies provided human resources in the form of representatives to the Management Conference and staff assistance. Governmental actors dominated the Policy Committee as well as the TAC. Moreover, as leaders of the effort, federal and state governmental actors were critical in deciding whom to invite to participate in the various committees. Over time, participation by representatives from several agencies diminished, and the program encountered difficulty involving local governmental actors throughout the process.

Federal funding and the participation of technical staff from state agencies gave the program access to significant technical resources. The decision to spend nearly half of the program's total budget on new research resulted in a significant accumulation of knowledge about the estuary. But because much of this research was devoted to improving the basic understanding of the estuary, rather than to resolving specific management questions, the program could not use this research extensively in writing its CCMP. At several stages of the program, scientific experts from academic institutions and government agencies were called together to summarize data to address various management questions.

Federal and state governments provided the financial resources of the program – about $11 million over seven years—through a 1:3 local-to-federal cost share. In addition, several federal agencies devoted special funding projects to the Albemarle–Pamlico system. Nearly half of the funds were spent on new research. Although the nongovernmental participants had a say in which research was funded, the initial decision about how much to allocate to research versus other activities was made before their involvement.

GROUP STRUCTURE AND DECISION-MAKING PROCESSES

Most of the decisions about the structure for APES were dominated by government. Within the flexible institutional framework of the NEP, governmental actors, along with the academic members of the Policy Committee, created the system of committees, decision-making processes, and plans that constituted APES. They established a majority decision rule, although most decisions were made by de facto consensus. The decision-making process was more collaborative than hierarchical, as recommendations of the TAC and CACs were supposed to be considered equally by the Policy Committee. Because the Policy Committee selected initial members of the TAC and CACs, the TAC reflected the governmental actors' view of the problem as essentially a scientific one—lack of coordinated understanding of how the estuary functions—rather than a primarily human problem of education, behavior, management, and politics.

As a result of the Policy Committee's sensitivity to partisan concerns, the CACs initially represented an interest group and political balance. Over time, however, they became dominated by those most motivated to participate in the extended planning processes, primarily environmentalists.

Thus, although the NEP institution set forth a framework intended to ensure balanced input and a collaborative decision-making process, decisions made by the actors in APES eventually led to a process dominated by scientists, technically trained governmental actors, and environmental interests.

COLLABORATIVE OUTCOMES

Government as an institution required the development of a plan based on science through a collaborative structure; however, the actual process and outcomes of APES were significantly affected by how the governmental actors interpreted this general mandate. Because the governmental actors and scientists involved in structuring the program agreed that it should enhance scientific understanding of the estuary, APES largely avoided difficult issues such as acting in the face of uncertainty, land- and water-use conflicts, and trade-offs among opposing values.

Environmental Outcomes

Environmental management outcomes for this collaborative planning program center on plan recommendations and subsequent changes in management. Many of the APES recommendations have been implemented, primarily by state agencies. Water quality protection efforts now are carried out on a basinwide basis throughout the state, as recommended in the plan, and the state completely overhauled its fishery management system. Participants from state agencies also cited several examples of ongoing collaboration between agencies that arose from partnering in the APES process (Korfmacher 1998).

Social Outcomes

APES contributed significantly to social outcomes, particularly the ability of local citizens to participate in estuarine management. For example, it aided the growth of numerous coastal environmental groups, which remain active in coastal environmental management (Korfmacher 1998). In some cases, however, their experience with APES contributed to citizens' hesitancy to become involved in future collaborative efforts. Without authority for plan implementation, the impact of APES "on the ground" was limited, and many participants who were optimistic at the beginning were disappointed at the end. This may have reduced their enthusiasm for involvement in future collaborative efforts. In addition, a number of citizens felt that the Management Conference ignored them, and therefore the time they invested in meetings over as many as eight years was wasted. Moreover, at least in part because of their experience in APES, several prominent environmental groups in North Carolina have drawn up conditions under which they will agree to participate in a government partnership to ensure that their involvement is taken seriously. On the whole, however, APES taught participants how to participate in environmental policymaking more effectively.

Another important social outcome is the development of new networks related to estuarine policy. Scientists in particular reported that participation in APES helped them better understand the decision-making process and how they could be more effectively involved. The active roles played by many state and federal agency actors led to a rich network of government divisions that had not existed before APES. This network led to better communication and several new coordinated programs (Korfmacher 1998). For example, the state Divisions of Environmental Management and Coastal Management used the GIS capacity developed by APES to develop a program for mapping and managing coastal watersheds.

CONCLUSIONS

Nongovernmental actors had significant roles in APES, and many governmental actors were personally committed to partnering with them. Nevertheless, most of the important decisions about issue definition, resources, structure, and processes were influenced strongly by governmental institutions and actors in the collaborative effort. These initial decisions had ongoing implications for the incentives of various participants and their ability to influence the outcomes of the collaborative process. In particular, the decision to focus on increasing scientific understanding as a prerequisite to planning had lasting implications for resource use, participation, and outcomes. This approach reduced the power and relevance of nontechnical participants, which in turn undermined the program's ability to develop consensus and buy in despite its collaborative structure.

The question of whether science-based collaborative planning can overcome the different agendas of various governmental agencies, interest groups, and members of the public is particularly important because so many collaborative efforts are built on the assumption that more knowledge will lead to better accord. Although APES tried to gain credibility and achieve consensus by improving understanding of the estuary, the funded science did not address key barriers to collaboration in managing the estuarine system. These barriers came from many sources, not just a lack of scientific knowledge. This case shows that although government may build credibility through science, it is still necessary to address the underlying sources of conflict both between governmental and nongovernmental participants and within various jurisdictions of government itself.

CHAPTER 7

GOVERNMENT-LED COMMUNITY COLLABORATION

The Animas River Stakeholder Group

Like the Albemarle–Pamlico Estuarine Study (APES) in Chapter 6, the Animas River Stakeholder Group (ARSG) is a case of government-led collaboration, but the two cases differ significantly. Whereas federal governmental actors and institutions initiated APES and served the dominant purpose of planning activities in the Albemarle–Pamlico Sound, state governmental actors initiated the ARSG and defined its purpose to encompass both planning and management activities in the Animas watershed, a much smaller area than the sound. Additionally, ARSG members faced fewer organizational constraints imposed by governmental actors than did participants in APES. In the APES case, interest already existed among organized communities, but with the Animas watershed, little organized community interest in undertaking an extensive remediation effort existed before the creation of the stakeholder group. In the end, the ARSG was able to agree on and promulgate new regulations to improve its watershed, unlike the more frustrated efforts in APES. In the case of the ARSG, governmental actors played a more active convening role in a collaborative environmental management effort than in any other case in this book.

COMMUNITY-BASED ENVIRONMENTAL MANAGEMENT

To understand the ARSG case, we first need to consider community-based environmental management (CBEM). Closely related to collaborative environmental management, CBEM is an approach that centers on community interests playing an active role in managing resources. Community-based environmental management would seem to imply the active involvement of communities engaged in or driving environmental management processes. Yet in one study, Kenney (1999) identified that communities were the lead coordinating entity in only 20 percent of 400 local watershed initiatives, while state agencies took the lead in 40 percent of the cases, and federal and local agencies each took the lead in 20 percent.

Community-based environmental management can originate with either a community organization or a local, state, or federal governmental agency. A community that is organized and looking to play an active role in managing its resources may serve as the catalyst for cultivating agency interest, or a governmental agency may serve as the driving force. These are two poles on a diverse continuum of options that involve various combinations of relationships between agencies and communities as they seek to manage resources that are important to them (Seymour 1994). The ability to integrate and involve community-based organizations in management solutions, then, is dependent at least partly on the willingness of these agencies to empower local actors (Berry et al. 1989; Kweit and Kweit 1980). Consequently, the potential for successful community-based environmental management hinges not only on the ability of a community-based group to take an active part in the management of the resource, but also on the organizational culture and institutional incentives within the managing agency (Romzek and Dubnick 1994). But if governmental actors often are the lead conveners in an effort to collaborate, and usually possess technical, financial, or other resources that are essential to the management task at hand, at what point does a government-led, community-based management effort cease to be community-based?

Agency actors can play important roles in cultivating organizational capacity at the local level and enabling strong local responses through the channeling of needed resources. The approaches agencies can take to drive community-based efforts are numerous. Agency actors can be involved in and even drive a community-based effort, but this association calls for a different role than agency actors have played traditionally. In contrast to the top-down, command-and-control, inflexible bureaucracies that have been associated with environmental management, community-based efforts require flexible responses and a more decentralized approach within a collaborative setting (Chess et al. 2000; McGinnis et al. 1999). Consequently, in a community-based management scenario, agency actors have to employ different skill sets, behaviors, and attitudes. Likewise, they must recognize the limits of their roles and the potentially negative force they can have if perceived as too domineering. The goal of this chapter is to demonstrate the constructive role agency actors can play in community-based management through a case study of the Animas River Stakeholder Group. Government-led, community-based management need not be an oxymoron. In circumstances where the community is unorganized governmental agencies can help stimulate and support collaboration. But governmental actors also must recognize the limits of their ability to control a legitimately community-based effort once it has developed.

THE ANIMAS RIVER STAKEHOLDER GROUP

The upper Animas watershed is located near the town of Silverton, Colorado, and ranges from 9,000 to 13,800 feet in altitude. Known as the "avalanche capital of the world," its steep mountains see approximately 40 to 50 inches of precipitation a year, mostly in the form of snow. The watershed is 186 square miles in size and is drained by the upper Animas River, which is fed by two tributaries, Mineral Creek and Cement Creek. The upper Animas turns into the lower Animas near Durango, Colorado. Because of the harsh winters, the population of San Juan County, in which the watershed lies, varies considerably throughout the year, with approximately 500 year-round residents and an additional 3,500 tourists and temporary residents in summer (Robinson 2000).

As part of a highly mineralized geologic zone, the San Juan Mountains long have been famous for the mining that has taken place throughout the spectacular red peaks. Gold, silver, lead, zinc, and copper have been excavated from the more than 1,500 mines that honeycomb the region (Blair 1996; Robinson 2000). Mining practices, as well as natural geologic processes, have contributed to heavy metal loading in the headwaters of the Animas. For decades, if not centuries or millennia, copper, iron, aluminum, manganese, lead, and cadmium have rendered the waters of the Animas virtually lifeless.

In 1991, the Colorado Water Quality Control Division (WQCD), the state agency charged with regulating surface water and groundwater quality, began a biological and water quality sampling program in the upper Animas watershed that lasted until 1993. Members of the Non Point Source Program in the WQCD were looking to work in a watershed that could demonstrate successful control of and improvement in water quality, and they believed that the Animas was an ideal target (Parsons 2001). Beginning in 1991, the WQCD sought to establish baseline data for the watershed. Field crews from more than 14 local, state, and federal agencies sampled over 100 sites throughout the watershed during high and low flows for three years (Robinson 2000). Biological and chemical sampling revealed that dissolved aluminum, cadmium, copper, and zinc in the river and its tributaries were toxic to most forms of aquatic life and resulted in an abnormal reduction in diversity and abundance of these flora and fauna (Robinson 2000). Armed with empirical evidence to support its initial premise, the WQCD advocated that the upper Animas River basin held great potential for improved water quality.

The Colorado Water Quality Control Commission (WQCC) is the primary institution in Colorado that sets water quality standards and use classifications on rivers and water bodies throughout the state, as part of fulfilling the requirements of the federal Clean Water Act (CWA).[1] The U.S. Environmental Protection Agency (EPA) has final jurisdiction over the CWA, but it grants primacy to state and tribal authorities to set designated use standards for water bodies. Use standards describe the desired conditions for the water resources in question. For instance, standards might be set for industrial uses, water supply, or recreation and fish and wildlife habitat.

In 1979, the WQCC first set water quality standards on the upper Animas as ambient (McAllister 1999). This meant that, given the poor water quality and the fact that the waters were not used as a source of drinking water, no use standards would be applied to the rivers. The ambient standards held until 1993, when the WQCC asked the WQCD to make a new recommendation for the upper reaches of the Animas River. The WQCD studies from 1991 to 1993 suggested that water quality in the Animas could be improved, but it was unclear how this might be accomplished.

The WQCD faced two options. The agency could impose new use standards for the watershed, but it understood that stakeholders in the region, especially Sunnyside Gold Mine, would resist more stringent water quality standards forced on them. In the late 1980s, Sunnyside Gold, the largest employer in the region, had conducted its own studies to substantiate the poor quality in the region. As a result, the WQCD feared that if it imposed higher standards, Sunnyside would counter with its own data and argue for lower standards. Foreseeing a regulatory deadlock, the WQCD was loath to engage in legal and technical battles that would leave the watershed no better off despite great expenditures of resources.

The second option for the agency was to use community-based environmental management, involving local stakeholders, including the gold-mining industry, in a process to determine collectively what standards would work best for the varied interests in the watershed. In this manner, the WQCD might avoid a data war and foster a more workable outcome. But no group or organization existed that could coordinate such an effort.

The problem facing the WQCD was how to craft a community-based process in an area where no organized community existed. The technical nature of determining water quality standards meant that those participating would need to devote significant time to the process and commit to mastering the expertise needed for sound management. States often perform a use attainability analysis (UAA) to determine the specific uses for a water body, and the institution that shapes water body use is a Total Maximum Daily Load (TMDL) program. A TMDL is a calculation of the maximum amount of a pollutant that a water body can receive and still meet water quality standards, and an allocation of that amount among the pollutant's sources.

To initiate the collaborative endeavor, the WQCD retained the services of the Colorado Center for Environmental Management (CCEM) to coordinate the creation of the Animas River Stakeholder Group (ARSG). A list of stakeholders was assembled by the CCEM and the WQCD for the first time in early 1994 (Table 7-1). From the outset, defining who constituted the relevant community for the process was a challenge. San Juan County has only about 500 permanent residents, so the initial local community from which stakeholders could be drawn was small. Additionally, because of the high percentage of public lands in the Animas watershed, various public agencies responsible for the management of those lands were designated as important members of the relevant political community that needed to be involved in a successful effort.

Absentee landlords own many of the mines in the region, and local people were apprehensive about the collaboration, as it involved the EPA and was coordinated by an unknown outside group, the CCEM. The initial par-

Table 7-1. Animas River Stakeholder Group Members

Federal government agencies	*Nonprofit organizations*
U.S. Bureau of Land Management	Colorado River Watch
U.S. Bureau of Reclamation	Friends of the Animas River
U.S. Corps of Engineers	River Watch Network
U.S. Environmental Protection Agency	San Juan County Historical Society
USDA Forest Service	
U.S. Geological Survey	*Industries*
	Durango and Silverton Narrow Gauge Railway
State government agencies	Echo Bay Mines Company
Colorado Department of Public Health and	Gold King Mines
the Environment	Little Nation Mining Company
Colorado Water Quality Control Division	The Mining Remedial Recovery Company
Colorado Department of Minerals and	Asarco
Geology	The OSIRIS Gold Company
Colorado Division of Wildlife	The Root and Norton Assayers
Colorado Geological Survey	St. Paul Lodge
	The Sunnyside Gold Corporation
Local government agencies	Silver Wing Company
City of Durango	The District Tusco Company
San Juan County Commissioners	Hydrosphere
Town of Silverton	
Southern Ute Tribe	
Southwest Colorado Water Conservation	
District	

ticipants coalesced around the process only after the state of Colorado made it clear that the standards would be determined with or without their involvement, and the EPA intimated that it otherwise would invoke the Comprehensive Environmental Response, Compensation, and Liability Act (CERCLA) and designate the area a Superfund site (Broetzman 1996). The threat of Superfund designation made WQCD's collaborative proposition seem comparatively appealing. Seeing the alternatives framed in this manner, the stakeholders exercised enlightened self-interest to undertake the collaborative ARSG process, which would more directly involve the populations most affected by new standards.

After the ARSG met for the first time in early 1994, its members had seven months to demonstrate to the WQCC that they could develop a reasonable regulatory alternative to a top-down, imposed standard (Parsons 2001). In September 1994, the WQCC held a hearing in Silverton, which was extraordinarily well attended by the stakeholders. After that meeting, the WQCC decided to grant authority to the ARSG to characterize existing sources of pollution, determine the feasibility for remediation, demonstrate the appropriate use classes and standards for implementation, and begin remediation (Simon n.d.). Without formal regulatory authority, the ARSG was to provide technical expertise and community-supported recommendations to regulatory entities—the WQCD, WQCC, and EPA.

The WQCC set a three-year deadline for the ARSG to accomplish its objectives, and the ARSG devised a three-phase plan to accomplish its goals (McAllister 1999). First, the ARSG wanted to establish baseline data for water quality in the upper Animas basin. The results of the 1991–1993 sampling program pointed to metal loading and acidity as the main factors limiting aquatic health and habitat (Simon n.d.). In 1995, the group began a long-term program to establish or reestablish gauging stations along the various stretches of the Animas to provide reliable water samples and flow determinations. Second, the ARSG sought to prioritize the most serious sources of contamination for cleanup. In 1995, the group began a program to determine sites that were the most significant loaders of metals that limited aquatic life and habitat. Prioritization of sites was an ongoing process that depended on various criteria, including feasibility, funding, cost-effectiveness, and overcoming regulatory disincentives for cleanup. Third, the group wished to undertake remediation projects. In 1998, when the initial deadline was reached, the necessary work had not yet been completed. But the ARSG was making good progress, and the WQCC extended the deadline to 2001.

GOVERNMENTAL IMPACT

Government played a dual role in the ARSG. Government was an actor, present in the form of different federal- and state-level agency personnel within the collaborative effort. Government also was present as institutions influencing the framework of rules and laws within which the ARSG stakeholder process played out.

Governmental actors were essential to group creation. The WQCD played a seminal role in the formation of the ARSG, as did the EPA. The WQCD had been through several conflict-ridden mine cleanups in the recent past and was seeking a new approach to cleanup efforts (Robinson 2000). To remove itself from a leadership position, it sought out a neutral party that could facilitate the initial meeting of the group and pull the stakeholders together. The WQCD envisioned itself as another stakeholder rather than the main driver of the process and wanted to create a situation in which it could make a credible claim to this role (Parsons 2001).

Governmental institutions, such as the CWA and the TMDL framework, provided a broader, rule-bound context in which the collaborative effort of the ARSG operated. These rules were necessary to mesh the community-based process with the larger regulatory schedule and operations. While the ARSG was deliberating its actions during the three years it had to determine use standards for the watershed, the existing ambient standards remained in place. When the three years ended in 1998, the ARSG process came up for review before the WQCC. The ARSG had not yet completed its UAA, so it could not make any determinations about setting use-designation standards. The group asked for an additional three years to continue to collect data to complete the UAA to make appropriate use-designation standards. The WQCC agreed unanimously to give the ARSG until March 2001 to come up with its recommendations (McAllister 1999, 41). If the ARSG could not provide adequate standards in 2001, then the WQCC would impose numerical standards. Because the ARSG was granted no formal authority for rulemaking, the final decision to accept its UAA and recommendations rested with the WQCC. At some level, because an external authority maintained control over the final regulations, the group ran the risk of having its recommendations rejected.

One of the largest challenges for the group was reconciling the existing and external environmental statutory structure suggested by the institutions of government with a cooperative, community-based structure embodied in the ARSG approach (Robinson 2000; Johnson 2001). The standards that emerged from the stakeholder process have been politically acceptable to the stakeholders, but they have been less well received by some within the WQCD, which is the regulatory entity responsible for the long-term management of the resource. Changes, turnover, and reorganization within the WQCD meant that the staff who originally participated in the ARSG effort in 1994 had left by the conclusion of the process in 2001. Without these governmental actors in place as part of the stakeholder effort, opportunities to mesh the investigation and findings from the ARSG process with the institutions of governance were lost. Much as was the case in the Albemarle–Pamlico Estuarine Study (Chapter 6), as government personnel changed, the expectations for what the ARSG process would produce also shifted. For example, the ARSG had to adhere to the formalities imposed when putting together a UAA, and different government staff had different expectations for this process and its product (Johnson 2001).

Likewise, the group was required to stay within the regulatory boundaries imposed by the CWA. A fundamental lesson here is that a politically acceptable process in the form of a stakeholder group and its outcomes can diverge from what is acceptable within the existing regulatory structure. Although this divergence has not been insurmountable in the ARSG case, it does underscore the difficulties of meshing two different cultures within a community-based but regulatory-approved process.

Liability issues related to cleaning up abandoned mines in the region have been an additional institutional influence on the group. Regulations associated with the CWA and CERCLA mean that the third-party provision of the CWA may curtail abandoned mines from being cleaned up voluntarily (Broetzman 1998). Recently ARSG has begun to deal with this problem by pursuing a Good Samaritan Provision that would permit third-party cleanups of historic mines and would limit liabilities for these volunteer cleanups to gross negligence and misconduct (Butler 2001).

CERCLA also played an important role in coalescing the group. Hanging over the group was the EPA's threat that the area could be designated a Superfund site. Superfund designation would have meant that different types of resources could be harnessed to tackle the water quality issues in the basin, and it also would have changed the focus of the group from a self-determined strategy of remediating the watershed as a means to serve varied interests to a more litigious one that gave decision control to lawyers and the courts. In other words, EPA used the threat of CERCLA regulations to rally the group, fortifying the ARSG's resolve to find a solution more positive than a Superfund designation (Parsons 2001).

State and federal agencies were responsible for following different institutional mandates, and the ARSG needed to adhere to these legal frameworks to produce effective and valid standards. Having stakeholders within the group who were knowledgeable about the various statutory requirements and bureaucratic machinations helped the ARSG members learn about and navigate these institutional requirements. Having regular contact within the group with the agencies responsible for the external rules reduced the possibility that expectations would go unfulfilled, especially early in the process. As the ARSG process unfolded over time, staff turnover and changes meant that expectations diverged, although not so severely as to jeopardize the final outcome of the process.

Issue Definition

Issue definition in the ARSG effort was influenced by government both as an actor and as an institution. WQCD personnel, as governmental actors, identified the need for a stakeholder group to improve water quality in the region. Consequently, WQCD members promoted the formation of the ARSG. A watershed biophysical scale was imposed through a problem definition that encompassed the entire watershed. In this manner, government led the creation of a collaborative effort. Government also played a role in encouraging collaboration through the EPA's threat of a Superfund designation. In this way, the EPA also shaped the way the problem was framed by providing a clear alternative, which was rejected by the residents of the watershed.

Resources

A variety of resources were crucial to the ARSG in accomplishing its goals, and some resources mattered more than others at different times during the group's development. Initially, the ARSG used financial resources to leverage human resources toward accomplishing its goals. As the group matured, it relied on relationships to leverage extensive technical resources among its member stakeholders. Because of the dominant presence of multiple governmental agencies, the group's legitimacy ultimately was called into question.

Financial Resources. The ARSG channeled a total of $19.2 million dollars to the watershed, including $5.9 million on watershed characterization, $13.1 million on reclamation, and $200,000 on cultural mitigation. Of this, Sunnyside Gold Company contributed the largest amount, with $10 million in its own reclamation effort, or 54 percent of the total, and the federal government contributed 40 percent (Robinson 2000). Thus it is fair to say that government did not dominate in the provision of financial resources, and private industry in particular played an important role in this regard.

Because it was the brainchild of the WQCD and the EPA, the ARSG had access to governmental financial resources that otherwise might not have been forthcoming. In this respect, the ARSG relied most heavily on financial resources from the EPA's Rocky Mountain Headwaters Mining Waste Initiative to fund its work. The EPA, in conjunction with the WQCD, also funneled money to the ARSG though the Section 319 program.[2] In 1999, the ARSG received nearly $450,000, a full 35 percent of the EPA's Section 319 grant money for the state of Colorado (McAllister 1999, 59). Technically, the EPA makes Section 319 grants to the WQCD, which then designates the moneys for use by the ARSG (Butler 2001). These financial resources were used to leverage human resources for the ARSG.

Other governmental agencies also contributed to financial resources through direct or indirect means, but they did not play as dominant a role as the EPA or WQCD. The Forest Service, Bureau of Land Management (BLM), and Colorado Division of Wildlife provided funding to the ARSG effort. San Juan County donated office space to the group. Local mining corporations and the Southwest Water Conservation District underwrote a small portion of the administrative costs. In recent years, the Southwest Water Conservation District has picked up a portion of the tab for the salary of the watershed coordinator (Butler 2001).

Human Resources. Governmental agency members were important participants in the ARSG, but they worked with nongovernmental actors to achieve their objectives. A core group of approximately 30 stakeholders met monthly to share their understanding about the state's water quality control standards and regulations, as well as new knowledge they had gained about factors contributing to the contamination. The ARSG has been notable in its success at building a well-functioning network of stakeholder members. Many of the original members remained involved, attending at least two meetings per year. Some were more active than others, with some members playing leadership roles. Representatives of federal and state governmental agencies were the most persistent members, along with some individual community members who served as representatives from local governments, nonprofit organizations, and industry.

Additionally, in 1994, the ARSG submitted a grant proposal to the EPA with the assistance of the WQCD and secured funding to hire Bill Simon as the watershed coordinator (Broetzman 1996). A longtime resident of the basin with a mining and environmental background, Simon was a good choice for the position and oversaw many administrative and fund-raising tasks while also acting as a spokesperson for the group. He participated in research and data collection for the UAA and the TMDL framework that was submitted to the state in 2000 (McAllister 1999). To help him handle his many activities, the ARSG obtained additional funding in 1998 from the EPA to hire a staff assistant, and several members of the group volunteered to head up various committees.

In 1999, the EPA began to reevaluate its financial support for these staff positions. Preferring instead to support remediation projects, the agency backed away from providing support for human resources, citing that the positions should be supported by the community or through other resources (Butler 2001). Since that time, the ARSG has lost its staff assistant but has managed to scrape together funding for Simon's position from various local sources. In this manner, the EPA has encouraged other community members to support the effort.

Technical Resources. State and federal governmental actors clearly dominated in the provision of technical resources in the ARSG. Because the ARSG possessed capable human resources, there was little need to search for additional technical resources apart from the immediate stakeholders, whose networks provided important technical resources (Steelman and Carmin 2002). In addition to Simon's technical training in mining remediation and environmental issues, various state and federal agencies conducted the initial stages of research in the upper Animas. In 1995, the Colorado Division of Mining and Geology began a study of one of the tributaries of the upper Animas, Mineral Creek. The EPA funded this effort with Section 319 moneys, and the Forest Service and the Colorado Geological Survey (CGS) provided technical assistance. In 1996, the ARSG initiated a similar study on another tributary, Cement Creek. Also that year, the ARSG began an evaluation of the Animas River Canyon to determine aquatic habitat limitations (McAllister 1999, 40). The Forest Service, which manages most of the federal lands in the watershed, provided technical help and contracted with the CGS to conduct an inventory of mines on Forest Service lands. The Forest Service has conducted biological studies in the area, as have the BLM and CDW.

GROUP STRUCTURE AND DECISION-MAKING PROCESS

The structure of the ARSG was defined by the group itself, with little influence from the EPA or WQCD, other than as actors within the group. Governmental actors are notable in this case for *not* having exerted undue authority on the collaboration. Agency members influenced how the group would be structured, but only as stakeholder members, not as entities driving the process. Consequently, governmental actors facilitated the development of structures and processes that served the group, rather than the government. The biggest impact the WQCD had on the structure of the ARSG was the role it played in contracting the CCEM to pull together the salient participants in the group.

The ARSG created three working groups and several subgroups, including the Monitoring Work Group, which coordinated the collection, assessment, and management of the watershed characterization information and the identification of source areas contributing to heavy metal contamination; the Feasibility Working Group, which conducted feasibility studies to identify alternatives for remediating mines and implementing remediation projects; and the Regulatory Working Group, which tracked the changes in relevant statutes and regulations and provided information about the group's work to various regulatory agencies, such as the WQCC.

The full group, as well as the working groups and subgroups, met on the third Thursday of every month in Silverton, Colorado. Working groups met immediately before the monthly meetings, and then presented action items to the group at large. A fourth group met in Denver, where many of the technical and agency staff were located, to coordinate multiagency activities and disseminate information to those who could not attend the regular stakeholder meetings in Silverton (Robinson 2000). Typed minutes from each monthly meeting were sent to all stakeholders and interested parties to inform those who had not been present. To encourage the inclusion of all stakeholder interests, decision making was by consensus rather than more formal majority-rule voting.

COLLABORATIVE OUTCOMES

The UAA provided the basis for determining standards for water uses in the watershed, and it was heavily influenced by an institution of government, the regulatory process of the WQCC. In January 2001, the ARSG completed the UAA, a composite of all studies conducted in the basin. Because of various revisions and the need to make all of the data available for adequate review, the WQCC postponed the hearing from March until May 2001. At that time, the ARSG submitted its work, and the WQCC took preliminary final actions to accept the proposed regulations while asking for clarification on a few remaining items (Frohardt 2001). On October 9, 2001, the WQCC formally accepted the ARSG's UAA. This was a victory for the ARSG in two ways: A diverse stakeholder group had agreed on use standards, and because of this agreement, the standards stood a much greater chance of being implemented by the various stakeholders involved in the process.

Environmental Outcomes

The ARSG was the catalyst for approximately $20 million spent on site characterization, prioritization, and remediation projects within the watershed (McAllister 1999, *40*). Since 1995, the ARSG coordinated or participated in nearly 50 individual site characterization studies of the geology, hydrology, and biology of the region in conjunction with various state and federal agencies (McAllister 1999, *65*). One of the notable findings from the site characterization studies was that a relatively small percentage of mines out of the 1,500 in the area actually contributed significant acid and metal loading to the watershed. Consequently, only about 100 mines were targeted for remediation, significantly fewer than initially anticipated (Robinson 2000). In addition to site characterization and prioritization, the ARSG has channeled remediation projects to the area. Nearly 35 projects have been completed already, and more are planned (Robinson 2000). Nonetheless, remediation is anticipated to take another 20 years or more.

Following the remediation projects, fish populations in the area are showing improvement. In 1996, naturally reproducing trout were recorded in the lower Animas River for the first time. Electrofishing surveys conducted in 1992 and 1998 indicated that trout populations had increased in the cleaner segments of the upper Animas watershed (Robinson 2000).

Social Outcomes

As a social outcome, the ARSG created trust among the various stakeholders. Having the government involved in the form of stakeholder members changed the perceptions of some nonagency participants. As one ARSG member recalled, "I used to see the federal government and state government as very much obstructionist. Now I hear their very legitimate concerns. They want to do the right thing" (Belsten 1996, *172–73*). Moreover, trust worked as a catalyst to accomplish other goals or reduce friction that may have prevented some from reaching out to others. Another ARSG participant reflected, "I think this process [has] ... built up a lot of trust. Solutions are locally generated. And I know I can pick up the phone and talk with anyone in the group between meetings" (Belsten 1996, *174*).

Many people in the group felt as though they understood not only the processes involved in standard setting, but also the data that accompanies such efforts. As one stakeholder noted, "It's a much more complicated issue than I think people initially realized. You do have to spend a great deal of time studying all the options before you can take any steps, finalize any solutions" (Belsten 1996, *172*). In meetings and working groups, different participants expressed their concerns and preferences, and the other stakeholders took them seriously. Efforts at joint data gathering and research helped foster collective understanding of the problems (Belsten 1996). Over time, the group gained a better understanding of the implications of setting specific water quality standards and a greater appreciation for environmental technologies and cleanup strategies, as well as a more thorough understanding of the long-term consequences of applying standards, technologies, and cleanup strategies.

Government involvement led to questions about the ARSG's legitimacy as a "community" group. In 1995, some local citizens criticized the group because they felt overwhelmed by the many governmental agencies that were part of the stakeholder process (Broetzman 1996, *10*; McAllister 1999, *50*). In 1996, a report on the group encouraged the ARSG to "maintain continuous contacts with the local population at large and to seek expanded local participation and/or acceptance in the process" (Broetzman 1996, *12*). Simon and others within the group promoted ARSG activities to involve more of the local public. Nonetheless, confusion about the intent of the ARSG and concern about the involvement of locals persisted. Attendance among locals increased whenever the group addressed controversial issues (ARSG 1999).

The charge of too little lay community involvement must be considered in light of who is appropriately considered to be in the community. *Community* can be defined in multiple ways (Hillery 1955). Members of a community may have similar identities, reside in a common geographic locale, or belong to a group that has related interests. An additional definition is those participants who are politically relevant to a decision or a decision-making process (Lasswell and McDougal 1992). Within the context of the ARSG, public agencies had a big stake in the designation of water quality standards, given the high percentage of public lands in the watershed, and thus rightfully were considered part of the community.

CONCLUSIONS

Government influenced the creation, activities, and accomplishments of the ARSG in important ways. Government, in the form of the WQCD, played a formative role in the genesis of the ARSG. Without the WQCD, it is unlikely that a stakeholder group would have formed within the watershed to address and improve water quality issues. In addition, both the WQCD and EPA played key roles in providing the group with initial financial resources, which the group used to secure a variety of resources that otherwise would have been more difficult to acquire, if not unavailable altogether. The financial resources allowed additional financial, human, and technical resources to be leveraged in generating important environmental and social outcomes. For instance, the EPA, WQCD, and other agencies contributed financial and technical assistance to provide the foundation for the UAA, site characterization, prioritization, and remediation studies, which have contributed to improvement in environmental quality in the region.

Although the ARSG was founded through an external process involving the WQCD and CCEM, internally determined group structure and processes such as regular meetings, consensus-based decision making, well-functioning working groups and regular interaction allowed varied parties to gain trust and attain common understandings about their surroundings and the many challenges involved in regulatory standard setting. Importantly, the WQCD did not impose external rules on the group, other than those necessitated by regulatory standard-setting practices. The WQCD relinquished its control over the process to give great discretion to the ARSG in determining its own rules for operating. This passive government involvement was just as important as the more active government involvement that led to the group's formation. Through the internal organizational processes, various participants learned to trust and learn from each other. Had an external government entity imposed these internal structures and decision-making rules, members may have had greater difficulty in trusting each other, thereby hindering their collective understanding of various aspects associated with establishing regulations.

In spite of the internally determined structure, the group's legitimacy was questioned based on inadequate representation within the broader local community. In this manner, government involvement may have left the group vulnerable to this claim, but it is unclear whether it had any detrimental impact on the outcome of the overall process. If the ARSG had been completely representative of the local community and lacked involvement of various governmental entities, the group would have been challenged to navigate the complicated terrain of regulatory and rule-making standards, likely making it less effective in the long run. The trade-off of more government involvement and resources for less representation by the local community was appropriate in this case, because the outcome was not compromised in the trade-off, and the salient political parties were involved to devise meaningful and workable outcomes.

The ARSG has demonstrated that a government-led, community-based effort need not be an oxymoron. The process was decidedly more community-based than if the WQCD had imposed standards. The WQCD did not dominate the process, but was an active participant in the process, as were other governmental and nongovernmental participants.

What criteria help determine whether an effort is truly community-based? To answer this question, it is instructive to consider why community-based approaches are preferable over a more command-and-control regulatory strategy. Drawing from the ARSG experience, Greg Parsons, the WQCD nonpoint-source coordinator who initiated the ARSG process, stated that community-based approaches are more appropriate for dealing with complex, unclear pollution sources that involve many actors, and that command-and-control rulemaking options "are no more appealing, because they just land you in legal fights and tie up the process through other channels .... If you have a clear point source of pollution, then you have adequate regulatory tools with which to establish your regulatory goals. However, if the situation is ambiguous then you need a different tool set." As part of this new tool set, community-based efforts can result in more readily implementable solutions than can traditional command-and-control strategies. And yet how is it possible to determine whether an effort is community-based?

Four elements from this case are instructive. First, the temporal dynamism of the group has to be considered in any statement about the degree to which it is community-based. Over time, the ARSG became less an artificial creation of the CCEM and more of an authentic community-based group. As such, the ARSG started as agency-driven but grew into a more community-driven exercise. Just because a group starts out as a government-led effort does not preclude it from becoming more community-based over time. The opposite also can be true, with groups beginning as community-driven efforts but gravitating toward agency-dominated processes.

Second, *community* is an elastic term. The degree to which an effort can be considered community-based rests on who is considered the relevant community. Not surprisingly, the determination of who constitutes the community is a contextual decision based on the nature of the problem and the social characteristics that surround it. In this sense, the ARSG stretches the definition of community. Community can be defined by interests, geography, and identity. In the case of the ARSG, however, these definitions do not necessarily serve the goal of determining water quality standards in the watershed. Here community representation was embodied in those participants who demonstrated an active interest and willingness to be involved and possessed or cultivated appropriate expertise. Importantly, this definition of community is not exclusionary. Others were not prevented from participating if they were interested in joining the effort. Many people opted not to be involved because of other competing outlets for their time and interests.

Third, *community-based* is a relative term. An agency-inspired stakeholder process is certainly more participatory and community-based than is a process in which an agency determines use standards without any input from those who would be most affected by them. Although the legitimacy of the group has been questioned because of its close ties to the agencies involved with its formation and the lack of more lay community involvement, the legitimacy of the ARSG as a community-based effort can be understood only when compared with the other available alternatives in this case—imposing standards in a top-down manner by the WQCD and the WQCC or designating the area a Superfund site. Consequently, it may be more appropriate to discuss the varying degrees to which an effort is or is not community-based. In all cases, it seems fair to compare the existing effort with other regulatory alternatives that might be pursued.

Fourth, the role for an agency in community-based management is one of participant, not boss. Understanding the role the agency plays in the process is important to understanding the degree to which the effort is community-based. Formed in response to a request from the WQCD, the ARSG was tasked to devise water quality use standards for the Animas River. The WQCD played an active role in instigating group formation, but it did so in a deliberate way to ensure that its representatives were not controlling the process. Agency personnel sought out a neutral facilitating organization and were content to be a stakeholder member rather than the lead organization. They did not impose extraneous external rules but placed trust in group members to determine their own sound, internal structural resources. The EPA also played an important formative role in the creation of the ARSG through its funding and technical support. Likewise, the EPA understood the importance of remaining a low-key player. As recalled by Peter Butler, an ARSG member, "The EPA and the [Water Quality Control] Division were very sensitive to the need to stay in the background" (Butler 2001). In more metaphorical terms, the EPA and WQCD understood the importance of being a passenger on the community-based management bus rather than the driver.

In summary, government-led, community-based environmental management appears to have been an appropriate choice in this case, given the complexity of the environmental problem, the need to involve the stakeholders who were affected most by water quality standards, the specific nature of the task, and the thinness of the lay community around the issue. This does not imply that government-led, community-based environmental management is appropriate for all circumstances. Rather, it should be reserved for instances where the conditions suggest that alternative approaches, such as command-and-control regulations, might be less appropriate and potential exists for cultivating organizational capacity to initiate an effort within the relevant community. Some agency personnel no doubt have cloaked themselves in community-based rhetoric to accomplish their regulatory objectives at the local level in other places, but careful analysis reveals that this has not been the case with the ARSG. The sincerity of effort and respect for the process on behalf of the WQCD, WQCC, EPA, and other agency personnel kept the government-led, community-based ARSG effort from being a contradiction in terms.

PART IV

RECONSIDERING GOVERNMENTAL ROLES

CHAPTER 8

GOVERNMENT AS ACTOR
AND AS INSTITUTION

Collaboration has become a popular idea touted by governmental and nongovernmental actors alike as a means to foster better environmental management through decentralization and public involvement. Although numerous studies have focused on collaborative environmental management, none have explored systematically the role of government in these processes. The six case studies of environmental planning processes and outcomes presented in this book provide greater insight into collaborative environmental management. Using a consistent set of factors to guide this inquiry, the case chapters explored how government as actor and as institution affected collaborations across situations where government took the lead, encouraged collaboration, or followed the efforts of nongovernmental actors.

IMPACT OF GOVERNMENT

Governments can play many roles in collaborative environmental management. In the cases examined, government participation and commitment helped shape the formation, functioning, and maintenance of collaborative endeavors. As actors, government personnel often took the role of stakeholders and frequently were just one voice among many. These individuals sometimes acted independently of their governmental agencies. At other times, they served as agency representatives, and thus the roles they played as actors in the process were bounded by institutional mandates and forces. As a set of institutions, government established rules and norms that influenced many facets of collaboration. Each case in this volume examined the ways that government as actor and as institution influenced issue definition, resources for collaboration, group structure and decision-making processes, and collaborative outcomes. Cross-case analysis of these factors provides a basis for understanding how governmental actors and institutions leave their mark on collaborative environmental management.

Issue Definition

Issue definition refers to the biophysical scale and the way that a particular problem is framed. Together, these two elements of issue definition provide a rationale for action and a foundation on which collaborative initiatives are built. In instances where government encouraged or led the collaboration, governmental institutions established the biophysical scale of the collaborative efforts (see Table 8-1). In the cases of the Ohio Farmland Preservation Planning Program (OFPPP), Albemarle–Pamlico Estuarine Study (APES), and Animas River Stakeholder Group (ARSG), institutional stipulations required that funds be spent on planning focused at a particular scale (county, estuary, and watershed, respectively). In the case of habitat conservation plans (HCPs), federal institutions did not specify the scale, either in funding HCPs or in other rules governing the process. Thus participants could conceptualize HCPs at any scale within the habitat of a threatened or endangered species. But because federal officials provided technical assistance, based on scientific evidence about habitat extent, government influenced the biophysical scale of the collaborative planning effort in the form of actors, not institutions. In the Applegate and Darby cases, tensions existed between institutional conceptualizations of the appropriate management scale and the views maintained by governmental actors. With Applegate, for instance, the Forest Service and Bureau of Land Management (BLM) were organized into discrete units that reflected structural decisions made many years earlier within these agencies. The existing structures did not facilitate interagency coordination at the scale of a watershed, even though many governmental actors believed that this was the appropriate

Table 8-1. Summary of Governmental Impact on Issue Definition

Case study	Biophysical scale		Issue framing	
	Actor	Institution	Actor	Institution
Applegate	BLM and Forest Service personnel worked to manage resources at watershed scales	Forest Service and BLM organized into non–watershed-based management units	Forest Service and BLM personnel framed issue as need to increase public participation, reduce conflict, and undertake ecosystem management	Forest Service and BLM reinforced hierarchical and segmented approaches; federal rules allowing Partnership One to be appealed led the group to broaden its issue focus
Darby	Governmental actors viewed scale as ecosystem rather than political jurisdiction	Little impact, although scale coincided with existing HUA government program	Governmental actors framed issue as problem with institutional water management practices	Little impact: Partners broadened issues beyond traditional government focus
HCP	FWS personnel advised how much habitat each HCP should cover	Little impact, as HCPs can cover a subset of habitat area	Local and state governmental actors (like private actors) developed HCPs as means to comply with federal endangered species rules	Federal ESA and implementing rules framed issue as need to protect listed species and their habitat
OFPPP	No impact	State program set scale based on county boundaries	No impact	State program framed issue as need to encourage collaborative approach to farmland conservation; local governmental zoning rules affected feasible alternatives
APES	Federal and state actors in Policy Committee helped refine aspects of estuary focus	Federal program set scale as estuary	State and local governmental actors in Policy Committee helped frame issue as need to reduce scientific uncertainty through collaborative effort	Federal program framed issue as need for greater collaboration and ecosystem approach to protect threatened estuaries
ARSG	State and federal governmental actors set scale at the watershed level	WQCD set scale as watershed to match UAA requirements in federal law and state regulations	Federal and state actors argued that Superfund designation could be avoided by taking a collaborative approach to watershed management	Clean Water Act required use designation; federal Superfund regulations framed unappealing alternative to collaboration

management unit. The result was that agency officials associated with the partnership held a different view of the appropriate biophysical scale than what was being advanced by their institutions.

Similarly, the cases demonstrate that the way an issue is framed by governmental institutions is not always aligned with the way it is framed by affiliated governmental actors. In both the Applegate and Darby Partnerships, institutional pressures reinforced ingrained management practices. Nongovernmental actors were free to take an alternative stance, asserting that management practices should be directed toward an ecosystem scale and that the issue should be reframed as a problem with highly fragmented approaches to forest or watershed management promoted by the prevailing institutions. By embracing this problem definition, the governmental actors who participated in these collaborations, at times, placed themselves at odds with or went beyond their institutions.

In contrast, in the government-led and government-encouraged collaborations, government institutions and actors were more closely aligned in their views and actions. The HCP program, for example, provided explicit parameters for acceptable HCPs. Rather than take independent action and initiative, federal officials implemented the program by granting permits only to those applicants whose plans fell within these parameters, though the officials still had discretion to recommend that HCP participants consider certain things within these parameters. Governmental actors also demonstrated independence in some instances as they refined and extended the way their institutions framed the problem. For example, in the case of the ARSG, federal regulations established a basis for Superfund designation. Rather than support the adoption of this designation, governmental actors promoted the formation of the collaboration as an alternative means for improving water quality in the Animas River.

Resources for Collaboration

Other investigations and discussions of collaboration have emphasized the importance of resources, particularly funding and human capital (e.g., Wondolleck and Yaffee 2000; Steelman and Carmin 2002). The cases in our analysis suggest that such resources are important for sustaining an initiative over time and can determine what outcomes realistically can be accomplished. Regardless of their role, governmental actors and institutions influence the availability and character of human, technical, and financial resources in these endeavors (see Table 8-2).

Table 8-2. Summary of Governmental Impact on Resources

Case study	Human resources		Technical resources		Financial resources	
	Actor	Institution	Actor	Institution	Actor	Institution
Applegate	Forest Service and BLM personnel comprised significant minority of active participants, even after FACA ruling	Industry used FACA to prohibit government membership on board of directors	Forest Service and BLM personnel provided information and expertise	No impact	Forest Service and BLM personnel provided in-kind support	Forest Service and BLM budgeting systems constrained implementation of partnership agreements
Darby	Majority of general and core membership was federal, state, and local agency personnel	No impact	Federal, state, and local agency personnel shared information and provided expertise	No impact	Several governmental actors secured funds for indirectly related projects	No impact
HCP	Number of local, state, and federal actors participating varied greatly across HCPs	Federal guidelines encouraged broad participation for some HCPs; FWS personnel must approve HCPs but need not participate in them	FWS personnel provided key technical information and expertise	No impact	FWS personnel used grants to encourage collaboration	The ESA authorized grants to local communities with matching requirements, which encouraged collaboration
OFPPP	Majority of participants in most task forces were local governmental actors	By delegating authority to county commissioners, program fostered participation of governmental actors	Some groups received assistance from local governmental agency experts	Program guidelines encouraged use of government information sources	Local governmental actors made additional contributions in some cases	State program was key funding source; flexibility led to varying ways funds were spent
APES	Majority of active participants were federal, state, and local governmental actors	Federal guidelines suggested broad inclusion of stakeholders; appointments determined by Policy Committee	Federal and state agency personnel conducted research, shared findings and technical expertise	Government grants and programs supported related projects and studies	State and local governmental actors garnered funding for basic research and additional spin-off projects	Federal program was primary funder, and significant portion was dedicated to research
ARSG	Majority of actors were federal and state agency personnel	EPA grant program funded watershed coordinator	Federal and state agency personnel collaborated with stakeholders on research	Federal and state agency programs funded agency personnel to conduct research	Federal agency personnel secured additional funds	Federal program and state agencies were significant funders

Human Resources. Human resources consist of personnel and the capabilities that they bring to the collaboration. Participation in the collaborative endeavors described in this book ranged from small groups consisting of 9 individuals in one OFPPP task force to 600 participants at the first public meeting in the APES process. Voluntary and paid staff participation are central to collaboration (Wondolleck and Yaffee 2000), with governmental actors often being significant human resources for the group.

Governmental institutions can, but do not always, influence the makeup of the collaborative group and the degree to which agency personnel are involved. In all of the government-led and government-encouraged cases, institutions in the forms of agency processes, programs, and official guidelines established the rules for membership selection and determined the degree to which governmental actors could become involved in the collaboration. At one extreme is the APES case, where the National Estuary Program (NEP) established a collaborative structure and made recommendations about the inclusion of specific groups of stakeholders. At the other extreme is the ARSG case, where agencies delegated membership selection to the group.

In most of the government-led and government-encouraged cases, governmental actors formed the majority of collaborative group membership. Governmental actors were present and active in the government-followed cases to varying degrees. In the Applegate case, they made up a minority of the participants. The composition of the general membership was somewhat fluid, as individuals from diverse stakeholder groups elected to come and go as they deemed appropriate. In the Darby case, governmental actors constituted three-fourths of the general membership and about two-thirds of the core group members.

Governmental actors are embedded in the institutions that they represent. As a result, their participation in collaborative environmental management initiatives can be constrained by policies, procedures, and politics. The impact of institutions on governmental actors was clearly seen in the Applegate case, where personnel from the Forest Service and BLM serving on the partnership's board were forced to resign from their board positions because of concerns over the Federal Advisory Committee Act.

Technical Resources. Technical resources refer to information and knowledge about the natural resource and its management that are available to the collaboration. In the government-led cases, governmental institutions provided a foundation for technical support. In the APES case, agency programs funded technical studies, whereas in the ARSG case, federal and state agencies funded government personnel as well as technical studies to conduct research. Similarly, in the OFPPP, a government-encouraged case, the program established guidelines that encouraged task force participants to use governmental information sources. In the HCP case, also government-encouraged, the U.S. Fish and Wildlife Service (FWS) published technical guidelines for HCP participants. In contrast, governmental institutions had less impact on the availability of and emphasis placed on the use of technical resources in the government-followed cases.

Although the roles of institutions in providing technical resources varied greatly, individual governmental actors played consistent roles across the cases. In all instances, they provided technical knowledge and information that helped the collaborative groups work toward their goals. Government representatives provided the ARSG with water quality data and understanding of chemical processes, state and federal agency technical staff conducted research for APES, and agency representatives provided technical advice and assistance to the Applegate and Darby Partnerships. In the HCP process, federal officials used technical resources not only to achieve goals, but also as a means to promote collaboration itself, by framing a collective-action problem based on information about the distribution of habitat and knowledge about the causal mechanisms of extinction. Finally, in some of the OFPPP task forces, governmental employees, especially local government officials, provided technical information about farmland and land-use planning.

Financial Resources. Financial resources consist of the funding that a collaborative environmental management initiative receives or is able to generate. Governmental institutions established the basis for the disbursement of financial resources in all of the government-led and government-encouraged cases, with each drawing from different combinations of federal, state, and local funding. The financial resources also were distributed in different ways. In some cases, government provided funds for planning but not for implementation, as in the OFPPP and APES. Distribution of government funds also may be tied to formal matching grant requirements, such as in the OFPPP (100 percent local match of state funds), APES (25 percent state match of federal funds), and HCP (variable matches). In the government-followed cases, institutional impacts on funding differed. In the Darby Partnership, governmental institutions had no impact on funding, whereas in the Applegate Partnership, the lack of financial support from the Forest Service at times hindered the ability to implement agreements.

Governmental financial resources can benefit collaboration by facilitating research, covering operating expenses, supporting staff, and creating plans. Although the quantity of financial contributions is certainly important, the cases suggest that governmental actors also exert substantial influence by controlling the collaborative effort's use of funds. In the OFPPP, the state of Ohio provided financial support for the task forces but placed few limitations on their activities and use of funds. Consequently, how these funds were used, and what they accomplished, varied greatly across groups. In contrast, a significant percentage of the funding received from the government for APES was dedicated to research. As a result, nongovernmental participants had little influence on the degree to which research versus nonresearch activities could be supported. Although the presence of substantial levels of funding for research was useful, some participants were frustrated at the lack of support available for management actions. At the same time, governmental actors in all of the cases helped locate and secure additional financial or in-kind resources. As with human and technical resources, governmental actors may be constrained by their institutions, but they may exercise some discretion toward supporting and sustaining the collaboration financially.

Group Structure and Decision-Making Processes

Group structure refers to the ways in which the activities of members are organized and administered. Structure influences collaborative processes not only by shaping interactions, but also by establishing a framework for coordinating activities. In the government-led and government-encouraged cases, governmental institutions defined parameters for the way the collaborative had to be organized (see Table 8-3). In the APES planning process, the NEP recommended several model committee structures and what types of stakeholders should be included in the membership. The ARSG was required to form a single stakeholder group, the OFPPP was organized around task forces, and HCPs were oriented to planning groups. In these cases, institutions provided a general framework for the group structure but then granted autonomy to the groups to determine many aspects of the membership and internal organization.

Scholars suggest that collaboration should provide equal, if not greater, opportunities for nongovernmental actors to participate in and influence decision making (Gray 1989; Mandell 1999; Milward and Provan 2000). The case studies suggest that governmental institutions play an influential

Table 8-3. Summary of Governmental Impact on Group Structure and Decision Making

Case study	Structure		Decision making	
	Actor	Institution	Actor	Institution
Applegate	Forest Service and BLM personnel shared leadership with other members of partnership	Little impact, although FACA did require federal personnel to step down from formal leadership positions	Forest Service and BLM personnel had same influence as other stakeholders; encouraged informal process	Federal laws and regulations gave no policy authority to the group
Darby	Governmental actors followed NGO leadership	No impact	Governmental actors had same influence as other stakeholders; encouraged informal process	Existing laws and policies gave no policy authority to the group
HCP	Leadership varied, with some HCPs led by private actors and others by local or state actors	FWS guidelines gave discretion to private actors and local and state governmental actors in designing group structures	Little influence by federal governmental actors; local and state actors had great influence in those HCPs for which they led the planning process	HCP regulations and guidelines delegated authority to private actors and local and state officials to develop and implement plans; once a permit is issued pursuant to the plan, the plan bears legal obligations
OFPPP	Local governmental actors assumed leadership role in many task forces	State grant program did not specify structure; allowed local flexibility	Local governmental actors played key role in some task forces	State grant did not specify decision processes; decisions were nonbinding
APES	Governmental actors on Policy Committee participated in final decisions on structure	Federal rules mandated general committee structure	Governmental actors were dominant on Policy Committee and TAC but not on CACs	Program delegated authority to the group to develop plan; left decision processes flexible; granted no policy authority to implement plan
ARSG	State and federal actors shared leadership and responsibility for establishing formal committee structure	Federal and state institutions encouraged stakeholder group formation but did not specify structures	State and federal actors had same influence as other stakeholders	No institutional specification of decision-making processes; ARSG was to recommend water quality standards to agencies with authority

role in how decision making is structured. Although it is clear that collaborative approaches afford new opportunities for involvement, governmental institutions still define how the participatory process will unfold and the extent to which power and influence are shared. In all of the cases, institutions determined the degree of policy authority that was held by the collaboration. Similar to traditional approaches to participation, opportunities were granted for input, but in most cases authority was not delegated and decisions were not binding.

The cases illustrate a wide range of contributions by governmental actors to moderate the impact of institutions on decision-making processes. Various governmental actors implemented, interpreted, extended, and confronted existing institutional mandates and perspectives. Many of them demonstrated independent thought and action and influenced both group structure and decision-making processes. Across the cases, even when governmental actors were the leaders and when institutional parameters placed limitations on the policy authority of group decisions, these individuals often mediated institutional influence by working to foster genuinely collaborative efforts. With the exception of the APES case, these efforts made it possible for stakeholders to have relatively equal levels of input and influence in group decision-making processes. In the ARSG, for example, governmental and nongovernmental group members alike participated in establishing the water quality standards for the watershed. It appears that the key to making the transition from traditional forms of participation to truly collaborative styles of environmental management may be rooted in the way decision making is enacted and the degree to which power and influence are distributed between governmental and nongovernmental actors.

Collaborative Outcomes

In the environmental arena, the process of collaboration is important, but achieving outcomes is essential. For some practitioners and researchers, collaborative environmental management holds the promise of better environmental solutions through the early and ongoing input of multiple stakeholders. For others, the social outcomes of collaboration are just as important, because the hope is that they will enhance social capital and civic discourse to strengthen democracy.

Because of the limited number and types of cases, our analysis does not indicate whether collaboration is more or less likely to achieve better outcomes than other approaches to environmental management. Further, the

Table 8-4. Summary of Environmental and Social Outcomes

Case study	Environmental outcomes	Social outcomes
Applegate	Restoration projects; alternative approaches to traditional land management	Increased social capital; new spin-off community groups tackling variety of problems
Darby	Environmental education; new information; new cooperative projects; more proenvironmental behavior by governmental actors	Forum for discussion and learning about other perspectives; increased collaborative capacity
HCP	Creation and implementation of HCPs, incidental take permits, implementation agreements, and a wide variety of conservation activities	Increased trust among participants on successful HCPs, with collaborative capacity carried over to other collaborative efforts in one documented case; reduced legitimacy of the ESA among some environmental groups
OFPPP	Plans with varying sophistication across the counties; public education about farmland preservation	Most counties built new social networks and encouraged community discussions to address issues
APES	Plan development; basic research; spin-off projects	Improved networks and coordination but increased conflict and distrust among some participants
ARSG	New standards; new restoration projects; improved fisheries; improved water quality	Increased trust and understanding among diverse participants; denser social networks; created sense among some citizens that decisions were not legitimately community based

time frame is too short to evaluate the long-term ecological outcomes of these collaborations. The cases do, however, illustrate some of the environmental and social outcomes that can result from these and similar types of collaborative efforts (see Table 8-4) and provide insight into the various ways in which governmental actors and institutions affect these planning processes.[1] For example, HCP collaborators were required to implement the plans they designed as a condition for receiving incidental take permits, and members of the Applegate Partnership completed restoration projects.

Environmental Outcomes. The environmental management activities in the cases centered largely on planning, but they also included monitoring, implementation, and enforcement. In addition, activities included standard setting, research, analysis, and education. For example, the OFPPP and APES created natural resource plans, the ARSG established water quality standards, and the Darby Partnership provided education on watershed management. In addition to its restoration efforts, the Applegate Partnership used meetings and outreach activities to address a wide variety of issues, including county-level land-use planning and agricultural and small-business development.

The internal dynamics of collaboration pose challenges to participants and place limitations on what the initiatives realistically can achieve. Most of the collaborative initiatives studied here satisfied their mandates and produced acceptable environmental management tools. Although the evidence is anecdotal, many of these initiatives appear to have produced tangible and consequential environmental quality changes. The Applegate Partnership promoted changes in forest management practices and ecosystem restoration projects. Participants in the Darby Partnership maintain that the education they received altered their behaviors and limited their negative impacts on the ecosystem while in APES, basinwide planning has been implemented. In the ARSG, in addition to establishing new standards, research findings helped target remediation efforts. Preliminary evidence from this remediation work suggests that there have been improvements in water quality and the fisheries in the watershed. Although we cannot demonstrate from any of these case studies that collaboration leads to particular environmental quality outcomes, it is apparent that collaborative activities can produce environmental management tools and promote environmental change.

Plans, standards, and educational activities are essential aspects of environmental management. Although the cases suggest that collaborative endeavors can achieve their goals, they also raise questions about the extent to which collectively generated recommendations, plans, and standards provide an appropriate foundation on which environmental management practices should be built and sustained, particularly as the quality of these outcomes was highly variable. Similar to challenges that arise with traditional approaches to environmental protection, a number of the groups had difficulty satisfying their mandates in the time period allocated. In the case of collaboration, this may be a reflection of the challenges of achieving agreement, let alone consensus, as well as the additional time required when participants lack expertise and experience. The OFPPP case suggests that the participation of diverse stakeholder groups contributed to a high level of variation in plan quality, and members of the ARSG found that the standards they developed were not as acceptable to regulators as to local stakeholders.

Social Outcomes. Although creating changes in environmental quality and management is the motivation for most collaborative environmental management endeavors, another consequence of these activities is that they can generate social outcomes which, in turn, are expected to indirectly influence future environmental outcomes. Social outcomes such as trust, enhanced communication, and improved policy awareness have previously been attributed to collaboration (e.g., Wondolleck and Yaffee 2000; Cortner and Moote 1999; Beierle 1999). Across the cases studied here, relatively consistent social outcomes emerged, including the building of trust, increased knowledge and understanding, network ties, and enhanced communication among different stakeholder groups. As a result, many of the cases, including Applegate, the ARSG, and the OFPPP, showed that collaborative efforts generated good relations and provided a first step for developing new and enduring partnerships.

Social outcomes such as new network ties, enhanced communication, greater knowledge, and better understanding of the policy process all suggest that collaborative environmental management can promote participatory democracy and deliberative practice. For example, in the Applegate Partnership, citizens and agency officials had been in conflict. In coming together, they began to learn about their differences in perspectives, and in the process, they were able to promote genuine communication that ultimately led to cooperative efforts. Similarly, members of the Darby Partnership, APES, and the ARSG reported that they developed greater insight into, and respect for, each other's views. Through the process of open and engaged exchange, these and other groups have been able to foster awareness of multiple perspectives and use them to make informed decisions.

Although collaborative participants expressed many positive sentiments related to the social outcomes of collaboration, feelings about collaboration were diverse, even within a given case. Some participants in the OFPPP reported that they were encouraged by the process and would participate in future collaborations, but others were far less enthusiastic. In the APES case, numerous participants were disappointed with the outcomes of collaboration and maintained that they now had a more realistic—and pessimistic—understanding of how policy processes work. This case shows that democratic practice can be enhanced through collaboration, but when participation takes place without empowerment or authority for implementation, it also can undermine trust in the system.

By focusing on governmental roles in the case studies, this analysis demonstrates that collaborative environmental management can alter the balance of power between communities and government officials. For example, the Applegate Partnership changed the nature of relationships between community members and governmental agencies. By promoting meaningful dialogue, members of the partnership were able to overcome conflict and promote working relationships and agreements. Similarly, members of the ARSG found that the process helped them understand and trust officials. Rather than resort to ingrained responses to each other, both community and government participants found that they were more open to each other's perspectives and, as a result, better able to respect and incorporate each other's views. By working in a collaborative fashion, the balance of power was altered to provide greater equity of input and influence. Such a result can have important "spillover" effects, fostering subsequent collaboration. For example, in the HCP case, collaboration in the Coachella Valley Fringe-Toed Lizard HCP built social capital that carried over to a larger, multiple-species HCP effort.

Governmental Impacts on Outcomes. The various environmental and social outcomes are linked to governmental roles. In all cases, governmental institutions and actors affected outcomes in important, though varied, ways.

As institutions, governmental mandates and guidelines substantially influenced environmental outcomes. For the government-led and government-encouraged collaborations, governmental institutions determined specific criteria or mandates that the collaborative effort was supposed to meet, such as the level of detail contained in plans, the final form of recommendations, and the authority (or lack thereof) to implement the plans (see Table 8-5). These institutions fostered collaboration in the four cases. Conversely, the lack of a mandate to work collaboratively in the two cases of government-followed collaboration constrained what the efforts were able to accomplish environmentally.

Across all six cases, governmental actors contributed to the efforts' environmental outcomes by helping participants be innovative, providing information, securing resources, or carrying forward collaborative plans to be implemented. This is not to say that their actions always fostered greater environmental outcomes. In the APES case, for example, the focus of agency members on basic science may have distracted the program from producing information relevant for making on-the-ground environmental improvements. Importantly, governmental actors contributed even in the cases where government was following an effort developed by nongovernmental actors. For instance, the Darby Partnership encouraged governmental actors to incorporate watershed management concepts into their ongoing management programs. Additionally, governmental actors across the

Table 8-5. Summary of Governmental Impacts on Environmental and Social Outcomes

Case study	Environmental outcomes		Social outcomes	
	Actor	Institution	Actor	Institution
Applegate	Forest Service and BLM personnel helped create innovative approaches to land management	Agency structures designed to support traditional approaches to land management impeded collaborative projects	Forest Service and BLM personnel increased community involvement in public land management	Top-down approach limited development of social capital
Darby	Federal, state, and local governmental actors provided information and fostered cooperative projects to restore watershed health	Lack of formal mandate to participate limited outcomes	Federal, state, and local governmental actors participated in discussion and learning	Agencies allowed, and in some cases encouraged, participation by staff, leading to better understanding among fellow participants
HCP	FWS personnel sometimes encouraged collaborators to adopt specific plan components	Federal guidelines provided broad outlines of planning process and expected content of plans	Some local, state, and federal governmental actors increased social capital and trust by bringing their expertise to the planning process	Incidental take permits allowed economic activities where they would not otherwise be permitted under the ESA
OFPPP	In many task forces, local governmental actors provided resources that affected plan contents	Program funding and guidelines shaped quality of data and analysis; local zoning influenced plan recommendations	Local governmental actors in some task forces contributed to the development of new network ties	Grant program promoted interaction among local stakeholders
APES	State governmental actors contributed to plan development and improved scientific understanding; actors' focus on science may have prevented more substantive environmental outcomes	Federal guidelines required comprehensive plan development but relied on local and state implementation	State and local government actors promoted networking and coordination among other participants; created conflict between different levels of government	The NEP promoted development of networks across governmental and nongovernmental actors
ARSG	Federal and state governmental actors ensured that data collection and regulations were relevant to government; participated in remediation projects that improved water quality and fish populations	Federal regulations shaped final form of water quality recommendations	Prevalence of state and federal actors in collaboration led to questions of legitimacy of effort; state and federal actors worked together with other participants to foster understanding, and working relationships	Delegation of group formation, operation of stakeholder group without undue influence from institutions allowed social capital to flourish

cases served as key voices for the agencies and institutions they were representing, as well as conduits between the collaborative efforts and those agencies and institutions.

Governmental institutions left their mark on social outcomes. In the two government-followed cases, the perceived inadequacy of governmental institutions was what spurred nongovernmental actors to initiate collaborative efforts. The Applegate Partnership experienced continuing institutional barriers that limited social outcomes, such as community-wide trust of the agencies. The Darby Partnership enjoyed changes in agency norms that allowed or encouraged staff participation in the collaborative effort, which facilitated the building of understanding among participants.

Institutions played a somewhat different role in spurring collaboration in the remaining cases. For the HCP program and the ARSG, the desire to avoid existing governmental institutions—Endangered Species Act prohibitions on taking listed species and Superfund designation, respectively—provided a strong incentive for stakeholders to try to work things out collaboratively. For APES and the OFPPP, a government program promising funding provided the major impetus for collaboration, spurring interactions among stakeholders who otherwise might not have communicated. In these four cases, governmental institutions not only spurred collaboration, but also drove issue definition, which affected the breadth of stakeholders who worked together. One of the government-led cases, the ARSG, is notable because although it represented a high degree of governmental leadership, in practice the governmental agency delegated facilitation to reduce its impact and allow social capital to flourish.

With ubiquitous governmental actor involvement in the collaborative efforts, it comes as no surprise that these individuals had substantial impacts on social outcomes across the cases. In the government-followed cases, governmental actors facilitated collaboration through efforts to increase community involvement, even in the face of institutional barriers that made this difficult (especially the Applegate case), or by their willingness to participate and learn from open discussions (highlighted in the Darby case). In a number of cases, governmental officials increased social capital and trust by bringing their expertise to the collaborative efforts, including scientific understanding (as in the HCP and ARSG cases) and regulatory knowledge (especially the ARSG and Applegate cases). In several instances, governmental actors provided the group with access to key networks beyond the group, as well as new networks with fellow group members that persisted outside the collaborative effort. At the same time, governmental actors' roles sometimes harmed social capital. For instance, because the ARSG community of government personnel worked largely with each other, this led to perceptions of low legitimacy among some citizens. With APES, the confluence of diverse federal, state, and local governmental actors led to conflicts both among government actors and with nongovernmental participants.

PATHWAYS AND VARIATIONS IN GOVERNMENTAL INFLUENCE

Across all six cases, government personnel participated in the collaborative efforts and demonstrated individual levels of commitment. Because of their institutional ties, however, government personnel varied in the level of independent action they could take, including the extent to which they comfortably could maintain positions that were distinct from prevailing institutional norms. At the same time, governmental institutions had a significant and pervasive impact on all of the collaborative endeavors. Consequently, these institutions not only limited the autonomy of governmental actors, but also extended across all aspects of the processes and outcomes of the collaborations studied. The cases examined here represent a range of activities along a spectrum from government-followed to government-led collaborations. Even though governmental institutions made their mark on all of the collaborations, the extent of this imprint depends on where a case is situated on this continuum.

Government as Follower

In both the Applegate and Darby cases, government participated actively, though not as conveners of the collaboration. The Applegate Partnership formed in response to the spotted owl crisis and timber harvest injunction in the Pacific Northwest. An individual who recognized the importance of having industry, interest groups, governmental agencies, and area residents work together to manage the Applegate Valley spearheaded the partnership. Governmental agency members assisted with meeting facilitation and contributed time and other resources. Throughout the process, governmental actors served as both official representatives and interested individuals, assuming leadership roles at times and acting as engaged participants in other instances. Although highly collaborative, the Applegate Partnership was not without its conflicts and power imbalances, particularly because federal land managers had decision-making authority, expertise, and financial resources. Nonetheless, government actors generally shared the vision that collaboration would lead to better outcomes for everyone in the Applegate Valley. This perspective helped foster a "culture of good faith participation," with agencies, organizations, and individuals adopting a problem-solving perspective. At the same time, governmental institutions were wedded to traditional approaches to forest management and organized in ways that made coordination difficult. The result was that, although individual governmental actors were responsive to community concerns and local residents were attentive to the constraints and needs of the agencies, tension between actors and institutions characterized this collaboration.

By contrast, the Darby Partnership involved governmental actors as participants in a more limited way. In this case, a nonprofit organization, The Nature Conservancy (TNC), approached a variety of stakeholders and encouraged them to work together to address environmental issues in the watershed. TNC typically purchased land to promote conservation, but the area was too large for acquisition, so the organization tried a different tactic: inviting governmental agencies, nongovernmental organizations, and private landowners to join it in a collaborative venture dedicated to protecting the watershed. Although a nonprofit organization initiated and sustained the partnership, governmental agency members were among the most highly involved actors in the process. Rather than government serving as a catalyst for the process or using the meetings to promote a particular view, TNC provided a forum to disseminate information and to promote exchange and interaction among all parties, including government representatives. Although governmental actors did not take leadership positions, a wide range of agency representatives maintained consistent participation and were actively involved and highly committed to the watershed.

In both of these government-followed cases, we see a reversal of the stereotypical roles that characterize many public participation processes and interactions between government representatives and nongovernmental actors. The traditional approach to public participation is that governmental agencies create plans and policies and serve as enforcement agents. Along the way, organizations and individuals may be invited to provide input or attend information sessions. Many of the interactions that ensue between government and nongovernmental representatives often are characterized by conflict, contention, and distrust. The Applegate and Darby cases demonstrate several important alternatives to these approaches and styles of interaction.

First, the cases show that individual citizens and nonprofit organizations can be the initiators and facilitators of collaborative processes. In both cases, nongovernmental actors recognized a void in environmental practices that needed to be filled. Rather than see this as a point of contention, they took the initiative and developed a means through which collaboration could take place. Second, the cases suggest that governmental actors can benefit by participating actively in collaboration. Tensions still may be present between governmental and nongovernmental actors and between the collaborative group and governmental institutions. Government participation in these types of collaborations can, however, provide access to new information and other forms of local knowledge, and foster community support for agency activities. Further, these cases demonstrate that governmental and nongovernmental actors can work as partners, engaging in collaborative problem solving and cooperative exchange.

In both the Applegate and Darby cases, governmental inaction created a vacuum into which nongovernmental actors stepped, taking the lead and forging bonds with governmental actors. Although the efforts of governmental actors were constrained by institutional parameters, the influence of these institutions was relatively limited. This meant that there was more room for flexibility and creativity. Members of the Applegate Partnership developed a new conception of how public lands could be managed, and members of the Darby Partnership envisioned integrated watershed management. At the same time, the very absence of institutional commitments and mandates constrained the outcomes of collaboration. For instance, the Applegate Partnership sought to transform the governmental institutions that defined public land management, but because governmental actors within the partnership also were situated within the governmental institutions that participants sought to change, they were limited in their ability to carry out the plans they devised. Without a broader mandate to effect change, the Applegate Partnership was unable to execute its vision. Thus the presence and absence of governmental institutions creates opportunities as well as limits in cases where government follows the lead of nongovernmental actors.

Government as Encourager

Governmental actors and institutions can serve as catalysts that foster collaboration among multiple stakeholders. The HCP case provides an important vantage point for viewing how governmental incentives offset traditional regulatory approaches to environmental management. The Endangered Species Act (ESA) is the critical piece of legislation for protecting endangered species because it limits uses of habitat on both public and private property. The ESA reflects elements of a traditional command-and-control framework. The establishment of the HCP program, however, has afforded government officials a means for promoting collaboration. Developing an HCP offers landowners, resource users, and local and state governments the opportunity to obtain a permit that will allow them to do what is otherwise prohibited by the ESA—develop part of the habitat of a listed species—provided that the HCP specifies in advance how sufficient habitat will be protected to maintain the long-term viability of the species. Although collaboration is not required by the rules governing the program, collaboration may benefit those seeking a permit as they prepare and implement an HCP, particularly in instances where habitat crosses multiple private parcels and public jurisdictions. One way that agency officials promote collaboration is by providing technical assistance that demonstrates to permit applicants the nature of interdependencies and how applicants can benefit from collective actions such as pooling land and resources for a common preserve system. Financial assistance also serves as an incentive for collaboration, as federal funds typically are disbursed to collaborative HCPs. While the ESA is often viewed as an institution that places the federal government in its traditional command-and-control role, the HCP program under the ESA expands the government's role from simply writing and enforcing command-and-control rules to creating incentives for collaboration. The program also shifts government's role as an actor from one of enforcement agent to that of expert advisor.

The OFPPP is a second example of how governmental institutions can offer incentives to foster collaboration. This state-level program provided grants to counties with the requirements that they match the grant amount either with funds or in-kind contributions and establish a task force including stakeholders with a cross section of interests. In addition to funding, the state government defined the program's objectives and established the overall structure of the planning process. Although governmental institutions offered incentives for initiating the process by providing funds and some basic guidelines, the internal dynamics of the task forces remained flexible. The groups were self-organized, going about their activities in a variety of ways. Governmental actors on the task forces included local officials from counties and townships as well as conservation districts. They worked alongside a handful of citizens and nongovernmental organizations, especially ones with agricultural interests.

These two cases suggest that in government-encouraged collaborations, governmental institutions structure the general design of a program and determine funding criteria, such as matching requirements, as well as access to governmental actors. Although consistent with top-down approaches to environmental management, these types of collaborations offer some levels of flexibility in the way the efforts are planned and executed. In the HCP program, for example, groups were empowered to develop their own decision-making processes and structures, which might have included steering committees, advisory boards, or existing organizations such as councils of local government. In the OFPPP case, a governmental institution, the state grant program, provided financial resources and structured the collaboration but placed few limitations on task force activities. Government representatives on the task forces served as equal participants, however, assuming leadership positions in some instances. In both the HCP and OFPPP cases, government as institution supplied incentives for collaboration, and then government as actor helped sustain and implement a planning process. Governmental institutions instigated these processes and also delegated overall control to governmental participants, who aided and assisted rather than adopted the more traditional roles of leader and manager.

A clear distinction between the influence of governmental actors and institutions emerged in these cases of government-encouraged collaboration. Unlike the government-followed cases, in which governmental institutions had relatively little influence on how collaborative activities played out once under way, governmental institutions had significant impacts on the contours of the HCP and OFPPP programs. The patterns that emerged from the case comparisons suggest that government incentives do more than just spark collaboration; they may leave an institutional imprint on all facets of collaborative structure and action. This is a critical finding, because grant activities supported by governmental agencies often are perceived as relying on market approaches and consequently are thought to be a hands-off tactic. In contrast, the OFPPP program illustrates that the financial incentives used to promote collaboration were tied to guidelines about program design and goals. Likewise, incentives in the HCP program promoted participation as a means to avoid the regulatory hammer of the ESA, but once the support was accepted, collaborative groups had to conform to institutionally defined outcomes, even as they were empowered to select their own structures and decision-making processes.

Government as Leader

Governmental institutions and actors loomed large in their influence on the two cases of government-led collaboration. The NEP defined the issues and provided financial resources for APES. State and federal governmental actors along with marine scientists in the Policy Committee defined the issue so that they could focus on the reduction of scientific uncertainty in the watershed. This issue definition suited the Policy Committee well, but not the Citizen Advisory Committees (CACs). Access to the Policy Committee by the CACs initially was funneled through the Technical Advisory Committee (TAC), which was dominated by government actors, although later in the program this changed at the insistence of the CACs. Members of the CACs were frustrated with their inability to influence the overall issue definition of the estuarine planning effort, let alone the research agenda dominated by the Policy Committee and the TAC. Whereas governmental institutions established a basis for the collaboration, governmental actors controlled the way that issues were defined within the initiative and ultimately prohibited it from attaining more significant environmental and social outcomes.

The final case, the ARSG, demonstrates that a governmental regulatory agency can initiate and sustain collaboration without dominating the group decision-making process. In the early 1990s, the CWQD indicated that the quality of the waters in the Animas River could be improved. The CWQD decided that the agency could either impose new standards on the community or develop them by means of a collaborative process with local stakeholders. In electing the latter approach, the CWQD set out to initiate an agency-driven collaborative process. Local residents initially were skeptical of this idea, but they ultimately came to regard the proposed collaboration as a better alternative to the agency determining the standards unilaterally. In this case, government proposed the collaborative process and took measures to ensure that it would be developed and implemented. The stakeholder group included numerous representatives from federal, state, and local agencies in addition to representatives from local nongovernmental organizations. The ARSG also received funding and other forms of governmental support. Governmental actors were instrumental in initiating and sustaining the collaboration, but they also regarded themselves as participating stakeholders. Consequently, rather than rely on a traditional top-down approach to environmental management, the government participants were flexible, delegating authority to the stakeholder group.

Governments led both the APES and ARSG processes, but there were critical differences in the roles that government representatives played in each case. Government officials structured and coordinated most aspects of the APES planning processes. Local scientists generally supported APES, but the program had authority only to plan, so the implementation of APES rested with government. Similarly to APES, governmental actors formed and provided resources for the ARSG. To overcome initial resistance to the proposed collaboration, they acted in a way that appeared to be more coercive than participatory. Once the process was under way, however, government representatives in the ARSG relinquished control and participated as informed partners rather than retaining a dominant position. These cases provide further evidence of the variations in governmental roles in collaborative environmental management. Importantly, they also suggest that even in situations where the government has relied on top-down approaches, collaboration took root and replaced some aspects of these more traditional environmental planning and management processes.

CONCLUSIONS

Patterns from our cross-case analysis can be viewed in light of trends in citizen participation and governmental environmental management. Beginning in the 1960s, governmental agencies began to create alternatives to regulatory, technical, and bureaucratic approaches to environmental policy, planning, and management. Driven by societal expectations for improved environmental quality and citizen desires to have input into public decisions, policymakers expanded opportunities for public participation in environmental decision making. Many of these approaches relied on formal methods for disseminating knowledge and on public comment on pending plans and policies. This style of input met with criticism, however, being perceived as tokenism rather than an empowered form of participation (Arnstein 1969; King et al. 1998). In response, collaborative approaches to environmental management were adopted in the late 1980s and 1990s. The desire to move environmental management closer to affected communities and to incorporate community sentiments and views into decisions more fully, in combination with increased awareness that environmental issues span geographic, organizational, and institutional boundaries, has led many governmental agencies to perceive collaboration as an appropriate management option. At the same time, many private firms and nonprofit organizations have altered their positions, maintaining that cooperation rather than conflict will result in more productive outcomes.

The shift in focus from participation to collaboration places new demands on governmental institutions and actors. As an institution, government embodies the rules, norms, and strategies that establish the institutional context of collective efforts. Many of the cases demonstrate the sweeping influence that governmental institutions have on collaborative efforts. Governmental institutions leave their mark on how issues are defined, what resources are used or are available, the structure of collaborative processes, and the outcomes that these endeavors produce. In many instances, institutional provisions determine the timing of the process and the degree of authority granted to participants. For example, in the ARSG, a governmental mandate served as a catalyst for initiating the group and established a time line for the project. Although the state agency ultimately could reject standards the ARSG created, the group did have the authority to recommend standards. Similar provisions and constraints were present in the OFPPP. In this situation, the agency program determined the time frame for the development of the plans and established basic guidelines for which issues the plans had to include.

Institutional provisions in statutes and regulations establish whether collaborative decisions and recommendations will be legally binding. Collaborative groups were given policy authority in just two of our cases: the HCP program and the ARSG. In the HCP program, participants were given legal authority to both plan and implement HCPs, subject to the conditions of the permit for each HCP. Although similarly subject to agency rejection, the ARSG was charged with establishing standards. In the remaining four cases, collaborative decisions did not carry any legal authority. The APES case illustrates tensions between making recommendations and implementation. In this instance, the initiative was centered around the development of a management plan. Collaborative planning without the authority to implement left many people disappointed and disillusioned with the process.

Whereas some cases illustrate the restrictions governmental institutions can place on collaboration, others reveal how these institutions can serve as a key resource and the spark that ignites collaboration in the first place. In the HCP and ARSG cases, the threat of existing statutes and administrative rules was the catalyst. In the Applegate case, institutions were the source of conflicts that led to the formation of the partnership. The injunction that prevented federal timber harvest led to a battle among interest groups and generated a virtual stalemate in federal forest management. In response, the partnership was formed to create economic opportunities and reestablish federal land management activities. As these examples suggest, institutions can establish limitations as well as create opportunities.

Government-led and government-encouraged collaborative efforts appear likely to have access to more resources than do government-followed efforts. The case studies suggest that resource availability is tied closely to the institutional commitment of government to a given collaborative effort. At the same time, however, government-followed efforts have greater autonomy over the use of their resources, as governments play a less prominent role in determining their group processes and decision-making structures. This autonomy, combined with broader goals, can stimulate government-followed efforts to innovate with new projects, ideas, and practices. Thus government as an institution providing resources and structuring processes generates a series of trade-offs. On one hand, institutional rules may help move an initiative toward a tangible result within a bounded period of time, and resources may ensure that a project can endure. On the other hand, by placing limitations on participants, rules and the associated resources may constrain the potential a collaborative initiative has for heading in new directions and generating creative solutions to environmental problems.

The pervasive influence of institutions calls into question whether a change has taken place in the effort to move from participation to collaborative forms of environmental management. Although institutions may constrain processes and outcomes, the six case studies in this volume demonstrate that governmental actors may moderate the impact of governmental institutions. Governmental actors are tied to the agencies they represent. At the same time, they have opportunities to act in ways that can foster equality in power and influence among stakeholder groups. The roles governmental actors played and their influence in determining group structure and decision-making processes suggest that these individuals largely determine the character of the collaboration.

One way they do so is by their willingness to engage stakeholder groups. It is often assumed that collaborative environmental management is initiated and sustained by nongovernmental actors and developed only in response to conflict. But as the Darby case demonstrates, citizen-initiated collaborations are not always rooted in conflict. Even though frustrations and tensions were present, rather than serving as the basis for interaction, this collaboration was rooted in a desire to proactively manage environmental resources. Moreover, both the Applegate and Darby cases show that government representatives can be willing and responsive participants even when local community members initiate interactions. In contrast to the antagonistic posture that has come to characterize many relationships between nongovernmental and government actors, these cases demonstrate that both sets of actors can collaborate and use their diverse perspectives and skills to promote the achievement of environmental and social outcomes.

A second way that governmental actors affect the nature of collaboration is the point at which they begin to interact with nongovernmental actors or work across agencies. In general, traditional government-sponsored initiatives tend to invite involvement late in the process. Frequently, governmental experts draft a plan or develop a project, and citizens are invited to comment or offer input on the documents that have been generated. It has been argued that this approach creates barriers to collaboration (Cortner and Moote 1999; Meidinger 1997). The four cases of government-encouraged and government-led collaboration suggest that collaborative environmental management efforts rely on comprehensive participation by relevant stakeholder groups from the earliest stages of development onward. Further, the HCP, OFPPP, APES, and ARSG cases demonstrate that rather than impede collaboration, governmental actors can be the catalyst for these endeavors, constructively developing planning and management programs that encourage stakeholder involvement.

Previous studies (Gray 1989) maintain that genuine forms of collaboration will be based on equal partnerships among all actors rather than be dominated by a single stakeholder. In some of the cases examined in this book, governmental actors served as agents who routinely implemented and enforced institutional mandates or took control of the collaborative process. The APES case, for instance, illustrates how government personnel and scientists constrained the framing of the problem to one of scientific uncertainty, thereby limiting input from a broad range of stakeholders and dominating the process of creating the estuarine management plan. In other instances, however, such as the Applegate and ARSG cases, governmental actors not only exhibited independent action and framed issues in ways that were distinct from institutional perspectives, but also worked as equal partners with other stakeholders. The patterns in the cases suggest that governmental institutions have a pervasive influence on collaborative endeavors. At the same time, genuine collaboration can emerge when governmental institutions delegate decision-making authority and when governmental actors respond to institutional requirements while promoting equal influence among stakeholder groups.

CHAPTER 9

ENVISIONING THE ROLES OF GOVERNMENT

The diffusion and availability of environmental information, growing emphasis on deliberative democracy, and the place-based nature of many environmental problems that resist command-and-control strategies have made collaborative environmental management an increasingly popular means for addressing environmental problems. Although the character of collaborative environmental management may change as new environmental issues emerge and as governmental and nongovernmental actors learn from their experiences, it is a trend that is unlikely to wane in the near future. Many environmental and natural resource activities, such as ecosystem management, endangered species protection, land-use planning, water quality improvement, and forest management, involve multiple participants interacting across environmental media. Whether a collaboration is led by a governmental agency, nongovernmental organization, or individual citizen, governmental actors in many settings have demonstrated a willingness to forge partnerships with a diverse spectrum of other governmental and nongovernmental actors as a means to address such challenges.

To understand governmental roles in collaborative environmental management, we assessed how government as actor and as institution affected problem definition, the provision of resources, group structure and deci-sion-making processes, and the outcomes that were realized. The case analyses suggest a revision of some commonly held notions about collabo-ration. For example, citizen-initiated collaborations are not always rooted in conflict, and governmental actors can participate along with many other stakeholders involved in the process, representing different agencies, differ-ent levels of government (state, local, federal), and both individual and institutional perspectives. As posited by other researchers, however, our analysis demonstrates that issue definition, resources, and group structure and processes are important factors shaping collaborative environmental management. The cases further indicate that the impact of governmental institutions and actors on these three sets of factors varies depending on their position in terms of following, encouraging, or leading the collabora-tive endeavor. However, examination of issue definition, resources, and group structure and processes across all of the cases reveals several general patterns. First, collaborations are subject to strong and pervasive influences from governmental institutions; second, individual governmental actors can moderate some of the effects of governmental institutions; and third, just as governmental institutions permeate collaborative activity, they also create parameters that make it possible for governmental actors to temper the impact of institutions on these activities.

It appears that the tipping point between governmental domination and genuine collaboration hinges on the extent to which these institutions grant decision-making authority and promote equal access and opportu-nity for governmental and nongovernmental actors alike to influence deci-sions. This insight becomes increasingly critical as more governmental agencies and representatives choose to engage in collaborative endeavors. Although there may be many reasons for government to dominate environ-mental management, if collaboration is desired, government representa-tives should be sensitive to ways in which their actions and institutional designs shape collaborative processes and outcomes.

GOVERNMENTAL CHOICES AND CHALLENGES

With roots extending over 40 years, collaborative environmental manage-ment is the fruition of policy experience while, at the same time, part of an ongoing policy learning process. The case studies indicate that although strides have been made in fostering collaborative relations and activities, a gap exists between what the literature portrays about the character of collaborative environmental management and the empirical reality. Governmental institutions and actors had a notable impact on the collaborative initiatives examined in this book. These patterns suggest that while government representatives are highly active in these processes and can take individual actions that shape the tenor of collaboration, governmental institutions imprint collaborative experiences in ways that are subtle and often difficult to discern. This raises questions about how much progress has been made to ensure equal power and influence for governmental and nongovernmental actors alike.

Collaborative environmental management requires that governmental and nongovernmental actors make choices and assess trade-offs among many different approaches that can be used to address environmental problems. In this section, we address some of the challenges and questions raised by the practice of collaborative environmental management. These challenges and questions do not constitute an exhaustive list. Rather, they highlight some of the issues faced by governmental institutions and actors in the case studies in this book.

Challenges to Governmental Institutions and Actors

Governmental institutions often establish the focus of the collaboration, the resource availability, and the structure and processes within which the group will operate. Governmental rules also influence the degree to which recommendations stemming from a collaborative effort are binding. In many of the cases analyzed in this book, the government granted participants authority to make recommendations, but in most instances, government policymakers were not required to adopt or implement these recommendations.

The extent to which recommendations are binding generally reflects the purpose and mandate of the collaboration. Governmental agencies and representatives face difficult challenges, however, when they solicit input with an ambiguous commitment to follow through. Alternatively, in instances where recommendations are binding, agency officials must wrestle with how to incorporate input from nongovernmental actors into a policy framework for which they are held accountable. Being clear on the policy objectives, how collaboration advances those objectives, and the extent to which stakeholder input will be implemented can help align stakeholder expectations with agency constraints. It is important to acknowledge that because governmental agencies are restricted by specific mandates and by their accountability to the public, they face different constraints than do their nongovernmental partners. For instance, governmental agencies often must comply with legislative mandates. Working within these constraints while responding to the concerns of a diverse array of nongovernmental collaborators, each with potentially different levels of experience and familiarity with legislative and regulatory processes, often creates challenges for collaborative processes. Accordingly, mutual acknowledgment of differing roles and clarity of the objectives of all parties can help overcome expectation gaps and result in more constructive working relationships.

Agency officials must make choices about when and under what conditions they should promote collaboration. Establishing a process and encouraging community members to invest their time and energy without ensuring that their proposals will be implemented can lead to dissatisfaction and dissent. Governmental institutions may protect governmental actors and even encourage prudent use of resources. Reliance on institutions as a means for control, however, may be indicative of government concerns about the ability of stakeholder groups to make technically sound and environmentally appropriate recommendations. Consequently, governmental agencies should assess the trade-offs that arise between following institutional rules and relying on technical experts, on the one hand, and ensuring flexibility and promoting citizen empowerment, on the other.

Traditional approaches to regulation are rooted in bureaucratic structures. Collaborative environmental management is more viable, however, when individual agencies and actors are willing to adopt more flexible approaches to environmental planning and policy implementation. In other words, collaborative environmental management requires different structures and practices than governments traditionally have used to implement regulatory measures. Government regulation firmly places power in the hands of the government. In contrast, collaborative environmental management generally requires that governmental agencies share power with other agencies and with nongovernmental actors.

Just as different agency structures and cultures will be receptive to initiating or participating in collaborative environmental management in varying degrees, different agency personnel will vary in their response to, and support of, collaboration. Even though dissatisfaction with entrenched regulatory approaches may spark the desire to pursue collaboration, individuals invested in bureaucratic structures and processes may view collaborative environmental management as a threat. Because some individuals and agencies may be uncomfortable if they are not fully in control, they may resist or be antagonistic to collaboration. For collaborative environmental management to succeed, governmental actors need to consider whether it will be supported and sustained within their particular agency culture.

Issue Definition Challenges

The biophysical scale and ways in which problems are framed and interpreted are constantly in flux, creating challenges for agency actors who must make decisions with regard to relatively static administrative boundaries and problem definition. Similarly, scientific and technical knowledge about how best to manage environmental issues is ever changing. New knowledge does not always align with prevailing technical beliefs or existing values or viewpoints. Collaborative environmental management offers a flexible structure that can be molded in response to emerging views and knowledge. Nevertheless, participants face an ongoing challenge regarding how to use this structure to effectively integrate and employ new information, values, and management techniques in the face of governmental institutions that tend to be more resistant to change. The breadth and scope of environmental problems, as conceived by those addressing them, have profound effects on which stakeholders are involved, over how wide an area, and for which issues. Because no single scale is appropriate for all cases of collaborative environmental management, participants must be open to working across multiple scales and issue frames.

Resource Challenges

Resources can shape both the short-term success and long-term effectiveness of collaborative environmental management. Although governmental institutions often determine resource availability and the parameters associated with their use, the efficacy of a collaborative initiative does not rest fully on the level or types of resources that are provided. Rather, it depends on the ways in which resources are used to pursue goals and objectives. Providing resources for narrowly defined tasks can generate tangible, specific environmental outcomes, such as standards and plans. On the other hand, allowing stakeholders to develop broader goals and try a variety of activities may result in innovative projects, ideas, and practices.

Collaboration calls upon governmental actors to promote strong social relations, including trust and respect. The technical expert who once regulated others may now need to acquire a new suite of managerial and social skills, including the ability to promote effective external and interpersonal communication, to follow as well as to lead, and to foster critical thinking. To facilitate a supportive and collaborative environmental management process also requires that participants be culturally sensitive and have a willingness to acknowledge and resolve their differences. Each participant will face decisions about how to advocate and support the practice of collaborative environmental management within his or her organization. Governmental agencies therefore must make choices about which types of personnel to hire and activities to reward.

In a resource-constrained world, agencies must carefully assess the limits and trade-offs involved in making resource commitments. Engaging in collaborative environmental management means consciously deciding how, where, and when to expend scarce and limited resources. Therefore, agencies must select strategically those situations in which they will participate intensively. The patterns that emerged in the case studies suggest that direct support and support services such as funding and technical expertise are resources that are readily influenced by governmental institutions and actors. The provision of these and other types of resources not only demonstrates commitment from governmental agencies to collaborative environmental management initiatives, but also makes possible the implementation of more resource-intensive projects, including those that need to endure over long periods of time.

Different levels and types of resources will vary in importance to different initiatives, depending on the environmental outcomes desired and the process pursued. In general, however, the judicious commitment and allocation of resources by governmental institutions will be tied to the long-term success of collaborative environmental management. To spread tangible resources thinly over multiple collaborative endeavors may weaken collaborative environmental management as a whole, particularly if a large number of efforts are unable to realize their goals or be maintained over time. Similarly, retaining control may limit the potential to be involved in multiple efforts, whereas relinquishing control may mean less intensive involvement for agency staff and perhaps the ability to engage in more collaborative activities. Governmental commitment and application of resources have an impact not only on environmental quality, but also on the creation and maintenance of the social infrastructure on which environmental initiatives increasingly depend. In short, the social and substantive success of collaborative environmental management hinges on the capacity of actors to recognize appropriate opportunities for government involvement and to use resources to foster constructive and effective collaboration.

Group Structure and Decision-Making Challenges

Collaborative environmental management taps into common conceptions associated with participatory democracy, especially the reliance on large numbers of citizens to provide input as a means to achieve equal representation of interests. This conventional notion of democracy does not always square with the realities of collaborative endeavors. Consequently, the normative appeal of collaboration must be considered along with the pragmatic limits of reasonable participation and the practicalities of efficient and effective involvement of relevant community members. Rather than involve large numbers, collaborative environmental management tends to include a limited, and ostensibly representative, number of participants. Limiting the size of the collaborative may make it easier for participants to engage fully in the process. But governmental actors sometimes are responsible for deciding which groups and individuals will or will not be invited to participate. Because the exclusionary nature of many collaborative endeavors poses challenges to conventional notions of participation and democratic governance, government personnel along with other participants must engage in a delicate balancing act, ensuring that a collaborative is small enough to accomplish its task but large enough to be regarded as representative of the relevant stakeholder groups.

The degree of autonomy granted to participants and the overall level of decentralization pose substantial challenges, affecting the very nature and legitimacy of each collaborative endeavor. Even in situations where government-led collaborations are relatively decentralized, it appears that governmental institutions place control on decision making and establish limitations on independent action. Alternatively, rather than retain decision-making authority or control all the dimensions of the collaboration, government representatives can delegate authority and share power with participants. Relinquishing control and sharing power are tied to two critical decisions that will determine which direction the scales will tip and whether a balance will be achieved. First, governmental actors make choices about leadership, determining the extent to which they are willing to participate in rather than dominate the process. Second, government representatives must not only recognize that local stakeholders bring knowledge, skills, and talents to collaborative environmental management, but also decide the degree to which they are willing to integrate and use the input of these participants. Yet even when governmental actors want to make these choices, they may be faced with institutional rules and norms that do not support them.

CONTRIBUTIONS, LIMITATIONS, AND FUTURE RESEARCH

The histories and traits of specific institutions, agencies, communities, organizations, and individuals make each collaborative environmental management initiative distinct. By relying on a deliberate method of case selection and a common framework to analyze the cases, this analysis provides a step forward in the study of collaborative environmental management. The approach adopted here facilitated the examination of influential factors while accounting for the complexities and context of each collaborative endeavor. Factors such as issue definition and resources are important sensitizing constructs that can be applied to other case studies as a means for understanding governmental roles in collaborative environmental management. Although our case analyses did not include close examination of factors such as individual attitudes and values, organizational culture, or the management of intergroup conflict, the three sets of factors assessed here can be used to orient and conduct such investigations. For example, the attitudes and values held by governmental actors participating in a collaboration might be studied from the perspective of human resources. Moreover, these factors may be useful to studies of environmental management that aim to understand how collaborative efforts play out, without focusing on governmental impacts. Such studies could be examined from the perspective of issue definition or resources for collaboration, without explicitly examining governmental institutions and actors.

Although collaborative environmental management undoubtedly involves many direct and indirect relationships among numerous factors, our cases and analysis did not fully explore all of these linkages. Further empirical and theoretical research is needed to identify other factors that affect collaboration and to develop a richer understanding of the relationships and interdependencies among these factors. In the meantime, the concepts presented here help illustrate how government serves both as actor and as institution and how these roles affect collaborative environmental management. Key contributions of this analysis are that it addresses questions about how governments might engage in collaborative efforts,

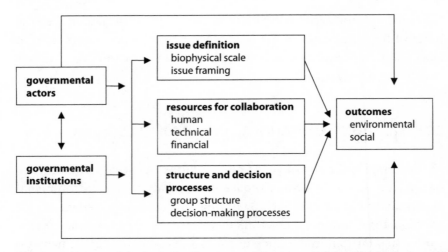

Figure 9-1. Framework for Analyzing Governmental Impacts on Collaborative Environmental Management

and it identifies several primary trends in and dynamics of the way governmental actors and institutions influence collaborative processes and outcomes (see Figure 9-1). Although governmental impacts on issue definition, resources, and structure and the decision-making process are likely to vary across contexts, we believe that these concepts represent three key sets of factors that an analyst should consider when examining the impacts of governments on collaborative environmental management.

Nevertheless, a number of important theoretical and practical questions remain unanswered. Each case examined in this book was selected to maximize variation in governmental roles in the collaborative process, especially in terms of who initiated the efforts. Although many key forms of collaborative environmental management are discussed, the full range of possibilities has not been explored. Therefore, additional research to gain further insight into the breadth of roles played by governments would be beneficial. The same concepts used here could guide an analysis of government-followed collaborations with high levels of government resources, or where, in its capacity as leader, government explicitly dominated the collaborative process. The cases in this book depict processes that took root and sometimes even flourished. It is also important to examine attempts at initiating collaborative environmental management that did not take hold, those that started but subsequently withered, and those where conflicting and inequitable relations dismantled the effort. Comparing successful collaborative initiatives with those that were not sustained or that had difficulty achieving their goals will lead to greater understanding of the factors most closely related to effective processes and provide insight into how government might alter its roles in different situations.

A critical question that plagues most environmental management initiatives in general, and collaborative ones in particular, is the relationship between processes and environmental outcomes. It is important to continue to expand quantitative, variable-based research in this arena. Here the investigation should not be limited to collaborative environmental management alone, but also should compare the processes and outcomes of different management regimes. At the same time, it is essential to recognize the path-dependent nature of collaborative environmental management and to conduct qualitative research that ensures that the assessment of outcomes remains embedded within the collaborative effort's social, political, and biophysical contexts.

As the study and practice of collaborative environmental management mature, additional issues not addressed in our analysis will become more important. This book focuses on the emergence of collaborative initiatives and their initial planning and implementation efforts. As an increasing number of collaborative endeavors persist, it will be essential to study the ongoing challenges associated with environmental implementation and monitoring, as well as with the maintenance of the collaborations. Although some initial attempts have been made to evaluate collaborative environmental management, there is neither consistency nor shared views about which types of data and criteria are most instructive and appropriate or how such evaluations should be conducted. In other words, the scholarly and the practitioner communities have not reached a consensus on whether such an evaluation should be done by participants or external evaluators, which evaluative criteria should be used, and what role evaluation should play in the design and management of environmental solutions. In addition, we know very little about how and why collaborative efforts end. Therefore, it would be useful to conduct longitudinal studies that investigate what happens to the participants when a collaborative initiative has achieved its goal, as well as the extent to which collaborations provide a latent or active network for addressing other problems and environmental issues. As the study of collaborative environmental management continues, and as these and other questions are answered, we will learn more not only about how to improve its design and implementation, but also about how it can enhance environmental quality and management.

CONCLUSIONS

As approaches to collaborative environmental management evolve and mature, governmental agencies and representatives will face new and emerging challenges. Perhaps the greatest contemporary challenge is that such collaboration requires governmental institutions and actors to share, and perhaps at times even relinquish, control over environmental management. If governmental institutions become more flexible and encourage governmental actors to participate in these processes, the balance of power and the ingrained relationships that have developed among agencies and communities may be transformed. Although this change could be interpreted as abrogating governmental obligations and abandoning legitimate roles, it also could be viewed as a means of enhancing democratic practice. Serving in different capacities and establishing relationships with community members contribute to the social outcomes. The interaction and shared deliberation inherent in collaboration may enhance relations both among and between nongovernment and government representatives by promoting trust, network development, and participatory democracy.

The patterns presented in this book suggest that over the past decade, important changes have taken place in the way that environmental management has been conceptualized and implemented. At the same time, these patterns raise lingering questions about whether collaboration is producing greater environmental gains or more genuine forms of participation than what has been achieved through traditional command-and-control regulation. A pivotal point that determines the nature of the collaboration appears to rest in the relationship between governmental institutions and actors. As an institution, government significantly imprints collaborative endeavors, determining the way the issue is framed, the nature and availability of resources, the way the process is organized, the goals and management tools that are produced, and even the actual roles that governmental actors play. But even though they must work within institutional parameters, it appears that governmental actors can moderate some of the impacts of institutions. The extent to which governmental actors strive to ensure an equitable distribution of power and influence among stakeholders affects the tenor of a collaboration and the perception of whether it is a true partnership or little more than a new label placed on government-dominated approaches to public participation.

METHODOLOGICAL
APPENDIX

To facilitate comparison and analysis, several criteria were used to guide the selection of the case studies included in this volume. First, all cases had to involve collaboration between governmental and nongovernmental actors. Even though interagency and interorganizational collaborations often take place and are important, to be included in the volume the cases could not be composed solely of governmental or nongovernmental actors. Second, the cases had to represent different degrees of explicit government control—leading, encouraging, or following—with two instances of each type of governmental role. Third, each case had to address an issue pertaining to natural resource management. Although numerous collaborative efforts focus on other types of environmental issues such as pollution, we limited the scope of the issues and management activities examined to ensure a reasonable basis for making cross-case comparisons. Finally, a primary focus (although not necessarily the sole focus) of the collaboration had to be planning.

APPLEGATE PARTNERSHIP STUDY METHODS (CHAPTER 2)

The Applegate Partnership research is based on participant observation, recorded interviews, and review of materials written between 1995 and 1998. The participant-observation approach included attending dozens of partnership meetings and field trips. The interviews were in depth and open ended and included Applegate Partnership participants from diverse backgrounds and other natural resource leaders from southern Oregon. Written sources such as meeting minutes, newspaper articles, and reports supplemented observations and interviews.

DARBY PARTNERSHIP STUDY METHODS (CHAPTER 3)

The case study of the Darby Partnership is based on participant observation, interviews, a survey of participants, and document analysis. Participant observation occurred at quarterly meetings of the partnership, on-site visits, and through discussions with The Nature Conservancy staff and interested citizens. Using a snowball sampling technique, more than a dozen interviews were conducted with key participants. A survey consisting of closed- and open-ended questions was sent to all 103 partners. The 42 percent response rate reflected an uneven distribution with the highest response rates from state and federal agency representatives and the lowest from local and county officials. Summary statistics were generated for the quantitative questions, and all qualitative answers were coded for common themes. A computer search of the *Columbus Dispatch* between 1991 and 1998 yielded nearly 150 articles related to Darby watershed protection efforts. Darby watershed–related publications by governmental agencies, academic researchers, and nonprofit groups also were collected.

HABITAT CONSERVATION PLANNING STUDY METHODS (CHAPTER 4)

Evidence about the federal HCP program is drawn largely from the U.S. Fish and Wildlife Service website, which contains links to laws and policies governing the HCP program, and to a database of HCPs. Articles and books about the HCP program and specific HCPs were consulted as well. These secondary materials included two important comparative studies: one on public participation in HCPs (Yaffee et al. 1998), and one on the use of science in HCPs (Kareiva et al. 1999). Evidence for the Coachella Valley Fringe-Toed Lizard HCP, gathered during two weeks of field research in June 1999, included tape-recorded interviews with 14 people who participated in or observed the planning or implementation processes for the HCP, as well as archival research in local libraries and public agencies. Evidence for Natural Communities Conservation Planning, which includes numerous HCPs, is based on field research conducted during 1994 and is supplemented with secondary sources. The field research included tape-recorded interviews with 20 people who participated in the planning process and observational work at numerous public meetings.

OHIO FARMLAND PRESERVATION STUDY METHODS (CHAPTER 5)

The study of the OFPPP investigated 15 of the 61 county task forces involved in preparing farmland preservation plans in Ohio. Cases were selected for variation in the level of county urbanization and geographic location, to represent a diverse range of counties. Information was collected about collaborative planning processes, as well as outcomes. For each task force, interviews were conducted with at least two key informants, with careful note taking and follow-up phone calls where appropriate to obtain accurate information. Additionally, a state official who worked closely with the county task forces was interviewed. The principal investigator attended a one-day conference on farmland preservation, sponsored by the Ohio Office of Farmland Preservation, in March 1999. Representatives from most of the 61 grant-receiving counties attended this conference, which included speakers from several state agencies and local government associations with land-use policy responsibilities. Finally, data were collected from content analysis of the completed farmland preservation plans. Each plan was coded for group process, contextual factors, and outcome variables. Additional documents provided by task force members included meeting attendance records and expenditure reports.

ALBEMARLE–PAMLICO ESTUARINE STUDY METHODS (CHAPTER 6)

The research on APES, which took place between 1994 and 1996 with additional data collected in 2004, is based on program documents, interviews, and survey results. Program documents, including all committee meeting minutes, progress reports, scientific reports, and budgets, were extensively analyzed. Interviews were conducted with 76 APES participants, including staff, researchers, and Management Conference members from all committees. Most interviews were conducted in person and lasted between 45 minutes and 2 hours. A mail survey about the goals, process, and accomplishments of the APES program was sent to all 162 Management Conference members, with a response rate of 77 percent.

ANIMAS RIVER STAKEHOLDER GROUP STUDY METHODS (CHAPTER 7)

The data for the ARSG study were collected over a period of several years, beginning in 1999. Analysis of archival documents, including the minutes from ARSG meetings, web pages, reports, book chapters, and articles, provided basic background information for the initial field visit to interview ARSG participants. A site visit in summer 1999 included in-person interviews with several participants. Participant observation through ARSG meeting attendance provided additional information. Follow-up interviews by e-mail and telephone were conducted in 2000 through 2002.

NOTES

Chapter 1. Governmental Roles in Collaborative Environmental Management

1. This vignette is derived from a larger study of NCCP in Thomas (2003b).

2. Water Pollution Control Act Amendments, 1972, 1977; Safe Drinking Water Act, 1974, 1977; Toxic Substances Control Act, 1976; Clean Air Act Amendments, 1970, 1977; Marine Protection Research and Sanctuaries Act, 1972; Resource Conservation and Recovery Act, 1976; Federal Land Policy Management Act, 1976; Coastal Zone Management Act, 1972, 1975; Forest and Rangeland Renewable Resources Planning Act, 1974; National Forest Management Act, 1976; Public Rangeland Improvement Act, 1978; Endangered Species Act, 1973, 1978 (compiled from Westman 1985, 54, 60, 66–67, 77).

3. In this discussion, "outcomes" refers to both "policy outcomes" and "policy outputs," as these terms are commonly used in the public policy literature.

4. Of course, this challenge is not limited to collaborative environmental management; the outcomes of traditional command-and-control policies are often difficult to assess and thus have been measured by proxy. See, e.g., Kettl (1983).

Chapter 3. Nonprofit Facilitation: The Darby Partnership

1. Early on, the partnership attendees tended to be senior staff of their organizations; later, field staff were often sent as delegates. TNC explains that this change was appropriate to

have "on-the-ground leadership discover problems and create strategies" (TNC 1996a, *11*) after the initial groundwork was laid by senior staff.

2. Indeed, the informal nature of the partnership sometimes caused confusion about its status as a public or private organization. Although meetings were open to anyone who had an interest in the Darby, lay citizens and members of the press seldom were present. When a reporter attended one contentious meeting in which the wildlife refuge was to be discussed, the facilitator tried to discourage him from taking pictures or making recordings. But then a local government official pointed out that the meeting was subject to the Sunshine Laws because some partners were there in an official capacity, and the reporter was allowed to continue.

3. Since 1991, TNC has had two to four staff members primarily devoted to its Darby-related activities, including the Darby bioreserve project director, a river steward, and a part-time administrative assistant. In addition, during the HUA program, TNC and the United States Department of Agriculture split the cost of an agricultural coordinator, and in 1997 TNC also hired an urban coordinator. Although these staff members do not work for the partnership, they help support it by organizing and facilitating meetings, gathering and presenting relevant information, and participating in joint projects with other partners.

4. This may reflect some response bias, since those who were available for interviews, came to meetings, and responded to the survey were more likely to be positively disposed toward the partnership. Because of this tendency, it may be easier to document the successes and positive views of ecosystem management institutions than failures and negative views (Griffin 1999). Nonetheless, key informants cited many positive outcomes.

Chapter 4. Encouragement through "Carrots" and "Sticks": Habitat Conservation Planning and the Endangered Species Act

1. Under the ESA, the National Marine Fisheries Service (NMFS) has regulatory authority over marine species. NMFS is relegated to citations and footnotes in this chapter because most habitat conservation plans are land based.

2. Sections 9(a)(1) and 3(18), Endangered Species Act of 1973, as amended. The Section 9 prohibition on take applies only to fish and wildlife species listed by the FWS as endangered (i.e., at imminent risk of extinction). It does not apply directly to plant species, or to species listed as threatened (i.e., likely to become endangered in the foreseeable future). Yet Section 9 does cover plant species indirectly because plants (such as old-growth forests) provide habitat for wildlife (such as spotted owls).

3. *Babbitt v. Sweet Home Chapter of Communities for a Great Oregon,* 515 U.S. 687 (1995).

4. Section 4 authorizes the FWS to list a species either as endangered, if it is at imminent risk of extinction, or as threatened, if it is likely to become endangered in the foreseeable future.

5. For example, The Nature Conservancy played a formal role in planning and implementing the second HCP, in the Coachella Valley near Palm Springs, California. It acquired and managed most of the designated preserve land in the HCP, using mitigation fees that developers paid to local governments. It later divested itself of these responsibilities by turning them over to a local nonprofit organization, the Center for Natural Lands Management.

Chapter 5. Encouragement through Grants: Ohio's Farmland Preservation Task Forces

1. Members of task forces on the low end of the spending scale indicated that they had received more money than they could figure out how to spend in developing their farmland preservation plans. Those on the high end obtained additional resources above the required 1:1 match.

Chapter 6. Science-Based Collaborative Management: The Albemarle–Pamlico Estuarine Study

1. At the time, the agency was called the Department of Natural Resources and Community Development (DNRCD). It has been renamed several times since then. For the sake of clarity, the current name of the agency—Department of Environment and Natural Resources (DENR)—is used throughout this chapter.
2. This ceremony occurred the day after state elections put a majority of Republicans in the North Carolina House of Representatives for the first time in decades. Many predicted this would make it more difficult to get APES-related legislation or appropriations approved by the legislature. This political shift made even the most optimistic participants acknowledge that the CCMP would not be immediately implemented in its entirety.

Chapter 7. Government-Led Community Collaboration: The Animas River Stakeholder Group

1. The Clean Water Act is the common name for a group of statutes and amendments. The Federal Water Pollution Control Act was passed in 1972, and the Clean Water Act in 1977. Both acts, with subsequent amendments in 1981, 1987, and 1993, together are referred to as the Clean Water Act.
2. Under Section 319 of the Clean Water Act, states, territories, and tribes can receive grants to support a wide variety of activities, including technical assistance, financial assistance, education, training, technology transfer, demonstration projects, and monitoring to assist the success of specific nonpoint-source implementation projects.

Chapter 8. Government as Actor and as Institution

1. As described in Chapter 1, we use the term "environmental outcomes" to include both environmental conditions on the ground and environmental management tools such as plans, and the term "social outcomes" to denote the enhancement of the capacity for individuals to work together to address their concerns.

REFERENCES

ACIR (Advisory Commission on Intergovernmental Relations). 1980. *Citizen Participation in the American Federal System.* Washington, DC: ACIR, U.S. Government Printing Office.

AFT (American Farmland Trust). 1998. http://www.farmland.org/Farmland/files/protect/why.htm (accessed June 13, 1998).

Agranoff, R., and A. Pattakos. 1979. *Dimensions of Services Integration: Service Delivery, Program Linkages, Policy Management, and Organizational Structure.* April. Washington, DC: Project SHARE.

Allan, K. 1991. One of the Last of the Best. *The Nature Conservancy Magazine* 41(1): 17–23.

Almond, Gabriel A., and Sidney Verba. 1963. *The Civic Culture: Political Attitudes and Democracy in Five Nations.* Princeton, NJ: Princeton University Press.

Alter, C., and J. Hage (eds.). 1993. *Organizations Working Together.* Sage Library of Social Research 191. London: Sage.

APES (Albemarle–Pamlico Estuarine Study). 1987. *Albemarle–Pamlico Estuarine Study Work Plan.* APES Report 87-02. Raleigh, NC: Department of Environment, Health, and Natural Resources.

———. 1992. *The First Public Draft of the Comprehensive Conservation and Management Plan of the Albemarle–Pamlico Estuarine Study, August 14, 1992.* Raleigh, NC: Department of Environment, Health, and Natural Resources.

———. 1994. *Comprehensive Conservation and Management Plan Technical Document: Albemarle–Pamlico Estuarine Study, November 1994.* Raleigh, NC: Department of Environment, Health, and Natural Resources.

Applegate Partnership. n.d. *Applegate Partnership: Practice Trust, Them Is Us.* N.p.

Archer, Jack H., and Robert W. Knecht. 1987. The U.S. National Coastal Zone Management Program—Problems and Opportunities in the Next Phase. *Coastal Management* 15(2): 103–20.

Armingeon, Neil (ed.). 1990. *Blueprint for Action: The Albemarle and Pamlico Citizens Advisory Committees' Resource Management Recommendations for the Albemarle–Pamlico Estuarine Study.* APES Report 90-26. Raleigh, NC: Department of Environment, Health, and Natural Resources.

Arnstein, Sherry R. 1969. A Ladder of Citizen Participation. *American Institute of Planners Journal* 35: 216–24.

ARSG (Animas River Stakeholder Group). 1999. Meeting Summary. http://www.waterinfo.org/arsg/mtgsummary.html (accessed October 15, 1999).

Barker, Paul D. 1990. The Chesapeake Bay Preservation Act: The Problem with State Land Regulation of Interstate Resources. *William and Mary Law Review* 31: 735–72.

Beatley, Timothy, David Brower, and Anna Schwab. 2002. *An Introduction to Coastal Zone Management.* Washington, DC: Island Press.

Beierle, Thomas C. 1999. Using Social Goals to Evaluate Public Participation in Environmental Decisions. *Policy Studies Review* 16(3–4): 75–103.

Belsten, Laura. 1996. Community Collaboration in Environmental Decision Making. PhD diss., University of Denver.

Berry, J.M., K.E. Portney, and K. Thompson. 1989. Empowering and Involving Citizens. In *Handbook of Public Administration*, edited by J.L. Perry. San Francisco: Jossey-Bass.

Blair, Rob (ed.). 1996. *The Western San Juan Mountains: Their Geology, Ecology and Human History.* Niwot, CO: University of Colorado Press.

Blomquist, William, and Edella Schlager. 1999. Political Pitfalls of Integrated Watershed Management. Paper presented at the Western Political Science Association annual meeting. March 24–26, 1999, San Jose, CA.

Bonnell, Joseph. 2001. Group Processes and Ecosystem Based Management: An In-Depth Qualitative Case Study of a Multi-Stakeholder Watershed Management Group. PhD diss., Ohio State University School of Natural Resources, Columbus.

Brick, Philip, Donald Snow, and Sarah Van De Wetering (eds.). 2001. *Across the Great Divide: Explorations in Collaborative Conservation and the American West.* Covelo, CA: Island Press.

Broetzman, Gary. 1996. *Animas River Collaborative Watershed Project: 1995 Status Report.* Denver: Colorado Center for Environmental Management.

————. 1998. *Barriers and Incentives to Voluntary Cleanup of Abandoned Hardrock Mine Sites*. Denver: Colorado Center for Environmental Management.

Brunner, Ronald D. 2000. Beyond Scientific Management. Roundtable presentation at the 22nd Annual Meeting of the Association for Public Policy Analysis and Management. November 2000, Seattle.

Brunner, Ronald D., Christine H. Colburn, Christina M. Cromley, Roberta A. Klein, and Elizabeth A. Olson. 2002. *Finding Common Ground: Governance and Natural Resources in the American West*. New Haven, CT: Yale University Press.

Buckle, Leonard G., and Suzann R. Thomas-Buckle. 1986. Placing Environmental Mediation in Context: Lessons from "Failed" Mediations. *Environmental Impact Assessment Review* 6(1): 55–70.

Butler, Peter. 2001. Telephone interview with Peter Butler, of Friends of the Animas River, by Toddi Steelman. October 3.

Carr, Deborah, Steven Selin, and Michael Schuett. 1998. Managing Public Forests: Understanding the Role of Collaborative Planning. *Environmental Management* 22(5): 767–76.

Chess, Caron, Billie Joe Hance, and Ginger Gibson. 2000. Adaptive Participation in Watershed Management. *Journal of Soil and Water Conservation* 55(3): 248–52.

Cicin-Sain, Biliana, and Robert W. Knecht. 2000. *The Future of U.S. Ocean Policy*. Washington, DC: Island Press.

Coggins, George Cameron. 1998. Of Californicators, Quislings and Crazies: Some Perils of Devolved Collaboration. *Chronicle of Community* 2: 27–33.

Coglianese, Cary. 1999. The Limits of Consensus. *Environment* 41: 28–33.

Collins, Alan, G. Constantz, S. Hunter, and S. Selin. 1998. Collaborative Watershed Planning: The West Virginia Experience. *Conservation Voices* 1(2): 31–35.

Conley, Alex, and Ann Moote. 2003. Evaluating Collaborative Natural Resource Management. *Society and Natural Resources* 16: 371–86.

Cortner, Hanna J., and Margaret A. Moote. 1999. *The Politics of Ecosystem Management*. Washington, DC: Island Press.

Crawford, Sue E.S., and Elinor Ostrom. 1995. A Grammar of Institutions. *American Political Science Review* 89(3): 582–600.

Cubbage, Frederick, Jay O'Laughlin, and Charles Bullock III. 1993. *Forest Resource Policy*. New York: John Wiley and Sons.

Culhane, Paul. 1981. *Public Lands Politics: Interest Group Influence on the Forest Service and the Bureau of Land Management*. Baltimore: Resources for the Future, Johns Hopkins University Press.

CVHCP (Coachella Valley Fringe-Toed Lizard Habitat Conservation Plan Steering Committee). 1985. *Coachella Valley Fringe-Toed Lizard Habitat Conservation Plan*. Palm Desert, CA: Coachella Valley Association of Governments.

Davis, Charles. 2001. Introduction: The Context of Public Lands Policy Change. In *Western Public Lands and Environmental Politics*, edited by Charles Davis. Boulder, CO: Westview Press.

Davis, David Howard. 1998. *American Environmental Politics*. Chicago: Nelson-Hall Publishers.

Davis, Stephen D., V.H. Heywood, O. Herrera-MacBryde, J. Villa-Lobos, and A.C. Hamilton. 1997. *Centers of Plant Diversity: A Guide and Strategy for their Conservation*. Volume 3. *The Americas*. Cambridge, UK: World Wide Fund for Nature and the IUCN–World Conservation Union.

Endicott, Eve. 1993. Preserving Natural Areas: The Nature Conservancy and Its Partners. In *Land Conservation through Public-Private Partnerships*, edited by Eve Endicott. Washington, DC: Island Press.

Ethridge, Marcus E. 1987. Procedures for Citizen Involvement in Environmental Policy: An Assessment of Policy Effects. In *Citizen Participation in Public Decision Making*, edited by Jack DeSario and Stuart Langton. New York: Greenwood Press.

Evans, Parthenia B. (ed.) 1994. *The Clean Water Act: A Handbook*. Chicago: American Bar Association.

Freeman, A. Myrick, III. 1990. Water Pollution Policy. In *Public Policies for Environmental Protection*, edited by Paul Portney. Washington, DC: Resources for the Future.

———. 2000. Economics, Incentives, and Environmental Regulation. In *Environmental Policy*, 4th ed., edited by Norman J. Vig and Michael E. Kraft. Washington, DC: CQ Press.

Frohardt, P. 2001. Telephone interview with Paul Frohardt, administrator of the Colorado Water Quality Control Commission, by Toddi Steelman. October 3.

Geddes, Barbara. 1990. How the Cases You Choose Affect the Answers You Get: Selection Bias in Comparative Cases. *Political Analysis* 2: 131–52.

Golden, Marissa Martino. 1998. Interest Groups in the Rule-Making Process: Who Participates? Whose Voices Get Heard? *Journal of Public Administration Research and Theory* 8(2), 245–70.

Graves, William J. 1998. *Farmland Preservation Plan Guidelines*. September 9. Memo to the Ohio Small Cities Community Development Block Grant Formula Allocation Program Grant Recipients. Columbus: Ohio Department of Development.

Gray, Barbara. 1989. *Collaborating: Finding Common Ground for Multiparty Problems*. San Francisco: Jossey-Bass.

Griffin, Carol B. 1999. Watershed Councils: An Emerging Form of Public Participation in Natural Resource Management. *Journal of the American Water Resources Association* 35(3): 505–18.

Grumbine, R. Edward. 1994. What Is Ecosystem Management? *Conservation Biology* 8(1): 27–38.

Hall, Peter. 1986. *Governing the Economy: The Politics of State Intervention in Britain and France*. New York: Oxford University Press.

Hall, Peter, and Rosemary C.R. Taylor. 1996. Political Science and the Three New Institutionalisms. *Political Studies* 44: 936–57.

Hays, Samuel. 1959. *Conservation and the Gospel of Efficiency: The Progressive Conservation Movement, 1890–1920*. Cambridge, MA: Harvard University Press.

———. 1987. *Beauty, Health, and Permanence: Environmental Politics in the United States, 1955–1985*. New York: Cambridge University Press.

Hillery, George A. 1955. Definitions of Community: Areas of Agreement. *Rural Sociology* 20: 111–23.

Hirt, Paul W. 1994. *A Conspiracy of Optimism: Management of the National Forests since World War II*. Lincoln, NE: University of Nebraska Press.

Hoberg, George. 1997. From Localism to Legalism: The Transformation of Federal Forest Policy. In *Western Public Lands and Environmental Politics*, edited by Charles Davis. Boulder, CO: Westview Press.

Jackson County Government. 1992. *O&C*. Medford, OR.

John, Dewitt. 1994. *Civic Environmentalism: Alternatives to Regulation in States and Communities*. Washington, DC: CQ Press.

Johnson, Sarah. 2001. Telephone interview with Sarah Johnson, manager of the Assessment Unit, Colorado Water Quality Control Division, by Toddi Steelman. October 11.

Kareiva, Peter, Sandy Andelman, Daniel Doak, Bret Elderd, Martha Groom, Jonathan Hoekstra, Laura Hood, Frances James, John Lamoreux, Gretchen LeBuhn, Charles McCulloch, James Regetz, Lisa Savage, Mary Ruckelshaus, David Skelly, Henry Wilbur, Kelly Zamudio, and NCEAS HCP working group. 1999. *Using Science in Habitat Conservation Plans*. Washington, DC: American Institute of Biological Sciences.

Karkkainen, Bradley C. 2003. Toward Ecologically Sustainable Democracy? In *Deepening Democracy: Institutional Innovations in Empowered Participatory Governance*, edited by Archon Fung and Erik Olin Wright. New York: Verso.

Kellogg, Wendy A. 1998. Adopting an Ecosystem Approach: Local Variability in Remedial Action Planning. *Society and Natural Resources* 11:465–83.

Kenney, Douglas S. 1999. Historical and Sociopolitical Context of the Western Watersheds Movement. *Journal of the American Water Resources Association* 35(3): 493–503.

Kenney, Douglas S., and William B. Lord. 1999. *Analysis of Institutional Innovation in the Natural Resources and Environmental Realm: The Emergence of Alternative Problem-Solving Strategies in the American West*. Research Report RR-21. Boulder, CO: Natural Resource Law Center, University of Colorado School of Law.

Kerwin, Cornelius M. 1999. *Rulemaking: How Government Agencies Write Law and Make Policy*. 2nd ed. Washington, DC: CQ Press.

Kettl, Donald F. 1983. *The Regulation of American Federalism*. Baton Rouge, LA: Louisiana State University Press.

Kickert, W.J.M., E.H. Klijn, and J.F.M. Koppenjan. 1997. Introduction: A Management Perspective on Policy Networks. In *Managing Complex Networks: Strategies for the Public Sector,* edited by W.J.M. Kickert, E.H. Klijn, and J.F.M Koppenjan. London: Sage Publications, 1–13.

King, Gary, Robert Keohane, and Sidney Verba. 1995. *Designing Social Inquiry.* Princeton, NJ: Princeton University Press.

King, Cheryl Simrell, Kathryn M. Feltey, and Bridget O'Neill Susel. 1998. The Question of Participation: Toward Authentic Public Participation in Public Administration. *Public Administration Review* 58(4): 317–26.

Klyza, Christopher McGrory. 1996. *Who Controls Public Lands? Mining, Forestry, and Grazing Policies, 1870–1990.* Chapel Hill, NC: University of North Carolina Press.

Kneese, Allen V., and Charles L. Schultze. 1975. *Pollution, Prices and Public Policy.* Washington, DC: Brookings Institution.

Koontz, Tomas M., and Katrina Smith Korfmacher. 2000. Community Collaboration in Farmland Preservation: How Local Advisory Groups Plan. Association for Public Policy Analysis and Management Annual Research Conference. November 2–4, Seattle, WA.

Korfmacher, Katrina Smith. 1998. Invisible Successes, Visible Failures: Paradoxes of Ecosystem Management in the Albemarle–Pamlico Estuarine Study. *Coastal Management* 26(3): 191–212.

———. 2000. Partnering for Ecosystem Management of the Darby Creek Watershed. *American Behavioral Scientist* 44(4): 548–64.

Korfmacher, Katrina Smith, and Tomas M. Koontz. 2003. Collaboration, Information, and Preservation: The Role of Expertise in Farmland Preservation Task Forces. *Policy Sciences* 36: 213–36.

Kweit, Robert W., and Mary Kweit. 1980. Bureaucratic Decision-Making: Impediments to Citizen Participation. *Polity* 12(4): 646–66.

Lamb, Berton L., ed. 1980. *Water Quality Administration: A Focus on Section 208.* Ann Arbor, MI: Ann Arbor Science Publishers.

Lasswell, Harold D., and M.S. McDougal. 1992. *Jurisprudence for a Free Society.* New Haven, CT: Kluwer Law International.

Lawrence, Barnett. 1988. Towards a National Coastal Policy. *Environmental Law* 8(3): 1–9.

Leach, William D., Neil W. Pelkey, and Paul A. Sabatier. 2002. Stakeholder Partnerships as Collaborative Policymaking: Evaluation Criteria Applied to Watershed Management in California and Washington. *Journal of Policy Analysis and Management* 21(4): 645–70.

Lohstroh, M. 1992. Ohio's Darby Creek Gains from Cooperation. *Soil and Water Conservation News* (May–June): 4–6.

Lubell, Mark, Mihriye Mete, Mark Schneider, and John Scholz. 1998. Cooperation, Transaction Costs, and the Emergence of Ecosystem Partnerships. Paper presented at the American Political Science Association annual meeting. September 3, Boston.

Lynn, Frances M. 1987. Citizen Involvement in Hazardous Waste Sites: Two North Carolina Success Stories. *Environmental Impact Assessment Review* 7: 347–61.

MacKenzie, Susan Hill. 1996. *Integrated Resource Planning and Management: The Ecosystem Approach in the Great Lakes Basin*. Covelo, CA: Island Press.

Malone, Charles R. 2000. State Governments, Ecosystem Management, and the Enlibra Doctrine in the US. *Ecological Economics* 34: 9–17.

Mandell, Myrna. 1990. Network Management: Strategic Behavior in the Public Sector. In *Strategies for Managing Intergovernmental Policies and Networks*, edited by Robert W. Gage and Myrna P. Mandell. New York: Praeger, 29–53.

———. 1999. Community Collaborations: Working through Network Structures. *Policy Studies Review* 16(1): 42–64.

March, James G., and Johan P. Olsen. 1989. *Rediscovering Institutions*. New York: Free Press.

McAllister, Sean. 1999. The Confluence of a River and a Community: An Experiment with Community-Based Watershed Management in Southwestern Colorado. Paper presented at the Advanced Natural Resources Seminar on San Juan Basin, University of Colorado Law School.

McCloskey, Michael. 1996. The Skeptic: Collaboration Has Its Limits. *High Country News* 28(9). http://www.hcn.org/1996/may13/dir/Opinion_The_skepti.html (accessed March 21, 2000).

McGinnis, Michael V., John Woolley, and John Gamman. 1999. Bioregional Conflict Resolution: Rebuilding Community in Watershed Planning and Organizing. *Environmental Management* 24(1): 1–12.

Meidinger, Errol E. 1997. Organizational and Legal Challenges for Ecosystem Management. In *Creating a Forestry for the 21st Century*, edited by Kathryn A. Kohm and Jerry F. Franklin. Washington, DC: Island Press, 361–79.

Mihaly, M. 1994. Farming for the Future. *Nature Conservancy Magazine* 44(5): 25–29.

Milward, H. Brinton, and Keith G. Provan. 2000. Governing the Hollow State. *Journal of Public Administration Research and Theory* 10(2): 359.

Morrison, Michael L., Bruce G. Marcot, and R. William Mannan. 1992. *Wildlife-Habitat Relationships: Concepts and Applications*. Madison, WI: The University of Wisconsin Press.

Morrissey, Wayne A., Jeffrey A. Zinn, and M. Lynne Corn. 1994. Ecosystem Management: Federal Agency Activities. Congressional Research Service Report for Congress, 94-339ENR.

Moseley, Cassandra. 1999. New Ideas, Old Institutions: Environment, Community, and State in the Pacific Northwest. PhD diss., Yale University.

Moseley, Cassandra, and Brett KenCairn. 2001. Institutional Problem Solving or Social Change: the Applegate and Grand Canyon Forests Partnerships. In *Ponderosa Pine Ecosystems Restoration and Conservation: Steps toward Stewardship*, edited by Regina Vance, Carleton Edminster, W. Wallace Covington, and Julia A.

Blake. Flagstaff, Arizona, April 25–27, 2000. Ogden UT: UDSA Forest Service, Rocky Mountain Research Station.

Mullner, Scott, Wayne Hubert, and Thomas Wesche. 2001. Evolving Paradigms for Landscape-Scale Renewable Resource Management in the United States. *Environmental Science and Policy* 4: 39–49.

Napier, Ted L. 1998a. Conservation Coalitions Cannot Overcome Poor Conservation Programming. *Journal of Soil and Water Conservation* 53(4): 300–3.

_____. 1998b. Impacts of Voluntary Conservation Initiatives in the Darby Creek Watershed of Ohio. *Journal of Soil and Water Conservation* 53(1): 78–84.

Noss, Reed F., and Allen Y. Cooperrider. 1994. *Saving Nature's Legacy: Protecting and Restoring Biodiversity*. Washington, DC: Island Press.

Noss, Reed F., Michael A. O'Connell, and Dennis D. Murphy. 1997. *The Science of Conservation Planning: Habitat Conservation under the Endangered Species Act*. Washington, DC: Island Press.

Ohio Watershed Network. n.d. Welcome to the Ohio Watershed Network. Columbus, OH: Ohio State University Extension. http://ohiowatersheds.osu.edu/ (accessed March 10, 2003).

Osborne, David, and Ted Gaebler. 1992. *Reinventing Government: How the Entrepreneurial Spirit is Transforming the Public Sector*. Reading, MA: Addison-Wesley.

Ostrom, Elinor, Roy Gardner, and James Walker. 1994. *Rules, Games, and Common-Pool Resources*. Ann Arbor: University of Michigan Press.

Owens, David W. 1987. Estuary Reports: Albemarle–Pamlico Sounds. *EPA Journal* (July–August): 26–27.

Parsons, G. 2001. Non Point Source Coordinator for Colorado Water Quality Control Division. Telephone interview with Toddi Steelman. October 4, 2001.

Patrick, Ruth. 1992. *Surface Water Quality: Have the Laws Been Successful?* Princeton, NJ: Princeton University Press.

Peters, B. Guy. 1999. *Institutional Theory in Political Science: The New Institutionalism*. London: Pinter.

Pierce, J., and H. Doerksen. 1976. Citizen Advisory Committees: The Impact of Recruitment on Representation and Responsiveness. In *Water Politics and Public Involvement*, edited by J. Pierce and H. Doerksen. Ann Arbor, MI: Science Publishers.

Press, Daniel. 1998. Local Environmental Policy Capacity: A Framework for Research. *Natural Resources Journal* 38(1): 29–52.

Rhoads, Bruce L., David Wilson, Michael Urban, and Edwin E. Hendricks. 1999. Interaction between Scientists and Nonscientists in Community-Based Watershed Management: Emergence of the Concept of Stream Naturalization. *Environmental Management* 24(3): 297–308.

Rhodes, Rod A.W. 1996. The New Governance: Governing without Government. *Political Studies* 44(3): 652–67.

Richardson, Elmo. 1980. *BLM's Billion-Dollar Checkerboard: Managing the O&C Lands.* Santa Cruz, CA: Forest History Society.

Robinson, Robert H. 2000. Upper Animas River Watershed Abandoned Mine Land Program. Report of the Bureau of Land Management, Minerals Program in Colorado. January 19. http://www.co.blm.gov/mines/upperanimas/upperanimas. htm (accessed May 14, 2001).

Romzek, Barbara, and Melvin J. Dubnick. 1994. Issues of Accountability in Flexible Personnel Systems. In *New Paradigms for Government,* edited by Patricia Ingraham and Barbara Romzek. San Francisco: Jossey-Bass.

Rose, Jerome G. 1983. *Legal Foundation of Environmental Planning: Textbook-Casebook and Materials on Environmental Law.* (Volume 1.) New Brunswick, NJ: Rutgers, State University of New Jersey, Center for Urban Policy Research.

Rosenbaum, Walter A. 1978. Public Involvement as Reform and Ritual: The Development of Federal Participation Programs. In *Citizen Participation in America,* edited by Stuart Langton. Lexington, MA: Lexington Books.

Schattschneider, Elmer E. 1960. *The Semisovereign People: A Realist's View of Democracy in America.* New York: Holt, Rinehart, and Winston.

Schweik, Charles, and Craig W. Thomas. 2002. Using Remote Sensing to Evaluate Environmental Institutional Designs: A Habitat Conservation Planning Example. *Social Science Quarterly* 83: 244–62.

Seymour, Frances J. 1994. Are Successful Community-Based Conservation Projects Designed or Discovered? In *Natural Connections: Perspectives in Community-based Conservation,* edited by David Western and R. Michael Wright. Washington, DC: Island Press.

Sher, Victor M. 1993. Travels with *Strix*: The Spotted Owl's Journey through the Federal Courts. *Public Land Law Review* 14(Spring): 41–79.

Simon, Bill. n.d. Upper Animas Watershed Restoration Action Strategy. Incomplete draft. On file with author.

Singleton, Sara. 2000. Co-operation or Capture? The Paradox of Co-management and Community Participation in Natural Resource Management and Environmental Policy-making. *Environmental Politics* 9(2): 1–21.

Smith, Rogers M. 1992. If Politics Matters: Implications for a "New Institutionalism." *Studies in American Political Development* 6: 1–36.

Snow, David A., and Robert D. Benford. 1988. Ideology, Frame Resonance, and Participant Mobilization. *International Social Movement Research* 1: 197–217.

Snow, Donald. 2001. Coming Home: An Introduction to Collaborative Conservation. In *Across the Great Divide: Explorations in Collaborative Conservation and the American West,* edited by Philip Brick, Donald Snow, and Sarah Van de Wetering. Washington, DC: Island Press, 1–11.

Steelman, Toddi A. 2000. Innovation in Local Land Protection: The Case of Great Outdoors Colorado. *American Behavioral Scientist* 44(4): 579–97.

Steelman, Toddi A., and JoAnn Carmin. 2002. Community Based Watershed Remediation: Connecting Organizational Resources to Social and Substantive Outcomes. In *Toxic Waste and Environmental Policy in the 21st Century United States*, edited by Diane Rahm. Jefferson, NC: McFarland Publishers.

Stenberg, Carl W. 1972. Citizens and the Administrative State: From Participation to Power. *Public Administration Review* 22(3): 190–97.

Thelen, Kathleen, and Sven Steinmo. 1992. Historical Institutionalism in Comparative Politics. In *Structuring Politics: Historical Instituionalism in Comparative Analysis*, edited by Sven Steinmo, Kathleen Thelen, and Frank Longstreth. Cambridge, UK: Cambridge University Press.

Thomas, Craig W. 1999. Linking Public Agencies with Community-Based Watershed Organizations: Lessons from California. *Policy Studies Journal* 27: 544–64.

———.2003a. Habitat Conservation Planning. In *Deepening Democracy: Institutional Innovations in Empowered Participatory Governance*, edited by Archon Fung and Erik Olin Wright. New York: Verso.

———. 2003b. *Bureaucratic Landscapes: Interagency Cooperation and the Preservation of Biodiversity*. Cambridge, MA: MIT Press.

Thomas, Craig W., and Charles Schweik. 1999. Regulatory Compliance under the Endangered Species Act: A Time-Series Analysis of Habitat Conservation Planning Using Remote-Sensing Data. Paper presented at the Association for Public Policy Analysis and Management (APPAM) Annual Research Conference. October, Washington, DC.

TNC (The Nature Conservancy). 1996a. *The Darby Bioreserve Project*. Draft report prepared by The Nature Conservancy–Ohio Chapter. Dublin, OH.

———. 1996b. *The Darby Book: A Guide for Residents of the Darby Creek Watershed*. The Nature Conservancy–Ohio Chapter. Dublin, OH.

Tripp, James T.B., and Michael Oppenheimer. 1988. Restoration of the Chesapeake Bay: A Multi-State Institutional Challenge. *Maryland Law Review* 47: 425–51.

USDA (Department of Agriculture). 1998a. *A Great Place … The Darby Creek Hydrologic Unit Area, Ohio*. Project #95-EHUA-1-0133.

———. 1998b. *1998 Agricultural Statistics*. National Agricultural Statistics Service. Table IX-10. http://www.usda.gov/nass/pubs/agr98/acro98.htm (accessed January 5, 2003).

USDA and U.S. DOC (Department of Commerce). 2000. Unified Federal Policy for a Watershed Approach to Federal Land and Resource Management. *Federal Register* 65(202): 62566–72.

U.S. EPA (Environmental Protection Agency). 1989. Saving Bays and Estuaries: A Primer for Establishing and Managing Estuary Projects. EPA/503/8-89-0001, Washington, DC: US Government Printing Office, 1989.

———. 1996. Big Darby Creek Watershed, Ecological Risk Assessment, Planning and Problem Formulation. *Risk Assessment Forum*. Draft, June 14, 1996.

———. 2003. The National Estuary Program: Which Estuaries Are in the NEP? http://www.epa.gov/owow/estuaries/find.htm (accessed December 1, 2003).

U.S. FWS (Fish and Wildlife Service). 2002. U.S. Fish and Wildlife Service Awards $68 Million in Grants to 16 States for Endangered Species Habitat Conservation Planning and Habitat Acquisition Projects. News release issued by fws-news listserver. September 13.

———. 2003. Environmental Conservation Online System. http://ecos.fws.gov (accessed November 21, 2003).

U.S. FWS and NMFS (National Marine Fisheries Service). 1996. *Habitat Conservation Planning Handbook*. Washington, DC: U.S. Fish and Wildlife Service and National Marine Fisheries Service.

———. 1998. "Habitat Conservation Plan Assurances ('No Surprises') Rule," *Federal Register* 63 (35): 8859–8873, March 25.

———. 2000. Notice of Availability of a Final Addendum to the Handbook for Habitat Conservation Planning and Incidental Take Permitting Process. *Federal Register* 65(106): 35241–57.

Vira, Bhaskar, and Roger Jeffrey (eds.). 2001. *Analytical Issues in Participatory Natural Resource Management*. New York: Palgrave Macmillan.

Vosick, D., and K. Cash. 1996. *The Role of Agriculture in Protecting Biological Diversity: United States*. Report prepared for the OECD Seminar on Environmental Benefits from a Sustainable Agriculture: Issues and Policies. COM/AGR/CA/ENV/EPOC (96)132. September 10–13, 1996, Helsinki.

Waters, Elizabeth B. 1993. *Albemarle Pamlico Estuarine Study Workshops*. Internal APES report. Raleigh, NC: Department of Environment, Health, and Natural Resource.

Weber, Edward P. 1998. *Pluralism by the Rules: Conflict and Cooperation in Environmental Regulation*. Washington, DC: Georgetown University Press.

———. 2003. *Bringing Society Back In: Grassroots Ecosystem Management, Accountability, and Sustainable Communities*. Cambridge, MA: MIT Press.

Weeks, W. William. 1997. *Beyond the Ark: Tools for an Ecosystem Approach to Conservation*. Washington, DC: Island Press.

Wengert, Norman. 1971. Public Participation in Water Planning: A Critique of Theory. *Water Resources Bulletin* 7(1): 26–32.

Westman, Walter E. 1985. *Ecology, Impact Assessment, and Environmental Planning*. New York: John Wiley & Sons.

Wondolleck, Julia M., and Steven L. Yaffee. 2000. *Making Collaboration Work: Lessons from Innovation in Natural Resource Management*. Washington, DC: Island Press.

Yaffee, Steven. L. 1994. *The Wisdom of the Spotted Owl: Policy Lessons for a New Century*. Covelo, CA: Island Press.

Yaffee, Steven L., P. Aengst, J. Chamberlin, C. Grunewald, S. Loucks, and E. Wheatley. 1998. *Balancing Public Trust and Private Interest: Public Participation in Habitat*

Conservation Planning. Ann Arbor, MI: School of Natural Resources and Environment, University of Michigan.

Yaffee, Steven, Ali F. Phillips, Irene C. Frentz, Paul W. Hardy, Sussanne M. Maleki, and Barbara E. Thorpe. 1996. *Ecosystem Management in the United States: An Assessment of Current Experience*. Washington DC: Island Press.

Yin, Robert K. 1994. *Case Study Research: Design and Methods*. Thousand Oaks, CA: Sage Publications.

Zwinger, Ann. 1994. Back Home Again. In *Heart of the Land: Essays on Last Great Places*, edited by Joseph Barbato and Lisa Winerman. New York: Pantheon, 151–60.

INDEX